# BEYOND BAGHDAD

## Books by Ralph Peters

*Nonfiction*

Beyond Baghdad
Beyond Terror
Fighting For The Future

*Fiction*

Traitor
The Devil's Garden
Twilight of Heroes
Flames of Heaven
The Perfect Soldier
The War in 2020
Red Army
Bravo Romeo

## Writing as Owen Parry

*Fiction*

Bold Sons of Erin
Honor's Kingdom (Hammett Award)
Call Each River Jordan
Shadows of Glory
Faded Coat of Blue (Herodotus Award)
Our Simple Gifts

# BEYOND BAGHDAD

*Postmodern War and Peace*

Ralph Peters

STACKPOLE
BOOKS

First published in paperback in 2005 by
STACKPOLE BOOKS
5067 Ritter Road
Mechanicsburg, PA 17055
www.stackpolebooks.com

Printed in the United States

First paperback edition

10  9  8  7  6  5  4  3  2  1

*Cover photo: AP Photo/Laura Rauch*
*Cover design: Caroline M. Stover*

**Library of Congress Cataloging-in-Publication Data**

Peters, Ralph, 1952-
  Beyond Baghdad : postmodern war and peace / Ralph Peters.– 1st ed.
    p. cm.
  ISBN 0-8117-0084-4; 0-8117-3233-9 (pbk.)
  1. National security—United States. 2. United States—Armed Forces. 3.
United States—Military policy. 4. War on Terrorism, 2001– 5. Iraq War,
2003. 6. World politics—1995–2005. 7. Military art and science—United
States. I. Title.

UA23 .P469 2003
355'.033073–dc22                                            2003015813

*To those with whom I served*
*And from whom I learned*

The ordinary Writers of Morality prescribe to their Readers after the Galenick Way; their Medicines are made up in large Quantities. An Essay Writer must practise in the Chymical Method, and give the Virtue of a full Draught in a few drops.

—Joseph Addison, the *Spectator*

# Contents

**CODA: Au Revoir, Marianne . . . Auf Wiedersehen, Lili Marleen**

# Foreword

by Barry R. McCaffrey, General, USA (Ret)

This powerful collection of essays by Ralph Peters is a joy to read. It will further extend his intellectual influence on the thinking of those in the defense community who are challenged by the new and very diverse threats posed by international terrorism, rogue states, the rapid proliferation of chemical, biological, and nuclear weapons, extremist hatred, and the convergence of international crime, drug money, and terrorist organizations.

The author is simply one of the most creative and stimulating writers on national security affairs we have produced in the post-WWII era. Ralph Peters has written a dozen successful and critically acclaimed novels. However, he has really made his mark as a uniquely qualified strategic analyst who combines a career of worldwide, tough, frontline military experience—rising from the rank of Army Private to Lieutenant Colonel—with the sensitivity of a gifted intelligence officer who has a lifetime of direct experience, observation, and travel in more than fifty nations. Ralph's intellectual underpinnings are strongly rooted in his sense of history, literature, and philosophy. His writing is hard-hitting, direct, and persuasive. The commentary entitled "Au Revoir, Marianne . . . Auf

Wiedersehen, Lily Marleen," dealing with the disruptive German and French strategy that so grievously hampered U.S. policy to liberate the 24 million Iraqis from the cruelty of the Saddam Hussein regime, may be one of the most powerful indictments of European political shamelessness ever written.

*Beyond Baghdad* builds upon the highly influential impact of his earlier book *Beyond Terror* and the widely praised work on strategy *Fighting for the Future*. The first portion of this book focuses primarily on strategic issues and includes a brilliant analysis done for the U.S. Marines, "Hidden Unities," that peers far into the out-years. The second portion of the book covers the long build-up to the recent war in Iraq, the war itself, the aftermath, and related national security issues. Ralph should be enormously proud of the prescient and accurate predictions he made on the nature and probable outcomes of the military operations in both Afghanistan and Iraq. He was dead on target in his thinking and judgments. The Bush Administration approached these powerful post-9/11 threats with a sense of moral and political courage that stepped beyond the failures of the preceding 15 years of political self-paralysis. The Lockerbie Bombing and the years of numbing losses and bloodshed by state-sponsored terrorism emanating from Iran, North Korea, Syria, Libya, Cuba, the Sudan, and, of course, Iraq had set up the American people for the tragedy of 9/11.

The Department of State website identified some thirty-five foreign terrorist organizations on the day that al Qa'eda operatives brutally murdered over 3,000 innocent Americans. On that terrible morning, we lost more Americans in the World Trade Towers, the Pentagon, and during the heroic struggle on an airliner over Pennsylvania than we had suffered in any 24-hour period since the Civil War. We are fortunate that the new and untested President of the United States and his senior team reacted with resolve, courage, and an unblinking focus to prevent the inexorable growth of terror—including the threat of future use of nuclear devices, chemical poisons, and biological toxins.

Ralph Peters and others (myself included—in the November 2002 issue of *Armed Forces Journal*) called correctly for decisive military action against Iraq. We argued that this despotic regime could be successfully brought down in a lightning air-ground-sea campaign that would shatter the power of an evil government that had murdered over 500,000 of its own citizens while wrapping the entire region in a quarter century of war and terror. No voice was more courageous and informed than that of Ralph Peters in this pre-war debate that threatened the American government with self-paralysis from the many, many voices agonizing about the real and imagined perils of pre-emptive action. Thankfully, the President and Congress acted, and the courageous Brits and Australians stood with America during this defining act of self preservation.

For the purpose of full disclosure, I should note that Ralph Peters has been a valued professional collaborator and partner—and a personal friend—for more than a decade. His reputation for brilliance, unvarnished candor, and logic was Army-wide. I asked to borrow him for the first of several collaborative and sensitive missions just following the first Gulf War, when I served as General Colin Powell's Strategic Planner on the Joint Staff in the Pentagon. At the time, we were trying to sort out the enormous challenge facing us in the Balkans as we verged on political-military intervention in Bosnia. Of the many experts I consulted from the Pentagon, the State Department, and the CIA, none was a greater help in forming my own strategic perspective than Ralph Peters. My personal travel and observations on the ground in beleaguered Bosnia, in the capitals of the warring states of Serbia and Croatia, and in the NATO-partner countries cemented a fundamental trust and admiration for his judgments.

In the following years I would return to the Army Chief of Staff several times to ask for the loan of this remarkable intelligence officer. During a tour as the U.S. Joint Commander for U.S. Forces in Latin America, I asked Ralph to carry out an extensive personal reconnaissance of the Andean Ridge cocaine threat—a task he performed at great personal risk and with unusual analytic clarity. While serving as the nation's Drug Policy Director in charge of our $19 billion effort to reduce the devastating impact of drug addiction, I asked Ralph to carry out personal missions on the Thailand-Burma border as well as a series of very complex missions involving the drug threat along the U.S.-Mexican border. His analytical work had a huge influence on our understanding of these extremely complex and dangerous problems.

His written reports were explosively direct in their powerful description of the corruption, incompetence, and incoherence we faced in these grave challenges to our security from narco-criminals. Ralph posed a difficult challenge to an interagency bureaucracy that frequently felt uncomfortable and threatened by his insights and analysis. I was proud to be associated with his creative work, which had a major effect on the development of our international drug strategy.

Ralph Peters and I also share a common belief that our Armed Forces should and will undergo a powerful and significant transformation in the coming years. The Bush Administration will shape a new national security and military strategy that will produce a very different defensive concept for the first quarter of the twenty-first century. Sweeping changes in technology (smart munitions, unmanned aerial vehicles, digital communications, stealth technology, satellites and computers, night vision devices, GPS, reactive armor, nanotechnologies, and new revolutionary sources of electrical power) will lead to a very different set of Joint Doctrines for our fighting forces. Air power will play a new and crucial role at the strategic, operational, and tactical levels. The Naval-Marine Expeditionary Team will become central to our range of responses for both deterrence and war fighting. Our global force-stationing concept will change dramatically in Korea, the Middle East, Western Europe, the Central Asian States, and in the Americas.

Yet despite the promise this new technology and doctrine offer, we need to approach this transformation with a sense of caution and humility. Congress must be central to this discussion—only it has the constitutional authority to define this future battle force. The media also must help the American people understand what is at stake. The lessons of Iraq Wars I and II and Afghanistan must be read cautiously. We face a broad range of threats in the coming years, which include enemy conventional and irregular forces of enormous power and determination. Military planners must again review the compelling historical arguments of books such as the seminal work on Korea, *This Kind of War* by T. R. Fehrenbach. At the end of the day, the successful employment of any military strategy will require the use of ground combat forces to carry out operations designed to close with enemy forces and kill them through direct fire and maneuver. American fighting men and women will be killed and maimed. Warfare is a nasty, brutish business.

If we intend to remain free and exercise our enormous economic, political, and moral power for the protection of the American people and the benefit of our allies, we must maintain strong, well-equipped, well-trained, and courageous Army and Marine combat forces. In my judgment, we did not give the ground force commanders in the recent liberation of Iraq adequate combat forces. Two Army Divisions and one Marine Division took on a 400,000-soldier Iraqi force in a country the size of California. We needed to shatter their combat units at the outset, dominate their capital, secure the alleged sites for WMD, root out the Ba'ath Party criminal leadership, suppress the Tikrit Sunni region as the base of Saddam's power, and jump-start the economy and oil industry. The force we used was adequate to win the initial battles, but its size put the start of the campaign unnecessarily at risk.

The 1991 Desert Storm Campaign used a massive force of nine U.S. Army and Marine Divisions to crush the Iraqis in a campaign that went roughly the same distance as the recent campaign. (XVIII Airborne Corps's left-hook attack versus the 3rd ID attack to the outskirts of Baghdad.) Both ground-air campaigns produced roughly the same number of American and British casualties; however, the operation took 28 days in 2003, but only 4 days in 1991. More importantly, the enormous courage and determination of the smaller Gulf War II forces were severely tested in battle. The outcome was not finalized until substantial reinforcements were rushed into theater to ratchet up and deploy a battle force of four Army divisions, two armored cavalry regiments, and substantial Military Police reinforcements. This war was won by the courage and determination of our combat forces and the brilliant leadership of the CENTCOM Joint Team commanded by General Tommy Franks. The planning was extremely creative, particularly in the employment of special operations forces and the clever use of deception and psychological operations. Nonetheless, at the conclusion of the initial land campaign, it was clear that our ground combat strength was inadequate.

Our purpose in warfare is not to win with barely adequate power. Our purpose must be to minimize the chance of a political disaster caused by bloody military setbacks during opening campaigns. This has been the American way of war through much of our history. We lose opening battles and then surge back to accomplish our objectives with a powerful second effort. Kasserine Pass in North Africa, the Marines at Guadalcanal, Task Force Smith in Korea, the 7th Cavalry in Vietnam in the battles of the Ia Drang—all are examples of inadequate initial combat power. Over the past 15 years, we have gotten it right through the application of overwhelming military force. On future battlefields we will fight enemies who will not be crippled by the shame and suffering inflicted during 23 years of cruelty by Saddam and his criminal regime. We must focus on the decisive use of air-land-sea combat power whenever we are finally forced to use military options to achieve our objectives.

This book of essays is a powerful and clear analysis of the key challenges facing our national security interests in the coming decades. Ralph Peters has done us a great service in helping to shape this crucial debate. We must build the future military forces and design the doctrine needed to confront the terrorist and conventional enemies that continue to menace us in this very dangerous world.

# Introduction

## A Matter of Identity

I write. I write essays and commentaries for a variety of publications, from the mildly fusty to the gleefully feisty. I write books, including novels set during our Civil War (under my pen name, Owen Parry) and volumes on military policy, strategy and security affairs, such as this one. I have written fiction about the drug trade as well as Christmas stories, argued the strategic utility of equal rights for women, and examined the violence inherent in monotheist faiths.

The differences between my flirtations with "serious" journals and my affairs with populist newspapers, the variety of themes I romance and discard, and my refusal to wed any partisan ideology all disconcert those proper souls who abhor such promiscuity. But writing is, indeed, like dating and mating: Honesty is essential, while monogamy is a matter of taste.

Writers are typecast as firmly as are actors. I refuse to cooperate.

There are two essential types of writers, just as there are two basic types of actors. We have the stars who simply present themselves, preening in film after film or in column after column, predictable and reassuring, and we have character actors who take their craft seriously, who can slip into startlingly different roles, yet convince us of the authenticity of each voice and the validity of each persona. I like to imagine myself among the latter.

Some writers write for themselves. Others write for their audience, to inform, entertain, convince, and when necessary, enrage. I would much rather have someone remember my ideas than my name.

Nor is entertaining the reader the least important part of a writer's mission, although it is the quality most readily dismissed by would-be intellectuals. You cannot persuade someone you are too self-important to interest. The notion that "serious" writing has to be as dull as mortgage paperwork has been foisted upon us by academics who couldn't write a grocery list without ten pages of footnotes.

A writer's goal should not be to stretch out one small, frail conceit into a book the reader can barely lift, but to pack as many fierce ideas into one cleanly written essay or column as he or she can do. If you cannot say a thing simply and clearly, it simply means you have no clear idea of what you want to say.

Of course, different audiences have various needs and differing expectations—which only a fool would ignore. Consider three of the newspapers in which I have been privileged to publish occasional commentaries: *The Wall Street Journal, The Washington Post,* and the *New York Post.* When you write for *The Wall Street Journal,* you write for people with investments. When you write for *The Washington Post,* you write for people with positions. And when you write for the *New York Post,* you write for people with jobs. None of these audiences is more important than the others (although, as a coal-miner's son and a career soldier, my heart will always be with those who labor for their paychecks). To engage and convince, you must write in a style and vocabulary appropriate to the specific readership, patrician or populist (and in 900 words, as editors sternly remind me).

It is not a matter, as many imagine, of reaching the "most important" audience. Each audience is important in our country. Each citizen has value and deserves the writer's respect and best efforts. I am bewildered by those self-important scribblers willing to write off millions of Americans as unworthy of the products of their pens. My goal is to reach the man driving the car, as well as the passenger with the briefcase in the backseat.

As a far better writer than I shall ever be once put it, "Only connect."


This book was assembled because I was annoyed. Our Secretary of Defense and his fawning train of courtiers had carried their self-adoration a step too far. During and immediately after our recent, noble war to depose the regime of Saddam Hussein, a number of Donald Rumsfeld's posse of commissars, creatures with no first-hand experience either of the military or of the savage harshness of this world, insisted that none of our generals or admirals or military veterans were worth a damn and that civilians who had never tied on a combat boot knew best how to wield our military. They ridiculed the voices of experience, even implying that those in uniform had a yellow streak, while the civilian lions safe at their Washington desks were models not only of wisdom but of courage.

Sorry, your three-button majesties, but those of us who served *did* get it right—and called the game far more accurately than those who declared that Iraq might be conquered with airpower alone, while a handful of troops took a Sunday drive to Baghdad. I offer what I wrote, unaltered, as evidence.

But those who had been too important to serve in uniform when they were young and ambitious were far too important to listen now that they were older and powerful. General Eric Shinseki, an honest and admirable soldier, was mocked in the courtyard of the neo-con temple for suggesting that it might take as many as two hundred thousand soldiers to occupy Iraq. Yet, as I write, there are nearly that many troops on the Tigris and Euphrates. We may decide to send more.

General Shinseki was right, and the SecDef's blustering scalawags were wrong. But we will never hear an admission or an apology from any of those gods of war in size-48 trousers.

During our recent war, we heard a great deal of dishonest criticism of retired military officers from our Secretary of Defense and his Kmart KGB. A man of deeply flawed greatness (but of greatness, nonetheless), Donald Rumsfeld himself was the worst offender. Piqued that retired officers dared to criticize any aspect of his performance, and forgetting that we live in America, not in the Spain of Philip II, Rumsfeld dismissed our veterans with a degree of contempt even greater than that he shows to those who remain on active duty. Men who had bled in battle and earned our nation's highest honors were ridiculed as "armchair generals" in an Orwellian twist of language meant to disguise the fact that *all* of Rumsfeld's immediate subordinates were, in fact, armchair generals, with the crumbs of lunatic theories strewn across soft, expansive laps.

America may, indeed, be the new Rome, but Secretary Rumsfeld has not yet been hailed as Caesar. He might show a hint of humility to the Senate and the people, as well as to the legions guarding the barbarian frontier.

Who better to explain to the American people what military operations mean than those who have served in uniform?

Yes, a few former military officers, new to television, got camera fever and fell under the spell of the newsroom's excitement, making dire pronouncements that soon embarrassed them. But the real veterans, men such as retired Generals Barry McCaffrey, Wes Clark, Al Gray, Charles Krulak, Gordon Sullivan, George Joulwan, Montgomery Meigs, David Grange, and numerous veterans of lesser rank did the public a worthy service by explaining war's complexities. Not every one of them judged each development correctly—but their batting average was vastly higher than that of the pundits who declared victory at night, only to insist we had been defeated the next morning.

It is not only the right but the duty of those who have served to make our voices heard, to speak for those still in uniform who cannot speak for themselves. If we do not explain our military's needs, dilemmas, limitations, and potential, we leave the debate to those who scorn our soldiers as the mere janitors of strategy. If war is too important to be left to the generals—a cheap platitude—then military policy is far too important to be left to political hacks. We speak no treason when we tell the truth to our fellow citizens.

This book is divided into one section that attempts to come to terms with the future's strategic demands upon our country and the emerging realities of a world in the midst of one of history's great transitions, and into another that addresses our post-9/11 wars. The latter section is drawn from newspaper commentaries. I have always been suspicious of books compiled from newspaper pieces (I'm eating a portion of crow, which should be featured on every menu in Washington), but most of the commentaries republished here were written not simply to comment on a given day's or week's events, but to try to explain, in the clearest terms possible, the conditions of modern warfare and the environment of contemporary strategy.

That said, the book you hold in your hand does *not* pretend to be a definitive account of our latest wars; on the contrary, my interests lie in the nature of conflict, now and in the future. The enduring accounts of our campaigns in Afghanistan and Iraq will be written by the soldiers and Marines who fought and won them so splendidly, and by those admirable journalists who went to war beside our troops, who shared their risks, and who possessed the humility to learn about war from nineteen-year-old soldiers and Marines. This is an attempt to understand, not to chronicle. For the high drama of battle and the inside stories of tactical engagements the reader will need to turn elsewhere. The great books will come, in time, from the eyewitnesses.

Lastly, I must thank General Barry McCaffrey for his generosity in contributing a few words to this book. His time is much in demand and his advice is sought by our highest elected and appointed officials. But he is as loyal to those who served with him as he was courageous when leading them. A genuine hero while in uniform, General McCaffrey has continued to work for the good of our country and our military after the end of his formal service. He is an exemplary American. I have been privileged to know him and to serve with him.

My sole criticism of General McCaffrey is that his remarks make me sound far braver than I ever was. I just wanted to be a good soldier, so I did what appeared to be necessary, to the best of my abilities. Most of it was great fun.

The praise reflects the man himself, not me. He led. I was proud to follow.

Ralph Peters
The summer solstice 2003

# PART I

## Our Future

# Rolling Back Radical Islam

## Parameters

*Autumn 2002*

You cannot win a war if you do not fight, and you cannot win a peace through inattention. In peace and war, the American response to the violent extremism that so damages the Islamic world has been as halting and reactive as it has been reluctant. We simply do not want to get involved more deeply than "necessary." But Muslim extremists are determined to remain involved with us.

We are not at war with Islam. But the most radical elements within the Muslim world are convinced that they are at war with us. Our fight is with the few, but our struggle must be with the many. For decades we have downplayed—or simply ignored—the hate-filled speech directed toward us, the monstrous lessons taught by extremists to children, and the duplicity of so many states we insisted were our friends. But nations do not have friends—at best, they have allies with a confluence of interests. We imagine a will to support our endeavors where there is only a pursuit of advantage. And we deal with cynical, corrupt old men who know which words to say to soothe our

3

diplomats, while the future lies with the discontented young, to whom the poison of blame is always delicious.

Hatred taught to the young seems an ineradicable cancer of the human condition. And the accusations leveled against us by terrified, embittered men fall upon the ears of those anxious for someone to blame for the ruin of their societies, for the local extermination of opportunity, and for the poverty guaranteed by the brute corruption of their compatriots and the selfish choices of their own leaders. Above all, those futureless masses yearn to excuse their profound individual inadequacies and to explain away the prison walls their beliefs have made of their lives.

In late spring 2002, headlines claimed that intelligence leads should have alerted President Bush to impending terrorist attacks prior to September 11, 2001. But a few tips from FBI field offices are easily lost in the colossal noise of government, their value clear only—ruefully so—in retrospect. Though important tactically, those memos were as nothing compared to the countless warnings we had been given as a strategic drama played out openly before us—while we willfully shut our eyes—for the last quarter of a century. Islamic extremists never made a secret of their general intent and often were specific in their threats. The tragedies of 9/11 were not so much the result of an intelligence failure as of a collective failure to face the reality confronting us.

Throughout much of the 1990s, intelligence personnel were not quite forbidden to consider religion as a strategic factor, but the issue was considered soft and nebulous—as well as potentially embarrassing in those years of epidemic political correctness. Now, of course, religion may be discussed in intelligence circles, if bracketed with careful disclaimers noting that all religions have problems and that we are not bigoted toward any one religion. But what if a great world religion is bigoted toward us? Might we, even now, just wish the hatred and prejudice away?

The time has come for a modest degree of honesty. The good news is that the Islamic world, on its populous, decisive frontiers, is far more hopeful than we might suspect in the wake of recent events. While we must deal with fanatical, soulless killers in the present, Islam's future is undecided. The door to a brighter tomorrow has not closed—far from it—and millions of Muslims are willing to keep that door open, despite the threats of a legion of fanatics. A struggle of immense proportions and immeasurable importance is under way for the soul of Islam, a mighty contest to decide between a humane, tolerant, and progressive faith, and a hangman's vision of a punitive God and a humankind defined by prohibitions. And we have not even noticed.


We have been looking in the wrong direction, because that is where we have been conditioned to look. This great battle—this war for the future of one of the world's great religions (and, certainly, its most restive and unfinished)—is not being fought in the Arab homelands, which insist upon our attention with the temper of spoiled children, distracting us from better prospects elsewhere. The contest between competing Muslim visions, between those who would turn back the clock and those who believe they must embrace the future, has already been lost in the sands of Arabia. Fortunately, the Arab homelands are far less critical than our policymakers and strategists unthinkingly believe.

Blinded by oil and riveted by the Arab-Israeli conflict, leaders and legislators alike have failed to reexamine their thinking for the past forty years. Now we must change our beliefs and our behaviors. It is time to write off the Arab homelands of Islam as lost. They are as incapable of constructive change as they are unwilling even to consider liberal transformations. They have been left behind by history and their response has been to blame everyone but themselves—and to sponsor terror (sometimes casually, but often officially). Much of the Arab world has withdrawn into a fortress of intolerance and self-righteousness as psychologically comfortable as it is practically destructive. They are, through their own fault, as close to hopeless as any societies and cultures upon this earth.

Of course, we need not call back our ambassadors from the Middle East, nor could we cease dealing with the oil states entirely. But it is time to shift our focus and our energies, to recognize, belatedly, that Islam's center of gravity lies far from Riyadh or Cairo, that it is in fact a complex series of centers of gravity, each more hopeful than the Arab homelands. On its frontiers, from Detroit to Jakarta, Islam is a vivid, dynamic, vibrant, effervescent religion of changing shape and gorgeous potential. But Islam's local identities are far from decided in its struggling borderlands, and, in times of tumult, any religion can turn toward the darkness as easily as toward the light.

We should make no mistake: This struggle between religious forms, between prescriptive, repressive doctrine and the sublime adventure of faith, is one of the two great strategic issues of our time—along with the redefinition of the socio-economic roles of women, their transition from being the property of men to being equal partners with men (which is the most profound social development in human history).

The United States will never be the decisive factor in the struggle for the future of Islam. That role is reserved for Muslims themselves. But we can play a far more constructive role than we have yet done—usually on the margins, but sometimes from within unfinished societies. Until now, we have not even bothered to participate.

Our focus on the Middle East has been so exclusive that we have come to see Islam largely through an Arab prism. But the Islam of the Middle East is as fixed, as unreflective, and ultimately as brittle as concrete. We have forgotten that Islam is the youngest of the world's great religions, that it is still very much a work-in-progress on its vast frontiers, and that its forms are at least as various as the myriad confessions and sects of Christendom.

Driven by the ferocity of events, we have begun to react militarily to the violence in Islam's borderlands, from the Caucasus to the Philippines, as well as in that eternal frontier state, Afghanistan. And much more military engagement will be necessary in the future. But our military can address only the problems of the moment, problems rooted in yesterday. We must begin to examine the dilemmas and opportunities of each new day with greater interest, so that we may help (to the degree we can) struggling societies discover paths to a more peaceful, cooperative tomorrow. Whatever we do or fail to do, our military will be busy throughout the lifetimes of anyone reading these freshly printed lines. Success will never be final, but always a matter of degree—though, sometimes, of high degree: the difference between a bloody contest of civilizations and the routine ebb and flow of lesser conflicts.

Our lack of involvement—indeed, our lack of interest—in Islam's efforts to define its character for the twenty-first century and beyond has abandoned the field to our mortal enemies. Over the past few decades, Middle Eastern oil wealth has been used by the most restrictive, oppressive states to export a regressive, ferociously intolerant and anti-Western form of Islam to mosques and *madrassas* abroad, from the immigrant quarters of London to the back-country of Indonesia. When we noticed anything at all, we dismissed it as no more than an annoyance, our attitude drifting between the Pollyanna notion that everyone is entitled to his or her own form of religion (no matter if it preaches hatred and praises mass murder) and the "serious" policymaker's view that religion is a tertiary issue, far less instructive and meaningful than GDP numbers or arms deals.

But no other factor is as important as belief in this disturbed and dangerous world. The ease with which today's Americans of diverse faiths interact in social settings has allowed us to forget that our ancestors, in their homelands, massacred one another over the contents of the communion cup, or slaughtered Jews and called it God's desire, or delivered their faith to their colonies with Bibles and breech-loading rifles. Some even brought their hatreds to our shores, but America conquered their bigotries over the generations—although even we have not vanquished intolerance completely. Still, for most contemporary Americans, religion has become as comfortable as it remains comforting. But human history is largely a violent contest of gods and the men who served them, and our age is the latest, intense serial in a saga that shaped our earliest myths and may predate the oldest scraps of folklore.

Religious intolerance always returns in times of doubt and disorder. Our age of immense possibilities is simultaneously one of the breakdown of old orders, of failure in those cultures whose formulae for social organization do not allow effective competition with the world's leading economic and cultural powers, and of the extreme fanaticism that fear of change sparks in the human heart. Fundamentalist terrorism has not arisen despite the progress the world has made, but because of it.

In times of tumult, men and women cling to what they know. They seek simple answers to daunting complexities. And religious extremists around the world, in every major religion, have been delighted to provide those simple answers. It does not matter if those answers are true, so long as they shift blame from the believer's shoulders and promise punishment to enemies, real or imagined. Throughout history, from the days of Jewish rebels against Rome and Islam's early and recurrent fractures, through sixteenth-century Spanish Catholicism alarmed at the advent of alternate paths to salvation, to nineteenth-century Protestantism startled by Charles Darwin, religions under siege invariably have responded by returning to doctrinal rigor and insisting upon the damnation of nonbelievers. Each major religion has known its share of threats to its philosophical and practical integrity. Our age happens to be a losing era for Islam, when its functionality as a mundane organizing tool has decayed in much of the world—just as European Christianity had done by the beginning of the sixteenth century.

Islam certainly is not hateful in its essence—but a disproportionate number of its current adherents need to hate to avoid the agony of self-knowledge. The basic problem is daunting: We face a failing civilization in the Middle East. But if we have the least spark of wisdom, we will do all that we can to ensure the failure does not spread from cultures that have made socioeconomic suicide pacts with themselves to lands that still might adapt to the demands of the modern and postmodern worlds.

Religions change, because men change them. Fundamentalists insist upon an ahistorical stasis, but evolution in the architecture of faith has always been essential to, and reflective of, human progress. Certainty is comforting, but a religion's capacity for adaptive behavior unleashes the energies necessary to renew both the faith and the society in which it flourishes. On its frontiers, Islam remains capable of the changes necessary to make it, once again, a healthy, luminous faith whose followers can compete globally on its own terms. But the hard men from that religion's ancient homelands are determined to frustrate every exploratory effort they can. The Muslim extremist diaspora from the Middle East has one consistent message: Return to the past, for that is what God wants. Beware, no matter his faith, of the man who presumes to tell you what God wants.

It cannot be accomplished, of course, this longed-for return to a golden age of sanctity and success that is nine parts myth and, at most, one part history. But the bloody-handed terrorists and their mentors are determined to pay any price to frustrate those Muslims who believe that God is capable of smiling, or that it is possible to change the earth without challenging Heaven.


Our strategic blunder has been to attempt to work outward from Islam's inner sanctum. But the greatest—in fact, the only—chance we have to positively influence this struggle over the future of Islam lies in precisely the opposite approach: We must realign our efforts to work inward from the edges. Our assets and our energies should be spent where change is still possible or already under way, not squandered where opposition to all that we value has hardened implacably.

We have not even gotten the numbers right. In terms both of population density and potential productivity, wealth, and power, Islam's center of gravity lies to the east of Afghanistan, not to the west. The world's most populous "Muslim" countries stretch far to the east of the Indus River: Indonesia, India, Bangladesh . . . Pakistan . . . and other regional states, such as Malaysia, make this the real cockpit of crisis. And, thus far, the view on the ground is more encouraging than baleful news reporting would have it.

While Pakistan has been wracked with phenomenal corruption and suffers from a ravaged education system that opened the door for the pernicious expansion of fundamentalist religious schools, and even though its economy is in exemplary shambles, that most-endangered state still has not strayed irretrievably into the extremist camp. It may—*may*— even have turned a corner toward some fitful progress. But the path to economic, social, and cultural health will be long and steep and, together with impoverished, hard-luck Bangladesh (once governed from Islamabad), Pakistan remains the least promising of the region's states. Elsewhere, the picture is much brighter, if only we had the clarity of vision to appreciate the plodding reality behind the sensational headlines.

India and Indonesia are the two countries with the largest Muslim populations (despite India's Hindu majority, more than 15 percent of its billion people are Muslims, outnumbering the Islamic population of Pakistan). Each state presents a reason for hope, though in rather different ways. While Islam's frontiers include states as diverse and dispersed as Nigeria and Azerbaijan, Kyrgyzstan, the pseudo-state of Kosova, and Turkey, the most powerful determinants of the future course of Islam will probably be the success or failure of modernizing forces in Indonesia and India. And, frankly, we haven't a clue about the on-the-ground reality in either country.

First, India. Currently, militants tolerated (if no longer actively sponsored) by Pakistan have staged yet another cross-border massacre in Indian-ruled Kashmir. New Delhi is pondering retaliation, despite U.S. anxieties over the effects another Indo-Pakistani conflict (perhaps with a nuclear exchange) would have on our war against terror. Recently, we saw another gruesome flare-up of interfaith violence within India, as aggressive Hindu fundamentalists got an unpleasant surprise in the northwestern Indian state of Gujarat when Muslims responded to their hooliganism by burning them alive in a railway passenger car. The Hindu response was to massacre hundreds of Muslims across the state. So we are left with the impression, intensified by the media's interest only in blood, disaster, and suffering on the subcontinent, that India remains locked in a hopeless struggle between Hindus and Muslims, both within and beyond its borders. The overarching reality is more complex, and far more encouraging.

Recurring violence between Hindus and Muslims within India is undeniably a serious problem. Widespread pogroms a decade ago killed Muslims by the thousands, as well as hundreds of Hindus. The founding of India and Pakistan was anointed with the blood of at least half a million Muslims and Hindus. But to gain an objective picture of the situation, we first need to consider the broad, enduring trends within multiconfessional India, and not merely the anomalies within those trends: In fact, the frequency and intensity of interfaith violence has decreased impressively over the past half century— despite the resurgence of virulent Hindu fundamentalism among a small minority of India's citizens. Then we need to consider the numbers. With Muslims composing almost a fifth of its billion people, and given the poverty that still afflicts as much as four-fifths of India's population, India looks more like a success story than a failure when it comes to tolerance. We may deplore the intermittent violence and death when it occurs, but today's India is, to a far greater degree, the story of the dog that didn't bark, of the hundreds of millions of Hindus and Muslims (as well as those of other faiths) who do *not* kill each other and who, despite seductive prejudices, work together as Indians first, whether in the government, in the military, or in business.

Overwhelmingly, India's Muslims have accepted an Indian identity. Islamic extremism has not made nearly the inroads it has across the border in Pakistan or even next door in Bangladesh. Indian Muslims realize, for the most part, that their faith cannot express itself in acts of aggression without paying a high price, and that reasonable accommodation is much to their advantage. For all its merciless corruption, India is a rule-of-law state, displaying surprising religious diversity within its government and armed forces. All this seems to have encouraged a more flexible, markedly more tolerant form of Islam. One should not paint the picture in pious, stained-glass hues—and some would argue that Muslim docility is the result of repression—but there is something to be said for a country where a Muslim can enjoy a beer in public, where the murder of a compromised woman by her relatives is not accepted as business as usual, and where local pogroms shock citizens throughout the country.

In a way, the situation of Muslims in India resembles that of Muslims in the United States (of which more below): Under competitive pressures, the religion adapts and evolves, no matter how fiercely an older generation digs in its heels or how appealing the radical pitch may be to the disoriented young. Despite the nagging violence that reappears like outbreaks of plague, the competitive aspects of Hinduism may, inadvertently, be doing more to keep Islam healthy than all the mosques between the Atlas and the Hindu Kush. States in which a single, repressive confession reigns are ill-equipped for change, while multi-confessional states, if governed by law, enjoy the dynamism sparked by competitive pressures. Where there is more than one religious option, no religion can afford to underperform.

India matters to the United States for a host of reasons, from the inevitability of a strategic compact between our two raucously democratic states—despite the inane bickering of the past, for which both sides bear their share of blame—to the long-term economic and human potential of the subcontinent. But the unremarked importance of a developing state in which Muslims live productively and equitably alongside citizens of other confessions may prove of the first importance. Above all, the Islamic world needs success stories to compete with its myths of persecution at the hands of others. Afghanistan, if only we are wise enough to commit adequate resources to its reconstruction, could surprise the world by becoming one small success story. But a deeper socioeconomic harmonization of Islam with other faiths in India would provide a beacon for all the lands lapped by the Indian Ocean and adjacent waters where Islam has come ashore.


The importance—and promise—of Indonesia is even greater than that of India as regards the future of Islam. Of all the many countries I have visited, none has been so grossly misrepresented in the media. If Indonesia shows up at all on our television screens or in our newspapers and journals the story likely will warn of Islamic terrorists. Even a very fine *New York Times* reporter, covering this nation of 200 million Muslims on a fly-through, wrote only of the dangers Muslims in Indonesia pose to the West, not of the promise of Indonesia's Islamic alternatives.

The truth is that Indonesian Islam poses no danger whatsoever to the United States or to its citizens—or to anyone else, except Muslim extremists. The radical fundamentalists and sponsors of terror in Indonesia are a small fraction of believers. The danger—real, if slight—comes not from the syncretic, humane, tolerant, homegrown forms of Islam. The danger comes from models of Islam exported from Saudi Arabia and elsewhere, and insinuated into Indonesia through infusions of cash, missionaries, and hateful propaganda, by the building of mosques and *madrassas* where secular schools and clinics are badly needed, and through bribes—bribery seeming to be Indonesia's national sport. Yet, as one friend put it, the unhappiest investors in the world are not those Americans whose fortunes burst with the dot-com bubble, but the Saudis who spent millions upon millions to bring extreme fundamentalism to Indonesia. As they do with everyone else, in matters of business or of belief, the Indonesians took the money, then did whatever they wanted to do. In a phrase well-known to regional hands and frustrated businessmen alike, "The Indonesians just won't stay bought."

You can go to showcase fundamentalist schools in Solo, in central Java, and hear all the denunciations of the West you can absorb between lunch and dinner. Terrorists, both Indonesians and deadly vagabonds from abroad, certainly use Indonesia as a base. Within Indonesia's sprawling territories (more than 17,000 islands, of which over 6,000 are inhabited to some degree), there are, undoubtedly, terrorist hideouts and training camps. And homegrown extremists have sparked or intensified civil strife in Ambon, Sulawesi, the Moluccas, Kalimantan, Aceh, etc., etc.

Yet, except for Aceh, where a long-term separatist struggle continues, the root causes of most of the interfaith violence in

Indonesia have been struggles over the control of territory, local power, and economic benefits, all triggered by government-sponsored internal migration from overpopulated, Muslim Java to less-developed islands where Islam was either a new or a minority faith. Extremists, both Muslim and Christian, have used these struggles to their own ends. But in Jogjakarta, the old cultural capital of Muslim Java, the elite and the middle class send their children to Christian-run schools for a better education, they use Christian-sponsored hospitals because of the higher-quality care, and they have far more interest in Britney Spears than in Osama bin Laden.

This is not a metaphorical statement—while I was recently in Indonesia, Miss Spears got far more air-time than Osama did, which made me wonder whether Mr. bin Laden doesn't have a point concerning the cultural brutality of the West. Now, hard-headed politicos may dismiss the Cult of Britney (and of bare-midriff blondes in general, for whom one cannot help feeling a certain admiration), but a society in which the girls and women have been watching Christina Aguilera's displays of life-affirming exuberance on video is unlikely ever to sign up for the whole fundamentalist package. Indeed, when confronted with the word "fundamentalist," the young women of Indonesia tend to concentrate on the first three letters.

Islam came to Indonesia approximately eight centuries ago, through trade, not conquest, but gathered force only about 500 years back, its sudden appeal contemporary with the Reformation in Europe. Hinduism and Buddhism (and animist folk religions, which persist indestructibly as part of Indonesian Islam) had longer reigns in the archipelago than Islam has yet enjoyed, and Indonesians have always taken a "wear what fits" attitude toward the Muslim faith. On Java, Indonesia's indisputable heartland, the mystical, questioning

Sufi form of Islam shaped the faith early on, and although the coastal regions grew cosmopolitan with international trade, inland Java and the interior of the other great islands long were isolated from the world, allowing Islam to digest, rather than fully suppress, the multiple forms of local belief.

Technically speaking, Indonesia may contain almost 200 million Muslims, but less than 20 percent of them—and that is a generous estimate—would begin to pass muster with the strict mullahs of the Middle East. Even Muslims who describe themselves as devout include a range of superstitions and religious borrowings in their practices, from a belief in saints and shrines (anathema to strict Sunni Islam) to the conviction in rural parts of Sulawesi that transvestites have an inside track with Allah. And then there is the Indonesian fondness for an occasional beer. One woman showing me about described her female employer (none of this sounds terribly Middle Eastern, does it?) as a "most devoted Muslim, very strict," then added approvingly, "she doesn't pray during the day or wear religious clothing, and she likes to drink a little bit, but she is really a very good Muslim."

This is not intended to belittle the devotion of Indonesians. On the contrary, they are often profoundly religious (nowhere more so than on Hindu Bali, though). But they have adapted Islam to their own culture, rather than adapting their culture to Islam. Certainly, some Indonesians are more conservative in their beliefs than others. But despite the inevitable outbreaks of violence that punctuate every history and the increasing popularity of making the Haj to Mecca (a combination pilgrimage, holiday, and shopping trip for those with whom I spoke), Indonesians tend to take a live-and-let-live attitude toward faith. It is enormously frustrating to the extremists.

There long have been efforts to "clean up" Islam in the archipelago, with reports dating back centuries of the execution of Sufis who preached a curiously Lutheran doctrine of salvation through faith alone, then went on to scorn prayers, religious doctrine, and mosque visits as inconsequential compared to the faith within one's heart. In the nineteenth century, as steamships made the journey to Mecca cheaper, swifter, and safer, ever more islanders made the Haj (today they travel by chartered jet, after riding to their local airport in convoys of buses). While Aceh always had a Sunni bent and enduring ties to the Arabian Peninsula—including a school and hostel maintained in Mecca for visiting scholars—this new exposure to the Islam of the religion's ancient homelands inspired a minority of Sumatrans, Javanese, and others to attempt to reform their religion at home. The movement gained some force early in the twentieth century, and remains very much alive today under the Muhammadiyah banner, whose followers number somewhere under 20 percent of the Islamic population.

But even these "fundamentalists" had a strong progressive wing that believed in education and argued that Islam was not incompatible with progress. While the numerous Muhammadiyah schools and universities the visitor sees scattered about today have campuses full of girls in conservative dress (though not veiled), the real point is that they have campuses full of girls. And the curricula are far more progressive than anything in the Arab homelands. Indonesian higher education is not competitive with Western university programs, but whether religious or state-sponsored, it beats an education that focuses exclusively on the Koran and its medieval commentators.

One enduring image of Indonesia is from a small "supermarket" on the dusty edge of Solo. The young cashier wore a mini-skirt that wasted no fabric on modesty, while the girl bagging groceries wore demure Islamic garb, including the local head scarf that resembles the hair covering worn by German women at the turn of the fifteenth century. The two girls were friends, and there was no tension in their interaction. While Indonesia remains a male-chauvinist society, the opportunities afforded to women have dramatically outpaced anything in the Middle East—and this is a country with a popular, elected female president. The extreme liberality of divorce laws harms families and women alike, but there is a spirit of independence and spunk among the younger, better-educated generation of Indonesian women that makes a striking, positive contrast to Turkey (another "Muslim" country for which one is hopeful in the long term).

Indonesia faces a long list of challenges, some of which may prove intractable, from ethnic and religious violence on the outer islands to the worst corruption between Lagos and Tijuana (corruption, not fundamentalism, is the country's primary obstacle to progress, and corruption may prove the unwitting ally of fundamentalism in Indonesia, as it has been elsewhere). Yet the manner in which the United States has alternately scolded and ignored this huge, strategically positioned country, without making any serious efforts to peer behind the occasional nasty headline, is simply remarkable. For all its many problems, this is a country where Islam has spited the fundamentalists thus far, where the overwhelming majority of Muslims want no part of violent extremism, and where Islam is still an evolving religion that may adapt to the demands of a new century better than it will anywhere else in Asia—despite Malaysia's economic headstart. Throw in its proximity to vital sea lanes, and our blithe dismissal of Indonesia's importance begins to anger anyone who thinks seriously about America's future interests.

Indonesians must solve their own problems, of course. They must determine the content and contours of their own faith. But we can help through patient, informed engagement. Our enemies, acknowledged or not, are present and active, fighting to drag Indonesian Islam down to a Middle Eastern oppressiveness. They have spent a great deal of money to persuade Indonesians that intolerance is a virtue, that Christians and Jews are devils, and that God is a stern disciplinarian who expects men to imitate him. Thus far, they have failed. But in these tumultuous times, as Indonesia struggles with democracy, economic depression, and the unprecedented pace of global change, the future remains uncertain.

We Americans have not even been in the game, when we should be engaging Indonesians—despite their excesses in East Timor during their nervous transition to democracy—to impress them with the benefits of the rule of law applied fairly to all citizens, electoral openness, and business done honestly in the global marketplace and at home. We should not go as pontificating crusaders, but as thoughtful, open-eyed counterparts. To use a preferred image, Indonesia does not need and will not tolerate the heroic surgery characteristic of American foreign policy, but demands a long treatment with strategic acupuncture. We should engage Indonesia with our goals set half a century out. It may be un-American to think in such long time spans, but we are already more than a quarter century into the active struggle for Islam's future. And no single country is more important to that future than Indonesia.

Islam—the newest, yet the most anxiously traditional, of the world's major religions—is under phenomenal stress, especially in those states and regions where its practices are the most conservative. Any culture which oppresses its women and excludes them from education and the workplace cannot possibly compete with the West and its intensifying human efficiency. The matter of women's freedom is the defining issue of our age. The most profound and fateful divide between human cultures today places the failures decisively on the side that would continue to deny women their basic human rights and equitable opportunities, with the successes on the side that realizes, at last, that women are better suited to be men's partners than their property.

Social and economic freedom for women constitutes the most sweeping revolution in human history, yet this enabling revolution has, thus far, passed by the core Muslim states of the Middle East. My own fondest hope, as the United States intervened in Afghanistan, was that a bomb dropped by a Navy fighter flown by a female pilot would kill Osama bin Laden. It would have been the perfect image of both the West's triumph and a crucial factor in that triumph. But whether Mr. bin Laden is alive or dead at this hour, we should not mistake his war for other than what it is—a war not merely against the West, but against half of mankind, against all women. The West's liberation of women (which has been, to a great degree, their self-liberation in the face of stubborn resistance) is the essential element that renders so many Muslims irreconcilable to us. This particular set of freedoms threatens not only the Muslim male's religious prejudices, but his central identity. Until it successfully addresses the issue of women's rights—full rights—Islam will not compete successfully, in any area, with the West. In that regard, too, Indonesia offers a hopeful example among foreign states.

Numerous other cultural factors, veiled with religious justifications, haunt the old Muslim heartlands. The situation is, indeed, so dire that one sometimes wonders if there is any hope at all. Yes, there is hope, but change must—and will—come first on Islam's frontiers.

Last, we come to a brief mention of what may prove the most vital frontier: North America. September 11 created a wide variety of stresses upon and distress for America's Muslim citizens and residents. This newest body of immigrants, some of whom still have not fitted themselves fully to a profoundly different society from that of their countries of origin, reacted with complex and varied emotions: horror; anger at the damage done to their adopted country as well as to their faith; alarm that their faith might be misunderstood by their fellow Americans; worries about blind retribution directed against them; anxiety to show that they, too, are good Americans; and, sometimes, defensiveness about the often-disastrous societies they had left behind, incendiary excuses for the inexcusable, and, among the most disappointed and disaffected, muted pleasure that the proud had been given a public blow by the weak. Every single emotion—these and more—felt by our fellow Americans who believe that "There is no God but God, and Muhammad is his Prophet," is understandable when we set aside our own emotions. American Muslims are in perhaps the most difficult situation of any immigrant group since the Irish fled the Great Famine. And yet there is cause to be more hopeful for them than for Muslims anywhere else in the world.

As so many religious or ethnic groups have done before them, America's Muslim immigrants will need to jettison some of the behaviors brought along in their baggage, especially as regards the regulation of women. Many of our Muslim citizens have long since integrated into American society—some have been fully Americanized for generations—while some new arrivals are still in the process of adapting. All of this is the normal stuff of the immigrant's experience, with its shocks, discords, and ultimate success. What matters not only to us but to the world is that the long-overdue, liberal reformation of Islam is likeliest to happen here, in the United States.

Just as every other major religion has adapted to the unique challenges and opportunities of American life, Islam will do so as well. To retain the devotion of the young, generation after generation, as the possibilities (and the temptations) of America wean them from old behaviors and antique prejudices, Islam will have to travel the humane route pioneered by American Protestantism, Catholicism, and Judaism. There will be great complaints and concerns. But the ultimate effect of American life is to humanize the practice of faith. The great debate in the Islamic world as the decades advance may well be between progressive American Islam and more conservative forms lingering abroad.


In the dark days of the Cold War, when the world made grisly sense, American strategists touted the notion of "rolling back" communism. In fact, we never rolled back much—at least until 1989—but did our best to hold the line. But roll-back may have been a strategy far ahead of its time, a concept waiting for more propitious circumstances. It appears to be eminently suited as an approach for dealing with violent Islamic extremism.

We did not imagine we could defeat Soviet communism starting in Moscow; likewise, Islamic extremism cannot be engaged most effectively where it was born and bred. We must work our way in from the hopeful, unsettled frontiers, from Africa through Asia, in the Balkans, and in North America. The complex, exasperating, and frequently inspiring world of Islam faces a historically unique challenge. An entire religious civilization, of remarkable variety, must change if it is to survive economically and culturally. We are foolish if we do not do what lies within our power to enable that change to occur.

# Who We Fight

## American Heritage

*August/September 2002*

"His temperament lacked joy and good will toward men . . . and his soul gorged on two dishes, his ego and his god. Egotism and religion formed the content and the contours of his life, and he felt no sympathy with other human beings, since his eyes looked only upward, never down. His faith was gruesome and dark, for his god was a terrifying being, and the only lesson he drew from religion was fear. His respect for his god was all the deeper and more profound since he lacked respect for every other creature. The common goal of despotism and religion for religion's sake is conformity, and conformity was ever the crutch of his impoverished spirit. [He] could imagine no higher achievement than regimented faith. . . ."

Each word above applies perfectly to Osama bin Laden, but those lines were written 200 years ago by Friedrich Schiller, the German man of letters, about Philip II of Spain, who had died two centuries earlier still, after a literal reign of terror. As we approach the first anniversary of the worst terrorist incident in American history—though far from the worst in the history of the world—a great deal has been said about historical precedents. But we are most apt to page through our books in search of parallels of plot and similarities of event, though parallels of character and recurring, inextinguishable forms of personality may prove at least as illuminating.

The only salient difference between Philip II and Osama bin Laden is that the former enjoyed—if he may be said to have enjoyed anything—official power and formal authority, while Osama bin Laden had to construct his power and convince men of his authority. But their bitter souls are twins.

Such men are an enduring human type, the fanatical, aggressive believer, driven by devils of his own devising. The study of their limited hearts and fear-gripped souls must be instructive to even the best among us, for in their deficiencies and deformities we see not only the enduring foes of liberty, of conscience and warm faith, but a reflection of the enemy who lurks within us all, of Cain.

Philip II and Osama bin Laden share an apocalyptic vision of man's fate with many another figure cast upon the shores of history by the seas of change, men like Thomas Müntzer, the utopian avenger of the Reformation who baptized Germany in blood, and John Brown of Bleeding Kansas and Harpers Ferry. Such men require a vengeful God and the belief that few are chosen for salvation, the conviction that this world is hopelessly sin-wracked and that the lives of others may be sacrificed in atonement. Each figure is ultimately a blasphemer against his own religion, having appointed himself God's instrument upon earth, assuming the license to kill by the tens or the tens of thousands those who do not share his vision, to purge, to punish, and to sanctify.

Much has been said—naively, if with good intent—to assure us that Islam is not the problem behind the tragedies of September 11, 2001. On the contrary, Islam is very much the problem, but the problem is not unique to Islam. Extreme and violent fundamentalism is the dark familiar of each of the great monotheist religions, as well as of Hinduism, whose origins we cannot trace, but which may well have been, in lost millennia, a monotheist religion too (our monotheist religions may simply be too young and insufficiently decayed to have spawned the myriad fractured gods of older religions). The comfort of faith is always a tenuous thing, in every civilization, and in times of tumult and upheaval, when systems of belief and social organization collapse and mutate, the fearful among us crave certainty.

The rise of intolerance during periods of accelerated change is as predictable as heightened selfishness in times of famine. When the familiar walls fall down, the weak fortify themselves with a faith of stone, impenetrable to reason, evidence, or mercy. Fanatics reap their most abundant harvest of followers in the deserts of fear. When their faith is under assault and the social order cracks apart, human beings do not want explanations; they want reassurance and someone to blame. The hour of change is the hour not only of the pioneer but of the demagogue as well. Human history is a series of struggles between those who believe in the future and those who believe in the past. Philip II insisted upon the imposition of past virtues—much exaggerated—on a struggling present, as Osama bin Laden does today. This is a mark of deeply frightened men.

One of the most enduring arguments to accompany humankind down the centuries is over whether the divine force is essentially benevolent or disciplinarian. In their craving for certainty, the weak want rules. But those rules reassure the terrified believer only if they are universal—not just applicable to all but enforced upon all. The possibility of doubt, of

alternative paths, is anathema to those who see only the abyss
beyond the reassuring bonds of ritual and regulation.


Our problems with religious tyrants and God-haunted terrorists are never with strong men but with weak men desperate to
prove their strength to their God. The man who, with alacrity
and even delight, sacrifices other human beings for his own
salvation is the most enduring enemy of all that we term
"humane." The Aztec priest and the punitive Catholic king,
the Protestant madman, the fanatical Muslim and the Hindu
assassin are all disciples of the same godhead. Faulty, bloody
isms come and go, as empires rise and fall, and each renaissance of the spirit or the arts leads to an eventual twilight. All
things created by man acquire a lifespan, be it short or long.
But there is no sign, on earth or in the heavens, that the character of man has evolved in the least down the millennia.

Cain is the enduring human archetype, the man who
lights the fire beneath the martyr and who sends passenger
jets crashing into office towers. On that hot day when Cain
first raised his hand against his brother, surely Abel's fate was
sealed, above all, by his desire to talk things over, to explain
and compromise. Fanatics hate the sound of reasoned words.

Philip II inherited an empire near its apogee, a world
within a world, so powerful and vast that its greatest threats
came not from without but within. Although the Turks chewed
upon Europe's extremities and English privateers nibbled at
Spain's treasure fleets, the body of Philip's empire should have
grown stronger during his reign, nourished by the vigorous
capitalism of his majesty's Netherlands and the silver wealth of
Spain's New World possessions. But Philip sacrificed the
brightest of his territories and condemned the greatest power

of the age to decline and ultimate failure to placate his cruel vision of his God.

Much has been made over the past half-century, by the *Annales* school of historians and others, of the irrelevance of individuals and the irresistible power of the mass to determine history's direction; to a degree, this was a needed corrective to the "great man" theory of history, but the critique was carried to insupportable extremes. Perhaps now, in a new century, we may find our way to a balanced view of history, recognizing that it is sometimes the mass and sometimes the man—and often both—that wrenches the future from the past. Osama bin Laden may be a man of great evil, but he is a great man, nonetheless, in his effect upon his times (like Philip, he will have brought calamity down upon his own kind, not upon his enemies). Certainly, Philip II was *the* great man of his age, although his achievements consistently benefited those whom he opposed. His intolerance drove the pacific Netherlands to learn the arts of war and fight a 40-year struggle for independence; the pious rigor he imposed on Spain discouraged commerce, creativity, and merit, relying on military power as unsustainable in the long term as it was ineffective in the shorter term; the wealth Spain's colonies poured into his treasury destroyed the ethics and initiative of his state, its population, and even its priests (as oil wealth has ravaged Arab civilization); and his uncompromising commitment to his faith, carried to extremes no other mass murderer acting in the name of ideology achieved until the twentieth century, finally ensured the survival of the Protestant faith he sought so long to exterminate. His only enthusiasm was for heaven, and he dutifully created hell on earth.

Were Osama bin Laden to realize the power for which he longs, his reign would be no less savage. Killing heretics and unbelievers—even brothers of less rigorous faith—is a form of prayer for fanatics in every religion. There is no more dangerous man on earth than the one who views killing as cleansing.

It has become fashionable among academic historians— those profound enemies of history—to discount the "black legend" of Spanish misbehavior. But Spain under Philip II was as grim as the vivid Protestant writers—not least Schiller—of the High Romantic era portrayed it. The most creative elements of Spain's population lived in terror, and subject peoples, in Europe and the Americas, suffered incalculably. Philip built nothing but the Escorial, the living tomb in which he buried himself, an edifice that does not even rise to the taste of a Hitler but languishes as the monument of that Ceaucescu among believers. Philip drained his empire and destroyed his own family. He crippled his religion and made it hated. And he died, as Osama bin Laden will (or, perhaps, already has), convinced that he had been God's humble tool.

Philip II offers a perfect example of what these harshest of believers inflict on humankind when granted power. In the Netherlands—his richest, most peaceable provinces—he led the Counter Reformation effort to suppress all forms of religious dissent, whether Lutheran, Calvinist, or of lesser sects. He imposed the Spanish Inquisition in place of the milder local form, torturing and burning men and women until fear touched every citizen, Catholic or Protestant. In the name of his God, Philip lied, cheated, betrayed, and devoured the flower of the Flemish, Walloon, and Dutch nobilities; his armies burned, raped, and murdered their way across the most prosperous landscape in the sixteenth-century world. Cities were sacked with a viciousness uncommon even in those days of looting military companies, and Philip's enemies— those hundreds of thousands he made into his enemies—

became convinced that he would grant no peace but the peace of death, and so they fought him with animal fury. His ritualized terror in the Netherlands convinced England it must resist him at all costs and made kings and princes wary whenever Philip's cold eye glanced their way. No monarch can long govern without trust, unless he has the power to enforce an endless reign of terror. Philip could terrorize, but he lacked the strength to triumph and sustain his victories. Moreover, each apparent victory only strengthened the convictions of his enemies that they were, indeed, in an apocalyptic struggle.

Whether we speak of Philip II or of Osama bin Laden, of kings or renegades, their strength lies in the rigor of their intolerance, but that strength contains the seeds of their destruction. They make it clear to their enemies that the struggle inflicted upon them is a battle for survival, and even their allies come to fear their willfulness and inhumanity.

As Ayatollah Khomeini did to his own country four centuries later, Philip II cut his people off from liberal, international culture. On the eve of its twentieth-century civil war, Spain was history's backwater, scorched by religion, barely literate, and less industrialized than Japan. And that is the essence of Osama bin Laden's prescription for the Muslim world. He speaks of a new golden age of Islam, but he longs for an iron, joyless conformity.

Bin Laden's vision of what the Islamic world must become and which values it should cherish are eerily akin to Philip's yearning for a static, disciplined, somber Spanish empire. Both men readily used the technological innovations of their times to strike their enemies, impressing the world with their ferocity but ultimately failing to achieve their goals (as Osama bin Laden shall fail). Both men disliked the company of women and viewed them as tools at best, unequal to the male before God's throne. Each affected a personal simplicity but spent fortunes on violent religious crusades. Each insisted that his vision of the faith was the only correct one and that the world must conform to that vision. Each man sought to limit sensual pleasures and restrict the arts to religious themes and orthodox forms (although Philip had a good eye for painting, perhaps his sole human virtue). Each feared—indeed hated—freedom and individuality and saw himself as fitted into a hierarchy with only his God above him and all humankind below. Both shared a preference for male company and a taste for blood sports. Neither could bear contradiction, but both served their fanatical vision with devotion, sacrifice, and absolute commitment. Each man saw and felt his God to be terrible, vengeful, and remorseless.

We shall see these men again, in other robes.

Our age is the perfect incubator for these terrorists of the spirit and the flesh. We will meet them, over and over again, throughout our lifetimes. Cain was, above all, a jealous man. And we shall encounter no end of jealous men. Some of them will call upon their God to justify the fist they raise to strike us. But if their persistence discourages us, we may be encouraged by their consistent record of failure. Even when they briefly manage to create their "kingdom of God on earth," it fails in the end. But that is, of course, small consolation to those who must endure the experiment.

These tormented men are always with us, but they come into their own in troubled times. And no age has been as confusing as our own, so full of dislocations and systemic failures. Certainly each succeeding age sees its own days as the most challenging and addled by change. But no preceding generation has faced such swift, complex, layered, liberating, empowering, and threatening changes as our own, and the pace of change will only accelerate from here. We in the United States are at the cutting edge of simultaneous revolutions not only in technologies and communications but in social freedoms, in the participatory roles of the elderly, in racial, religious, and ethnic harmonization, in the re-imagination of the patterns and possibilities of our working lives, in military affairs, and, above all else, in the equalization of relations between men and women. This last transition, which matured only in the past half-century, from woman as property to woman as partner, is not only the most fundamental change in the history of human social organization but also the most threatening to traditional cultures. If there is a single factor that makes our civilization hateful to Osama bin Laden and his acolytes, it is our acceptance of women as full-fledged human beings, threatening the most important power relationship within the conservative Muslim world. Bin Laden is not only terrified of God, but also scared of the girls.

We in the United States are pioneering the *transcendent society*, smashing hierarchies and antique bigotries as we go. It makes us ferociously efficient, just as it horrifies those who cling to yesteryear's verities. Anyone who fears change fears America. Without the least jingoism (since not all change is inherently good), we may fairly claim that the United States has been the most powerful engine of change in human history. But even in our own society many prefer the comfort of clinging to what they know. If change frightens some of our fellow Americans, imagine the terror it arouses abroad, among those who cherish a secure place in a stagnant society at the expense of progress and prosperity.

Yet the rest of the world wants more of what we have—especially the material wealth and power—but traditionalists refuse to pay the cultural price to earn it. If your family's ultimate wealth is the "virtue" of its women, if a woman is owned by the man placed above her by divine sanction, the casual freedom of American life, where men and women speak calmly to each other in public, inspires tremendous rage. It threatens to rob the male of his most enduring wealth, of his last shreds of power. But without that commitment to the rights of the female half of any population, to maximizing your society's human potential, you cannot compete with America. The math isn't hard.

We stand at the beginning of yet another American renaissance, jump-started by the events of September 11, 2001. But our successes will only magnify the failures of those who cannot abide tolerance, freedom, and competition based upon merit. If our country has entered a golden age, then it must also prove a fertile age for fanatics, since the pace and breadth of change will unnerve ever more of the human beings consigned to the realms of failure. Fortunately, we do not face as our enemy a Philip II, armed with the might of empire. The greatest empire of the age is our own, although it is a new, benign—even beneficent—form of empire. Osama bin Laden's imperium is one of hatred but not of competitive power or abilities. He, and those who follow him, will persist in trying to stop our march into the future, but they must fail, as Philip failed before them.

# God's Real Estate

New York Post

*April 13, 2003*

One of the greatest blessings enjoyed by the United States is that God hasn't claimed any local real estate. The insistence in so much of the world that one divinity or another cherishes a specific handful of dust remains one of humankind's great curses.

Viewed honestly, the competition between faiths and creeds over sacred ground remains a cancer of the human condition. Whether we speak of millennia of bloody contests for control of Jerusalem or the bloodshed over plans to build a Hindu temple on the site of a razed mosque in Ayodhya, the importance of Karbala in Iraq or the destruction of Sufi shrines by Muslim fundamentalists, competing claims over bits of earth have spawned the world's most enduring and inherently insoluble conflicts.

The amount of suffering human beings are willing to inflict on one another over a corner of dirt is impossible to reconcile with the basic tenets of any of the world's leading religions. Men will fight for their religion, but they will massacre for their religion's totems. And sacred earth is the greatest totem of all, the ultimate idol.

Certainly, some religious groups in the United States value specific pieces of land, from the national shrine of the Virgin in Emmitsburg, Maryland, to the grounds of the Mormon Temple in Salt Lake City. But the roots do not run sufficiently deep to tap history's underground rivers of blood and, still more vitally, the sanctified ground is not contested.

We Americans also benefit from religious diversity so great that no single group can bully the others any longer. Our civilization is young, its potential far from exhausted and our land is wide. But the ancient homelands of the world's dominant religions have produced successive systems of belief that cannot be reconciled with one another, all competing for validation in close proximity.

While most of us may yearn for peaceful, equitable solutions to enduring religious conflicts, realism demands that we ask whether or not these competitions over bits of earth can ever be brought to an end without catastrophe to one side, the other, or both.

Of course, we all want peace in the Middle East. But is peace a realistic expectation when the claims of each party to the same small portions of earth are as irreducible and divinely sanctioned as the claims of the other? Outsiders ask why a shrine cannot be shared, but the hard core of believers in every great religion equates compromise with blasphemy.

Still worse, the world's competitions over sacred plots of soil profoundly energize believers on all sides. In the endless contest between systems of belief, ruins, temples, and shrines are tangible manifestations of religion, far easier for fanatics to embrace than are otherworldly spirits and admonitions to charity. Men who barely understand the tenets of their faith will die blissfully for a half-acre of wasteland anointed by their god. But they would much rather slaughter the competition for it.

This focus on real estate above all drags God (by any name) out of the heavens and makes of Him little more than a merciless landlord. One cannot help suspecting that, no matter how devout the intention, insisting that God is more richly present in one locale than another reduces the divine to a human scale, making of faith little more than a range war. Fastening God to a plot of earth renders the incomprehensible a finite thing we can touch, but it replaces transcendent beauty with the greed of ownership.

I do not suggest a solution to this problem, since I see none. But we need to define the problem more clearly and honestly than we have yet done, if we Americans are to act wisely and incisively in this tumultuous world. We need to be extremely wary of embroiling ourselves in any conflict that centers on the claims of competing religions to mastery of a particular sliver of earth.

This leads the argument to Israel (although there is no end of other examples, if often on a lesser scale). I am a firm and determined supporter of Israel, out of moral obligation and deep conviction. The people of Israel are fighting for survival against enemies who seek to destroy them, and the prospect of genocide is intolerable. Yet I cannot help feeling that the promised land for every religion represented in the United States lies here in America, not in the ghost-ridden domains of history.

Doubtless, this view will be judged insensitive by many. But isn't it a reduction of the divine to insist that God resides particularly in St. Peter's Basilica, or in any one mosque or temple? We struggle to tie God down like Gulliver. Despite the insistence of dubious texts on the sanctity of one bit of ground or another, one suspects that the true Jerusalem abides within us.

When we see Hindus and Muslims butchering each other over a forsaken acre in India, or listen to the maddened voices on every side in the Middle East, as we witness Nigerian Muslims desecrating churches while Nigerian Christians defile mosques, how can we escape the feeling that we have done a poor job of reverence? We have elevated dust above divinity.

Such conflicts may define much of our new century.


There are many respects in which the United States differs wonderfully from the old worlds we Americans left behind. But is there any more important advantage in continuing to build our unprecedented multi-ethnic, multi-faith society than the inability of zealots in our midst to convince us that God favors one bit of earth over another?

When our congregations outgrow our churches, temples or mosques, we build anew on a bigger plot, either down the street or miles away in a suburb. Communion in the "little brown church in the vale" has always been a movable feast. This flexibility grants us a tremendous strategic and moral advantage.

Of course, we Americans have strong religious traditions. The vision of a "city on a hill" is part of the fabric of our national being. But that city has never been a physical place, except in the sense of the nation as a whole. The simple fact that God—again, by any name or names—doesn't do real estate in the United States is so great a blessing that one almost suspects that we are—all of us, no matter our faith— truly a chosen people.

# Girls! Girls! Girls!

New York Post

*September 20, 2002*

The greatest social change in the history of humanity happened in the United States over the past 50 years. Women broke their ancient chains and became men's partners instead of remaining men's property. This shift in the status of women is the decisive strategic factor of our time.

Women's self-emancipation is a primary source of America's present power, wealth, and social energy. It is also the fundamental reason why religious fanatics around the world hate us.

Because English-speaking women fought their way into the educational system and the workplace, our economy operates on a wartime basis every single day, with full mobilization of our human resources.

Rosie the Riveter is in the boardroom. She flies combat aircraft. She's a lawyer, a doctor, a cop, a journalist, and sometimes, still a factory worker. In every role she fills, she's the real hero of postmodern America.

We Americans have been blessed with the experience of several simultaneous revolutions over the past half century. We've seen the civil-rights revolution, a "geriatric revolution" that inspires the elderly to continue contributing to society, an education revolution that began with the GI Bill, an efficiency revolution in virtually every sphere and the shimmering information revolution. But unleashing the energies and talents of the female half of our population is the essential key to our success.

Never before has any society been so open to talent, no matter its gender, race, ethnicity, or religion. Certainly, there are still glass ceilings. But another one shatters each day. The salient fact of postmodern economies is so obvious that even doleful lefties like Robert Reich can spot it: Human capital is a nation's ultimate resource. And no society has ever used its human capital as efficiently and effectively as we do.

Yes, we still have years to go to mature the gender revolution. But we already have leapt centuries ahead of the majority of the world's states and societies in terms of the humane treatment of and equal opportunities for women.

Therein lies the problem.

The American juggernaut of the industrial age that won the great wars of the twentieth century and inspired no end of jealousy from dictators and demagogues possessed only a fraction of the power and potential of twenty-first-century America. During the smokestack era, other societies could fantasize about a local duplication of our success. Today, even the Japanese and the Europeans are adrift in the flood of history, unsteady, unsure, and unwilling to change sufficiently to compete in the ultimate world series.

For backward—that taboo word fits—societies, such as those that paralyze all hope in the Middle East, there isn't a chance of challenging America's pre-eminence. It's not just our head start: Our society is structured for ceaseless self-improvement. Much of the Arab world prefers self-delusion. And there's a "No Women or Dogs" sign above every doorway that could lead to national development.

The math isn't hard. No society that oppresses half its population—the female half—can compete with a society that exploits the majority of its talents.

Worse, countries that revel in gender oppression consistently waste even more talent by excluding males who weren't born into the right families or tribes from the possibility of social and economic advancement. Woman-hating cultures, such as those of Saudi Arabia or Pakistan, also fit a pattern of stifling the freedom of expression, shortchanging education, imposing a harsh religious orthodoxy, employing corruption as a tool of social control, and blaming others for home-grown ills. This is not a formula for success in the twenty-first century.

If there is any single indicator of which societies will succeed or fail in the coming decades, it is the status of women. Societies where the girls get a fair shot at beating the boys at soccer, university studies, or software writing are going to leave those whose sexual terrors are expressed in veils and an obsession with virginity in the dust.

Oh, and those 70 virgins? Sounds like a lot of dreary work to me. I'll take one American career-woman any day (ain't nothing like a major babe in a tailored suit who picks up the dinner tab).

American women kick ass. And that's the best news since humanity mastered fire, the wheel, and the process of fermentation.

Our enemies—those who seek to kill Americans and wound our society—will arise, consistently, from societies frightened by females. The mock-macho culture of the Middle East is all flimsiness. These are societies so scared of the girls that they have to cover them over from head to foot, lock 'em up and keep them from watching Oprah at all costs. It's not only counter-productive, it's hopelessly dull.

My personal idea of Hell would be to be born again as a male in an Islamic state: All fear, no fun. And you have to pal around with the world's most sexually insecure males this side of a child-molesters' convention.

Apart from all the wealth and power women's emancipation has generated in the USA, it's also made life a lot more enjoyable. Any of you old codgers really want to go back to the 1950s? Not this puppy. Not only is the dating process a lot swifter and cheaper these days, but, levity aside, for the first time in human history, men and women can be best friends. Not just lovers, or husband and wife. Best friends. That is social and moral progress of an incalculable degree.

Would anyone except a few hooker-hunting televangelists and over-the-hill golf jerks really want to return to a gender-segregated society?

Yes. Hundreds of millions of men around the world who are terrified of losing their power and authority over their wives, sisters, and daughters.

They are our enemies, those haters of women. Mohammed Atta, the 9/11 hijacker whose "testament" forbade

women to pollute his grave by their approach, is the patron
saint of sexually terrified males around the globe.

I doubt President Bush sees it quite my way, but the fact is that
the war on terrorism is also a war on behalf of the world's
women. Islamic terrorists want to turn back the clock to an
imaginary golden age, and that golden age does not include
rights or even medical treatment for the female half of society.

Our terrorist enemies claim to fear God, but females really
make them jumpy. Freud would have a field day with America's new enemies.

Even within the Islamic world, the most hopeful states and
societies are those in which women's rights are expanding,
from Indonesia to India to Azerbaijan to Kosovo to the Muslim citizens of North America.

That much-delayed liberal reformation of Islam is on the
way, and it's likeliest to happen right here in the United States,
driven by social pressures. Islam will become more tolerant
not because of some grand theory, but because the family's
teenage daughter, young Fatima, is going to demand to know
why her brother can date but she can't. America humanizes
religion, and no religion is immune.

Meanwhile, the full integration of women into all reaches
of American society is going to continue to enrich and
empower us all. Conservatives who choke over stories of the
excesses of campus feminists are suckers for silliness. The professional feminists on campus are among the least productive
of America's women, just as every other sort of bigot is crippled in his or her potential. Our liberal arts faculties are like
the United Nations: They give embittered failures the illusion
of empowerment. Our response should be a giggle, not a gasp.

The real story is in the success and contributions of the women reading this paper on their way to work, in the careers of the women I served beside in the military, and in the female president we're going to elect as soon as we decide we need a chief executive who can speak in complete sentences.

Because women won their war for social equality, we're going to become still richer, more powerful, and happier.

Thanks, Rosie. You're a doll.

# The New Warrior Class Revisited

*Non-State Threats and Future Wars*
(ed. Robert J. Bunker)
and *Small Wars and Insurgencies*

*Summer 2002*

History has a wicked sense of humor. On the morning of September 11, 2001, I sat down to write an essay reconsidering, after a decade's interval, "The New Warrior Class," a piece that had suggested the U.S. military pay just a bit more attention to irregular and unconventional threats such as ethnic bullies, terrorists, religious extremists, tribal warriors, narco-guerrillas, and the all-others category that interests adventurers and special operations soldiers, but unnerves diplomats, defense contractors, and generals yearning to fight massive tank battles against any armored patsy they might be lucky enough to conjure. The phone rang. It was my mother, whose appetite for disaster is insatiable. She recommended that I turn on the television.

It took four months for me to get back to the essay.

In the wake of 9/11/01, there is nothing I would delete from the original piece. I believe the intervening years have proven the accuracy of my observations (for such they were—observations—not ideas by any means, but simply a reporting of things noted on journeys through the world's backwaters).

44

Lest anyone find the preceding statement arrogant, I hasten to declare, with all the penitence of an old Bolshevik placed before the tribunal of the workers and peasants, what I got wrong, my clumsy sin of omission: Although the essay spoke of the threat from terrorists, and I maintained a long concern thereafter with our unwillingness to respond effectively to terrorist attacks against us, I still underestimated the enemy. That was unforgivable—especially for a former intelligence officer who spent much of his career warning others that they must never do precisely that.

Another essay of mine from the mid-nineties made the specific point that even a nuclear attack on lower Manhattan would not stop the stock market for very long, since we could quickly reconstruct the data from brokerage offices around the nation. Yet I simply assumed, without much thought, that we had to beware one big strike. In my mind, I did not credit Islamic terrorists, especially, with the ability to mount such a brilliant, elegant, and well-coordinated assault on multiple targets. I had preached, with great zeal, that every culture on earth produced geniuses, and that a proportion of those geniuses might be hostile to us and lethal. But, like many a preacher before me, I ignored my own homily. I said the words, but did not live them. Nor did I foresee the complex ramifications of such a successful and theatrical terrorist strike. I considered only the physical, not the psychological, consequences, another whopping mistake for an old intel hand (old, clearly, does not necessarily mean wise).

Because of my interest in irregular combatants (and plain old killers, those fundamentalists of human behavior), I was asked to participate in a number of discussions about the terrorist threat over the years. My consistent position was that our enemies were deadly and serious, but not a threat to the survival of our nation. Despite the hullabaloo about weapons of mass destruction, I still believe I was right about that. The great weakness of God-clutching terrorist movements, especially, is that, having sighted or even imagined a glimmer of success, they rush to overreach, and by the extremity of their deeds mobilize their enemies to an annihilating response. This was as true of Jewish zealots two millennia ago and of German anarcho-Protestant insurgents during the "Peasants War" of the 1520s as it is of apocalyptic Islamic terrorists at the beginning of the twenty-first century.

I consistently stressed that our culture, society, and economy were so robust that, for the terrorists, our ultimate invincibility must be terribly frustrating. And it is. The overwhelming majority of American lives, if not spirits, returned to normal by September 12. And in the following weeks and months, the spirits recovered, too. The paradoxical results of the attacks on the World Trade Towers and the Pentagon were to bring Americans together in a profound wave of patriotism, to excite a furious desire for vengeance—which we are taking—and to draw together a surprisingly broad, if unevenly committed, alliance against terrorism. Determination will fade, old squabbles will re-erupt, and other priorities will re-emerge. Yet, though we may see still more spectacular terrorist attacks in the future, in a deeper sense the high watermark of terrorism may have been reached and passed. Its seriousness is now reckoned. In the end, the terrorists appear to have done an even worse job of misunderstanding and underestimating us than we did in our misjudgment of them. And they are paying the price.

I would not alter the words I wrote, but I would add to them, putting in a bit more that I think I have learned about terrorism since "The New Warrior Class" went to press. Those interested in the subject break down terrorists in a number of ways. I divide them into two basic groups: *practical terrorists,* with relatively rational (if sometimes highly ambitious) political goals, and *apocalyptic terrorists,* men driven by religious, often messianic, visions—men who yearn toward Armageddon, and for whom no victory could be sufficient (the practical terrorist may one day sit in his country's parliament, if he is not killed in his youth, but the apocalyptic terrorist wants to expedite the Day of Judgment; the first fights for changes in "the system," while the second wants only to destroy it, no matter his rhetoric about earthly concerns). Our guard was down because we were accustomed to dealing with practical terrorists—even Timothy McVeigh had a finite, earthly end in mind, despite his warped perspective on the possible. Terrorists were expected to land hijacked airplanes and make demands. Instead, we faced terrorists cast from an ancient mold, men frustrated with the things of the earth and impatient with their god's tempo, men who flew airplanes into skyscrapers full of the innocent in the belief that their deeds served divine ends and who hoped to jumpstart a kingdom of god on earth. While the practical terrorist may be a man (or woman) of great and conscious courage, the apocalyptic terrorist is always a man terrified of life's demands—more afraid of living than of dying. For the practical terrorist, death is a sometimes-necessary misfortune, while for the apocalyptic terrorist it is an answer—which does tend to complicate the negotiated settlements that have become the pornography of choice for Western diplomats. Above all, the apocalyptic terrorist is an egotist, convinced that his god has chosen him as an instrument. He cannot be rehabilitated, and must be killed or forever locked away. And killing him is better.

But I have written elsewhere of that, too, and a writer who repeats himself is simply a plagiarist with poor taste (if you're going to lift something, lift something better than your own stuff, for God's sake). So let me turn again to that new warrior class, while striving to minimize the inevitable repetition. I believe the categories of warriors I described in that now-dusty essay then expanded by one more (to five) in a subsequent piece still hold solidly and describe the acolytes of terror and their supporters as well as they did Balkan thugs and Somali tribesmen. These archetypes are anthropological, or even Jungian, not an original concept of mine. Again, I only picked up the pieces lying about and slapped them together. The warriors had been out there killing, simply waiting for someone to call them by name.

In summary, I see these irregular combatants as drawn from five socio-psychological pools. The proportions of each type of warrior in any hostile group may vary widely, depending on the duration and environment of a given conflict, but each sort of enemy is always there, be it in a greater or lesser degree.

First, there are the warriors from the underclass, men without prospects in time of peace, who become "somebodies" through the exercise of violence and the totems of power. Whether social misfits who become Serb butchers, or Hitler's Brownshirts, or simply the gritty bastards who enjoy a good pogrom anywhere in the world, these men usually form the initial "infantry" around which a much larger organization may coalesce over time. Most will quit when the tides of conflict turn decisively against them, but others must be killed, unwilling to give up the only satisfying life they have ever known.

Second, we find "course-of-conflict" joiners, young men who only sign up for a program of violence when other options are closed off. Over time, they may provide the largest number of recruits to the cause, swelling the ranks to impressive, but ultimately hollow, numbers. Although some may acquire a taste for killing and destruction, most of these What-choice-did-I-have? fighters will gladly attempt to reintegrate into a society upon which peace has been imposed. Unless they evolve into a different category of warrior (and these categories are not fixed or exclusive), these men are not natural born killers and do not particularly want to die for their cause. But they will pull the trigger while their side is winning.

Third come the opportunists, the entrepreneurs of conflict, a group my analysis initially slighted. These are the What's-in-it-for-me? actors who, given their lack of scruples, can be viciously cruel when winning, but who will generally look for a way to jump from a losing side. Often highly intelligent, they can also be charismatic, inspiring a loyalty-to-the-death they never feel themselves.

Fourth come the hardcore believers, whether convinced nationalists, religious fanatics, or simply men who have succumbed entirely to a leader (and the leader is often more important than the cause—human bonds matter and routinely transcend logic). They will die for what they believe in, and the more exclusive, restrictive, and harsh the system of allegiance to which they have committed themselves, the more deadly—or, at least, the readier to die—they will be.

Fifth are the mercenaries, the demobilized or deserted soldiers, the men who know the formal trade of killing in combat. They polish the destructive power of the collective. Some of them will fight to the last from sheer pride, but others would rather live to fight another day. Many can be bought.

During the recent, innovative campaign in Afghanistan, all five types were in evidence. Although al Qa'eda, given its rigorous screening, appears to have had a higher proportion of genuine believers in its ranks, ongoing analysis of prisoners may show a more complex picture. And the Taliban's swift collapse as a governing power demonstrates how, given the absence of choices, a movement's ranks may be swelled by many lacking a commitment unto death—the Taliban fielded tens of thousands of young men who simply found no better choice. As I write, in January 2002, we have seen the warrior patterns borne out. The men whose trade is war, the mercenaries or lifelong fighters, switched sides when the time was ripe, either for money, or for survival, or because the opportunities had shifted. Many a warlord proved to be no more than an entrepreneur of conflict and, as soon as the Taliban had fallen, went back to collecting tolls along roads (or to outright banditry), to stealing food aid and extorting money from journalists (not necessarily an evil pursuit), and to grasping any advantages they could. The boys and men who had been drawn or forced into the Taliban's ranks gladly faded away, while the unskilled bully-boys shifted effortlessly into the role of providing muscle for the more promising warlords. Only the true believers fought to the last, or fled in hopes of fighting on a more promising future battlefield, or hid themselves in the hope that the storm would pass—or continue, even now, to fight on. But the sheer numbers tell a great deal about the importance of responding to warrior threats with resolve and overwhelming force. Initially, the Taliban was believed to number between 40,000 and 50,000 rifles, five times the estimated strength of the Northern Alliance, America's temporary proxies. But those committed unto death were only a small fraction of that force, and the numbers shifted from one side to the other as easily as mercury spills down an upended surface.

When dealing with warriors, whether Islamic extremists, or Latin American narcos and paramilitaries, or pirates in Malay or Indonesian waters, the critical factor is strength of will. Western states invariably have the raw power to defeat warriors, although conventional forces may not be the ideal choice to combat them (in Afghanistan, we used our own "irregulars," special operations forces, to tremendous effect—but, lacking proxies or in a bigger conflict, conventional forces would have to augment the effort). Our soldiers are very well trained for conventional conflicts and, over the past decade, a great deal more training has been devoted to irregular threats and "peace operations." But regular infantry—especially their leaders—are trained and expected to stop killing too soon. Special operations forces, far from reporters and cameras, can behave far more ruthlessly—and judicious savagery is essential in cracking apart warrior organizations and spinning off the rank and file who lack a mortal commitment to their cause. You cannot defeat warriors gently. And the hardcore believers must always be killed or imprisoned (again, killed is always better, no exceptions). You must kill them both to eliminate them as a threat and as an example. The worst advice that can be given is "Don't make them into martyrs." Better a dead martyr than a living inspiration. Even after the events of September 11, 2001, some readers may judge this advice cruel, or wanton, or gratuitous. But there always have been, and always will be, some of our fellow human beings who need killing for the common good of the rest.

But whether we speak of commandos or conventional infantrymen, strength of will is not lacking in our soldiers (I'm smug about my position in September, 2001, when pundits who had never laced up a combat boot warned us that all the Afghan tribesmen were ten feet tall and had never been conquered—anyone who knew history or had been to the region knew otherwise—and my own position was that we could win handily, if only we made up our minds to do it right). The difficulty lies in exciting and sustaining the requisite commit-

ment to destroy warriors on the part of democratic governments. Now, I am proud of the deliberate and effective
response of our government to the terror attacks of 9/11/01
(the same pundits who said it couldn't be done, now find fault
with the way the campaign in Afghanistan was run; doubtless,
these lions of the green room would have savaged Hannibal's
reputation for negligence after Cannae). I believe much has
changed—overnight—since the awful decade of Clintonian
cowardice and the previous administration's willful ignorance
of global reality. President Bush has continued to stress that
the war against terror will be a long struggle and that the campaign in Afghanistan was only a beginning. The months
between the writing and the publication of the collection for
which this piece has been promised will have taught us all a
great deal. But, be it in a year, or in five years, some of our
strength of will, alacrity and single-mindeness will diminish.
That is a law of human physics. We must hope that sufficient
will remains to do that which is needful, and that we will never
again wallow in the fecklessness of the Clinton years, when terrorists had carte blanche and dead American servicemen and
-women were merely annoyances to be forgotten at their President's convenience, not victims to be avenged. Of course, the
terrorists themselves will do their part to re-excite us when our
energies flag. But we have done a very impressive job so far of
relearning the brutality necessary to deal with terrorists and
other forms of warriors.

A great advantage, of course, was our enhanced ability to
attack our enemies from the air—especially after special operations forces hit the ground and began focusing our attacks,
which had been largely ineffective until then, despite hundreds of billions of dollars worth of strategic sensors available
to us. It long has been a curiosity to me that Westerners in

general will tolerate tremendous damage inflicted by technology, at a psychological remove, while they will take to the streets in protest when lesser harm is inflicted by soldiers on the ground (I speak primarily of Europeans, since Americans have a healthier tolerance for slaughtering their enemies than outraged academics would allow). Attempts by the Taliban and their supporters to convince the world that America was targeting civilians just did not work this time (the claims were not true, but that has never bothered Europeans, with their love of complaint, to say nothing of the Muslim world, with its addiction to delusion). The terrorist attacks shocked even German undergraduates and French intellectuals into a new appreciation of strategic reality. And when American airpower killed Taliban frontline troops by the hundreds and did its best to exterminate some thousands of al Qa'eda activists, there was no audible criticism from any source that mattered. My point is that "sterile killing" has long been acceptable to us—a pilot's bombs may kill civilians, but the pilot is not judged a criminal, while the soldier on the ground is always suspect. Soldiers are expected to show mercy and moderation, and to take prisoners. Machines are not. The pilot gets a superlative efficiency report for the same results that get an infantryman court-martialed. Yet, the system works, and that is the soul of the matter.

I remain convinced, nonetheless, that ground forces will have an enduring, major role to play against warriors, especially in urban areas and on other complex terrain (as I write, our special operators are rooting through cave complexes and Marines are helicoptering about in pursuit of fugitives in the Afghan wastes, and we see again the need for balanced forces). But if we are to allow ground troops to be as effective as we need them to be, we have to recognize that we dare not compromise with warriors, or attempt to impress them with military demonstrations, or wage a war measured out by teaspoons. You must fight them with overwhelming power and ceaseless effort, not with modulated attacks that seek to avoid giving offense to third parties. Our only weakness in Afghanistan—understandable, given the legacy of the last decade and all the myths that had to be cast aside—was that we did not hit hard enough early enough, using an even greater range of forces. But military operations are rarely perfect, and this was a "recovery" campaign for a government— our own—that had been sick with illusions, both about the role of the military and about the nature of our enemies. But I believe we have now learned the right lessons. The trick will be to avoid forgetting them.

And will there be more warriors? I wrote above that I believe terrorism may have reached and passed a high-watermark. But that means only that, in the words of an old Irish rebel tune, "The West's awake." The world's discontents and dislocations will supply more than adequate numbers of warriors, whether terrorists, genocidal tribesmen, ethnic bullies, international criminals, or "near-armies," those formations that fall between rude guerrilla movements and fully-organized military establishments. Warriors were here long before the first soldier—that disciplined, organized, legally bound representative of state power—and, if we are unlucky, warriors will be here after the last soldiers have gone. The warrior, the man who profits from violence, who is drawn to it and sometimes even loves it, is a basic human archetype. As long as there are men and women upon this earth, there will be men who kill and think their killing good.

During the next decades, the greatest number of warriors who annoy the West will continue to come from the Islamic world. We face a situation unique in human history: A vast, old civilization, reaching literally from the Atlantic to the Pacific in its home dominions, and with outposts virtually everywhere, is failing on every front that matters. An entire world-view, with its encompassing culture and insistent tradition, has proved non-competitive not only for postmodern, but even for modern times. As the dynamic states and peoples of the West and in East Asia fuse informational creativity, startling human efficiency, and adaptive industrialism into (recessions notwithstanding) systems of wealth generation and power unthinkable even a generation ago (remember the 1970s anybody?), Islam has yet to display the industrial-age competence of Britain in the mid-nineteenth century. And there is absolutely no formula for the core Muslim states to catch up, nor will there be any such program. So much that allows late-modern and postmodern economies and societies to triumph is anathema (in the true sense of that word) to the Muslim world: Human equality that transcends birth status, gender and race; free flows of information and a populace able to tell fact from fiction; the rule of law; protection from corruption; recognition of the popular will (democracy being its most evolved form); reliable governments; self-criticism; accurate accounting; liberal education; civic responsibility; the ability to operate socially and economically across family and ethnic lines; religious pluralism. . . .

Islam's collapse as a socio-economic and organizational system is hardly reason for gloating, since it portends continuing difficulties for the rest of us. Of course, it would be better for all were the Muslim world competitive in the production of goods and services, in social effervescence, and in the quality of life provided to the citizens of Islamic states. But it simply is not going to happen on a significant scale. As Bernard Lewis, the greatest scholar of the Arab world in our time, has pointed out, Muslims faced a fundamental choice when confronted with Western successes and their own failures: They could either ask what went wrong and how it might be fixed, or they could ask who they might blame. They chose the wonderful comfort of blaming others for their own failings. And now it is frankly too late for them to recover. They lag so far behind, while the accelerated progress of successful states and cultures races ahead at an ever-increasing velocity, that it is a mathematical, as well as a practical, impossibility for them ever to reach developmental parity or to even approach it.

What will happen? None of us can say with satisfactory precision. Some regions or individual cities, and certainly plenty of individuals, in the Islamic world may do very well indeed. But the majority of Islamic states between the Pillars of Hercules and the Hindu Kush—if not still farther afield—are going to continue to grow relatively (and some absolutely) poorer, as prospects falter and populations increase. This need not lead to a Malthusian cataclysm, and the likeliest scenario is for the realms of Islam to muddle on through in shabby mediocrity, never satisfied, but surviving on the cast-offs of the West. But it is certainly a guarantee of an ample supply of discontented young males (like those 19 "martyrs" of 9/11/01) with no satisfying vision of worldly success before them.

This situation—and the propensity for violence—is compounded by the psychological dysfunction that pervades the Islamic world. Although it is impermissible to mention such matters in "serious" strategic discussions, Muslim males, individually and collectively, are terrified of female sexuality, and the simultaneously seductive and horrifying images of women they glean from their distorted views of the West drive them into a madness for which we lack the specific vocabulary.

There is perhaps no creature—not even the unicorn—rarer than a sexually-contented terrorist, and many another warrior has never developed into any form of manhood a psychologist would recognize as healthy and mature. But this, too, has been discussed elsewhere and at length, so I will simply offer that, among the many factors we foolishly exclude from strategic analysis (religion only belatedly made it into the club of "discussables") is sexual neurosis, individual and collective. Of course, superficially puritanical (and, thus, hypocritical) societies always suffer such disorders, but never in the annals of humanity has it posed so massive a threat. If a single factor unified the terrorists of 9/11/01, it was not a strict adherence to Islam—given the lap dances and booze that pleased at least some of the hijackers. Rather, it was that, to a man, they were simply afraid of the girls. I would put it still more bluntly, were it not for the inevitability of censorship.

Certainly, threats will appear elsewhere, although they will nowhere prove as consistent, as inchoate, or as implacable as those emerging from the Muslim world. Warriors have despoiled much of Africa and likely will continue to do so. But African violence remains, at least for now, introverted and fratricidal. We need have no quarrel with Africa—although human ingenuity may yet invent one. But we likely will need to intervene occasionally, when local violence becomes intolerable. In Asia, the security situation is complex and mutable, with China as the great unknown. Asia, too, has produced its share of warriors down the centuries—as has every people and culture we might examine. Latin America has been a congenial home to *caudillos* and killers, from the Rio Grande to Patagonia, since at least the Spanish conquest—and perhaps longer still. But that hybrid civilization may have begun to turn a corner. It will not rival today's most successful states in wealth or social fairness, but, despite some current disappointments and turmoil, the region may emerge as a halfway success, with satisfactory lives on offer for an increasing number of its people, if never for all of them. Even Europe, civilized almost to inanity, harbors its ineradicable warriors, from Basque terrorists, to Corsican separatists, to the gunmen of Northern Ireland (who have proven, so graphically, that neither Catholics nor Protestants have an advantage of virtue). Until all of mankind reaches a true, impossible utopia, the warrior will be with us.

I am inexpressibly optimistic about the future of the United States, and expect positive tomorrows for most of the countries that share at least our practical, if not always our moral, values. Granted a few more decades of life, I expect to see a continued expansion of wealth, opportunity, and convenience (a quality too often underestimated in its importance—can't all of human progress really be measured as the march of convenience?). I expect our power to grow exponentially, in every sphere, from cultural and linguistic hegemony to an even now unthinkable military superiority. And I hope to delight in yet unimaginable technological innovations and creations. But I do not expect the darkness to leave the heart of man. Whether from the countless mutant forms of jealousy, from real or perceived need, from the fury of belief, or from the collective madness that haunts the long human experience, I know that we will face violent threats, from heartless, ruthless men, and that we will need to kill them.

The key to winning against warriors is strength of will, supported by valor, conviction, and physical power. I do not worry about the determination or courage of our soldiers. But our leaders will remain a cause for concern over the years and decades. It is usually easy—and briefly pleasant—to do less than necessary, then declare victory. But the warrior of implacable belief is deterred only by death, and early intervention is the only way to minimize his appeal and affect. If we truly wish to increase our domestic security and global safety, we would do well to cast aside a lovely, but utterly false Western myth: That human life is precious. Human life is incalculably cheap. And we must always make certain that the warrior's life is priced far lower than our own, since, though we may value the lives of our countrymen, he does not share our prejudice—as we have learned, again, so very painfully. Our security can never be bought solely with money or even with the most skilled diplomacy, and it certainly cannot be secured with good intentions. A healthy state must cultivate a discriminating appetite for killing.

# Hidden Unities

## Alternative Strategic Divisions

*Prepared for the Center for Emerging Threats and Opportunities in June 2002 and published here with the generous permission of the CETO and with thanks to the United States Marine Corps.*

**A More Unified World Than We Know**

Perhaps the finest painting of a prize fight hangs in the National Gallery of Art in Washington, D.C. Titled *Both Members of This Club,* the work is by the American painter George Bellows. The painting shows two old-fashioned sluggers, identical but for skin color, pounding each other to a pulp. Both the painting and its title might serve as a perfect metaphor for the long-enduring and now renewed violence between Muslim countries and those that are, by heredity, Christian, Jewish, or Judeo-Christian.

Everybody in the fight is a member of the same club: The grand and hyper-violent club of monotheist cultures.

The vast territory between Ireland in the west and Afghanistan in the east, between Scandinavia in the north and the long transition zone of the southern Sahara, is one "club," a single strategic zone (North America is an adjunct to it, but increasingly separate from this macro-region). The countless wars within those boundaries all have been family feuds within the dynamic and long-expansive domain of monotheism.

Centered historically on the eastern Mediterranean, this is a single civilization that has mutated, along its expanded frontiers, into a wide range of cultures that may claim, in some respects, to be civilizations in their own right. But the distinctive characteristic of this there-is-only-one-god strategic region has been its aggressiveness, both toward other "members of the club" and toward other civilizations.

This historical predisposition to conquer and convert shapes the behavior even of those members of this vast community who have turned their back on active religion, as is the case with the states of northern Europe. Europe's superficial pacifism of the moment lacks only the right provocation, the right historical circumstance, to turn again to violence directed at non-Europeans. One of the worst mistakes today's strategic analysts make is to assume that, since Europe is so piously anti-military and "soft" today, it will remain so tomorrow. This is the same assumption that the Japanese made about the United States six decades ago, and which Osama bin Laden made about America more recently.

Violence toward other cultures is deeply—ineradicably—embedded in the European branches of monotheist civilization. It is only a matter of when the violence will re-emerge, what form it will take, and whether that violence will prove antithetical to U.S. values and interests. The Europeans who pretend to the moral high ground today are the heirs of those Europeans who, in 1912, insisted that the continent's nations were too civilized ever to make war on one another again.

### The Club Rules

While we may recognize, at least in less-controversial historical terms, that both Christianity and Islam have been fierce, messianic, driven faiths, the long sweep of history has obscured the similar nature of the other great monotheist religion, Judaism. Long strategically dormant, Judaism has returned as a strategic factor with a vengeance in the Middle East, where, despite Israel's veneer of secularization, the deeper struggle remains one between two monotheist faiths—which are, by their essential nature, incapable of peaceful co-existence. While Judaism, unlike Islam or Christianity, does not seek to convert its enemies to its faith, it is psychologically programmed for exclusive violence as surely as are its sister religions. One God means one way, and one way means our way.

We tend to view Judaism as a passive faith suddenly converted to defensive violence by the Holocaust, but this is a short-sighted reading of history: All monotheist religions produce cultures that are furiously aggressive and missionary. Even after their societies secularize, the mindset lingers. Only the powerlessness of Jewish communities scattered in the Diaspora tempered their ingrained impulse to conquer and subjugate. Judaism hasn't re-imagined itself in Israel; rather, it has rejoined the club from which centuries of powerlessness had excluded it.

Prior to the Roman destruction of the Jewish state, whenever Jewish political entities were not subjugated by intrusive empires, they behaved very aggressively, indeed, toward their neighbors— as Israel has done in our lifetimes (and, of course, as its monotheist, Islamic neighbors do toward Israel, less rationally and far more vindictively). Each of the three great monotheist religions has a history of atrocity, if one goes back far enough. It appears to be only a matter of who held power when.

Today, "Western" cultures, Christian, Judeo-Christian, and Jewish, behave more humanely, as a rule, than do Muslim cultures. But that is, at least partly, because we are so powerful and wealthy we can afford this indulgence. Much of the Islamic world is in the throes of a complex, multi-layered, psychologically-devastating crisis. And, when in crisis, monotheist cultures default to collective violence toward nonbelievers, whether in their midst or abroad.

The United States (and Canada), with its uniquely intermingled society, is in the least danger of turning on its minorities. But any member of a religious or ethnic minority in Europe had best be doing all he or she can to prop up the wealth and social accord of the state and the rule of law. Europe does not, will not, and cannot assimilate immigrant communities from other cultures. While we should not exaggerate the power of current rightward trends in the European political environment (the danger is not short-term, unless a very great provocation occurs, such as a cataclysmic terrorist act), in the long term, European societies may become, at best, cellular and informally segregated. At worst, we may see the rigorous, even violent, exclusion of unassimilated minorities and the establishment of a buffer zone, with puppet regimes that serve Europe's security needs, along the Mediterranean littoral.

Without drawing any premature conclusions, Americans would be foolish not to recognize that Europe is far more volatile than those endless, soporific pronouncements from Brussels would have it.

### Crusades Without a God

All cultures generated by only-one-god religions—Christian, Muslim, or Jewish—believe in one path to the truth. The debate—often bloody—is over which path is best, not over the equivalent value of alternate paths. These are all-or-nothing cultures. This "one true path" mentality compels them to inflict their vision of both religious and secular order on others.

Even now, when Europe is "de-religioned," by and large, and the United States would find it inconceivable to launch an overt religious crusade, this our-way-is-the-only-way prejudice subconsciously informs our actions. We still want things our way and cannot really accept that the differing ways of others have full validity; rather, we assume that they are only less-developed and must, eventually, learn our way of doing things and come to appreciate that our approach is the only right approach. Our desire to create democracies and market economies abroad, laudable though such systems may be, is an inheritance from nineteenth century missionaries yearning to convert the "heathen Chinese" or the African tribesman. Our most bellicose armchair strategists make much of supposed Chinese aggressiveness, but, to date, no Chinese government has insisted that the United States or anyone else adopt Chinese behaviors, social views, governmental forms, and business practices: Our way may, indeed, be for the good of all, but the alacrity with which we insist on it is unmistakably intolerant and close-minded missionary behavior. We are programmed to insist.

The all-or-nothing nature of our current, postmodern war against terrorism is masked by diplomatic manners, and that, in turn, obscures the fundamental and fateful division between Judeo-Christian culture and Islamic culture today: The historic break over the role of women in society. This is the one truly irreconcilable difference between "Western" societies and Middle-Eastern Islam. Although it may appear absurd to many a strategist, the current war against terror, and the recent fighting in Afghanistan, is, essentially, a war over women's rights and women's roles. The alteration in women's roles in the West is the most profound advance in human social history—more revolutionary even than the advent of democracy—and the most unsettling change to traditional societies. A male in a traditional Islamic society can more easily accept a monstrous dictator above him than a wife who insists on standing beside him. Although Islam's complaints about the West are couched in terms of sin and corruption, the real fear is of female freedom.

The battle for hegemony between the great monotheist religions—the imposition of social order, when not religious practice—will continue to be the defining struggle of our time. It will wear a variety of disguises. But it is a struggle between stubborn, self-righteous cultures, our own included. Our great advantage is that our own culture evolves constantly and has not closed the door on change; still, we must be fair and note that no cultures except the monotheists are currently attempting to force their values on others beyond their borders, whether we speak of the terrorist's brutal, oppressive version of Islam, or of our own belief in democracy and markets for all. I do not suggest we are wrong in our prejudices, only that we must recognize them as prejudices if we want to understand the hostile reactions our proselytizing elicits from much of the world. We imagine ourselves as a sort of strategic Santa Claus, bearing a sack full of better ways to do things, but much of the world sees a fire and brimstone preacher with a Big Mac in one hand and a precision-guided bomb in the other.

## A Little More on Europe
In the short through midterm, at least, violence will continue to erupt primarily from the self-destructive, humiliated Muslim territories, but, in the grand historical arc, it would be folly to imagine that today's passive—when not pacifist—Europe will always remain so. Europe has turned inward before and it remained so through much of the Middle Ages, only to look outward with a vengeance during its five-hundred-year colo-

nial phase. And even the introverted Middle Ages produced the Crusades—so startling because they were a sudden, expansionist aberration during a period of strategic introspection. Because Europe is passive today does not mean Europe will be passive against future threats—or even in the face of future opportunities. If we examine history objectively, Europe has been the least consistent, least predictable sub-region of the world, full of nasty surprises for everyone else. Europe is history's manic-depressive. Contrary to the popular wisdom, Europe is far less steady and dependable than the United States. While Europeans view themselves as the masters of the arts of civilization, their historical behavior has more closely resembled that of today's soccer hooligans.

## The Great, Grim Zone of Monotheism

If we sweep our hand across the map, from the lands of the Celts to the extremes of Central Asia, we will not pass over a single people who have not, at one time or another, behaved with extreme aggression toward their neighbors and, in the European instance, toward the entire world.

In our anger at the savagery of Islamic terrorists and our disgust at the social orders in so many Middle Eastern states, we are best served by the cool-headed recognition that, for all its unacceptable brutality, Middle Eastern Islam is fighting a defensive battle against the overwhelming cultural superiority and practical power of the Judeo-Christian band of states and nations. This recognition does not excuse terrorism, but may help us better understand it. Islamic terrorism is the violence of extreme desperation, symptomatic of the startling failure of Middle Eastern Islamic culture to compete with "the West" on a single productive front. Their failure is not our fault, but it is certainly our problem.

For all their documented violence, the Crusades are a red herring when invoked by Muslims to explain away their contemporary failures. Compared to a thousand years of Muslim attacks against and occupation of Europe's borderlands, from the Iberian Peninsula to the gates of Vienna to the Crimean khanate—and the occupation of Greece, the "cradle" of Western civilization into the nineteenth century—the Crusades amounted to little more than a long weekend during which a loutish collection of European tourists behaved particularly badly. Of course, the role of the Crusades in Islamic myth is far more important than the historical reality, but the critical point, at a time when the word "crusade" is so geo-politically loaded, is that these three monotheist religions have all produced crusader cultures (and Israel's West Bank settlements should be viewed in this context), from Joshua leveling the walls of Jericho, to the early Muslims thrusting up into France, to British missionaries (and soldiers) in Africa, to Osama bin Laden.

Whatever our personal religious convictions, we would do well to recognize that, strategically, the exclusive nature of monotheist religions makes them particularly ferocious, messianic, and . . . prone to crusading, no matter the name with which they cover it over.

Our current war against terror is a civil war on a very grand level, fought against irreconcilable brothers. In Cain and Abel country.

### The Bogus Peril in Asia

As this paper proposes below, concerns about Asian superpowers and any Asian "will to conquest" beyond regional goals utterly misreads the relevant cultural and social dynamics. The violence of the coming decades will continue to be spawned primarily by monotheist cultures, between themselves and with others. The greatest danger from the *bete noir* of the last decade, China, is not from intercontinental ballistic missiles, but from the possibility that the spiritual vacuum left by the Communist interregnum may open the door to some new, contagious, messianic, monotheist cult. Again, we must lay our personal beliefs aside to recognize that the worst thing that could happen to this world, short of nuclear or natural cataclysm, would be the sudden rise of an aggressive new (or reinterpreted) monotheist religion in China, leading China to turn its back on thousands of years of introversion to become a religious crusader. While this remains, in 2002, only one remote possibility among many, it is the one about which we should worry most profoundly. When Beijing cracks down on Falun Gong, it is clearly an unacceptable violation of human rights. But it is also evidence that the old men in Beijing recognize far more clearly than do we that intense, exclusive belief is transformative.

And all monotheist religions begin their careers with bursts of violent conquest.

**A World Divided By Three**
For American purposes, the world beyond our home territories—the United States, Canada, and the northern two-thirds of Mexico—can be divided into three strategic zones, each with its distinct character, challenges and opportunities:

- *The Monotheist Zone,* with its source in the eastern Mediterranean
- *The Sino-Vedic Zone,* with its bipolar powers, China and India
- *The Postcolonial Zone,* encompassing sub-Saharan Africa and Latin America

Each of these zones will be described at greater length below. First, let us consider alternative ways to categorize states and their behavior.

## Bridges and Barriers, Survivors, Sleepwalkers and Pioneers

There are many valid terms used to classify states, whether as democracies, dictatorships, market economies, theocracies, constitutional monarchies, failed states, and so on. But these are political terms that tell us largely of a state's present condition and little or nothing of its purpose. The focus of this essay is on cultural affinities and functions, and on strategic roles. New, alternative terms will be introduced. They will not describe every state, but our focus is on key or exemplary states. While many more categories might be devised, the following five classifications will be used to describe states of particular interest:

*Bridge states* connect two civilizations or two cultures within a civilization, allowing the passage of everything from ideas to armies. While their native cultures usually reflect a great deal of fusion, their core identity associates, at varying points in history, with one civilization or culture or another. They may be conquered and converted by a given side, but their geographic location or temperament tends to keep them open to outside influences and to keep caravans, cargo trucks, or new concepts in transit across their territories. They may or may not be originators of new ideas, techniques or movements, but they always feel their impact. Our era of confrontations and sharply drawn lines is not an especially fertile one for bridge states, yet many of those territories which have served this function historically continue to do so today. Examples of traditional bridge states are the predecessor states that occupied the land composing today's Turkey, golden-age Persia, Poland, and perhaps the most important bridge states in history, sixteenth century Spain and Portugal (see below).

In the postmodern period, both Mexico and South Africa may evolve into crucial bridge states, with the process already well underway in Mexico; similarly, Brazil could prove to be an unexpected bridge state between the Americas and Africa in the out-years, as could the United States. Today's key bridge states are often smaller in scale (normal during a period of continental or global structural crisis): Singapore and the unofficial "city-states" of Miami—which has emerged as the media and financial capital of much of Latin America—and Hong Kong and Shanghai, with their unacknowledged degrees of practical autonomy. Bangalore and Hyderabad in India may be emerging as crucial "city states" that function as cultural bridges, although it is too early to judge whether their impact will remain local or expand regionally.

Of note, city-states and cities possessed of informal degrees of independence or particular power always seem to have served as cultural bridges, from ancient Alexandria and Ephesus, down through Venice, Toledo, late-Ottoman Istanbul, Mexico City, and Beirut, although the latter has plunged tragically backward, to modern-day Vancouver. Port cities and littoral countries are, of course, always most exposed to international movements of any kind; conversely, port cities and densely-populated littoral countries are evolutionary by nature and seem to suffer—or benefit from—a sort of cultural dilution that prevents them from generating new and powerful religious, philosophical, or political movements.

The most powerful, as well as the most destructive, ideas tend to germinate and burst forth from inland areas where they can grow in the safety of relative isolation during their fragile infancy. The proximity to the sea, when measured by modern standards, of the lands that generated Judaism, then Christianity and Islam, obscures the relative poverty and isolation in which these violent faiths developed. While the cosmopolitan nature of the Roman Empire enabled the spread of Christianity, it had nothing to do with its creation, which was inherently anti-cosmopolitan, millenarian, and culturally reactionary in its original tenets. Likewise, deserts protected Islam in its infancy, while the relative openness and vast, indefensible borders of surrounding empires enabled its spread.

Bridge countries, at their best, temper the human impulse to exclusivity and devastating violence. In practical terms, there are fewer true bridge countries today than there were a hundred years ago, in the waning decades of colonialism, when imperial forces kept their colonies open, at least to influences from the empire's homelands. Despite a great deal of nonsense spouted about the information age breaking down barriers, many countries are struggling to build their cultural barriers ever higher. They may not succeed in the long run, but a retreat to exclusivity is the trend in many of the least successful or most threatened regions of the world.

*Barrier States* are those which block either invading armies or invading ideas. There is a natural tendency to associate barrier states with forbidding mountain ranges, deserts or other physical obstacles, but ideological impenetrability is often a more effective wall of resistance—and it is certainly more dangerous in our time. Barrier states can either keep ideas from their own people, serve as a wall to the transmission of ideas beyond their territory, or both. Some states may serve as both barriers and bridges, simultaneously or at different points in history.

There have been, in fact, a surprising number of dual-function states. For example, Poland, a state crucial to European development—and a barrier state despite its lack of defensible borders—served alternately as a bridge state funneling European ideas eastward and a barrier that decisively thwarted threats to Europe from the east, from the defeat at Liegnitz that nonetheless turned back the Mongols, through the repeated deflections of Turkish and Tartar Islamic threats that climaxed in King Jan Sobieski's rescue of Vienna, to the "Miracle on the Vistula" when a scraped-together Polish army defeated the Bolshevik invasion that aimed through Poland toward sympathetic millions in Germany. Today, Poland again serves as a bridge between Europe and unsettled Russia and Ukraine to the east— and, if the E.U. has its way, it will serve as a barrier against illegal immigration. To a remarkable extent, this country that disappeared from the map for over a century continues to play the role it did in the Europe of five hundred years ago.

Spain, too, served for centuries as a barrier to Muslim expansion northward into Europe, while serving as a bridge that allowed the passage of Muslim scholarship and the revived Greek classics northward, as the forces of Castille, Navarre and Aragon slowly rolled back the borders of Muslim Spain until, in 1492, the last Moors were expelled (along with Spain's Jews and much of the peninsula's cultural dynamism). Thereafter, Spain played a fateful, eccentric role first of transmitting European culture—and religion—to the New World, while, increasingly, serving as a barrier to later European cultural developments and keeping its empire (as did Portugal) frozen in cultural time. But more of Spain below. . . .

An impressive number of the world's recent conflicts occurred in old barrier states and territories, such as Serbia and Croatia, Georgia and Armenia, Chechnya and Afghanistan. These all are or once served as frontier states between cultures or civilizations, and Samuel Huntington's description of the fault lines between civilizations applies, of course, to the frontiers of faith, above all. To a powerful extent, belief is the decisive factor in creating a civilization's identity, not only in the religious sense but in the broader sense of values and identities.

Religion is culture, and culture is fate.

Certainly, in speaking of modern barrier states, religion is the number one determinant within the monotheist world and on its frontiers. While those frontiers shift with historical reallocations of power, the most notable development is the recreation of an Arabic Islamic world that is erecting its barriers higher each day. The Arab territories had begun, in the nineteenth century, to open up to western influences, but the process over the last half century has been one of closing doors, of re-building the old walls of the Islamic world of a thousand years ago—though without the long-gone dynamism and power. A broad belt of states across North Africa and the Arabian Peninsula into the Levant and eastward to Mesopotamia has turned inward, refusing to accept the demands either of modernity or postmodernity. Even Lebanon, which seemed so promising a generation ago, has gone backward, and "liberal" Arab states, such as Jordan and Morocco, may be living on borrowed time. Egypt, once something of a bridge state, has become a barrier to outside ideas and has chosen repression and a marginal economy over openness and progress.

Of course, this belt of barrier states reaches even farther east, at present, through Iran, unsettled Afghanistan, and into

Pakistan, touching distant, undecided Bangladesh. Although, for now, Islam's retreat from the modern world ends there, it is difficult to find many historical examples of so vast a region erecting barriers against the influence and ideas of the rest of the world. Only the Spanish Empire, from Phillip II until the occupation of Spain by Napoleon's armies, came close. And the lesson of the Spanish attempt to hermetically seal a vast empire is that the results are deformed economies and stunted cultures. Latin America is still fighting that hermetic, colonial legacy. It is difficult, given the accelerated pace of global development, to see how Islam's homelands will ever recover from their attempt at cultural secession.

Other barrier states—those which focused on protecting their own people from outside influences—include China and Japan through much of their histories, Russia between the lifting of the Mongol Yoke and the reign of Peter the Great (some would argue beyond him, as well), and the northern states of medieval India, whose complex behavior failed to save them from conquest, but preserved the integral Hindu states of southern, inland India from monotheist expansionism (other than some limited missionary successes). Curiously, France has made half-hearted attempts to become Europe's barrier state against American power and influence, but lacks the will and wherewithal to do so successfully.

Successful barrier states must be willing to kill—and, above all, to kill their own people.


*Survivor states,* for the purposes of this study, are those which contain a people that has suffered attempted genocide, or that perceives itself as having been so threatened. While the first type deals with reality and the second largely with self-created myth, all survivor states are ferocious when they perceive themselves in danger; expansive where lost historical territory, *Lebensraum*, or the need for defensible borders are concerned; intolerant to the degree that they view neighboring populations as less fully human than themselves; and obsessed with the notion of a historical mission. While such states are almost always small (Russia offers the only partial, great exception to this rule), they are disproportionately volatile and tend to spark larger conflicts than mere border wars. When survivor states are located next to one another, the situation is impossible to defuse completely and the maintenance of peace requires ceaseless external pressure or outright occupation.

In their do-anything-to-survive obsession, survivor states often will abrogate the rule of law, cut deals with criminals or even terrorists, and commit war crimes themselves—justifying their actions by all that their people have suffered in the past. Some survivor states may be democracies and have thriving economies but most maintain a self defeating siege mentality disproportionate to real and immediate threats. Wherever there is a survivor state on the map, planners can expect eventual trouble.

Obvious survivor states include Rwanda, Armenia, and Israel, but the list becomes much longer when nascent states and those who have mythologized threats to themselves are added on. Then the list includes Bosnia, Croatia, Serbia, Greece (which behaves as though the Turkish occupation ended last week), Turkey (in a grand and peculiar sense, viewing itself as the battle-hardened remnant of the Ottoman Empire, forged in its own war of liberation against the Levantine Greeks, under Kemal Ataturk's near-messianic leadership), the non-state state of Kosova, and the Palestinian state-to-be. An eventual Kurdish state, perhaps created unintentionally with the fall, through whatever means, of Saddam Hussein, would certainly qualify, as might spin-off, ethnic states from a failed effort to re-unite Afghanistan. Paraguay, still suffering from the effects of a disastrous war over a century ago, also displays limited survivor-state characteristics. So might East Timor, if its democracy and economic development fail to take hold. Cambodia has the potential to become a classic survivor state, but here, too, the jury is still out. Chechnya, should it ever gain its independence, undoubtedly would behave as a survivor state. Perhaps the mildest form of survivor behavior is exemplified by South Korea, although its occupation by Japan remains a highly-charged issue. The war-ravaged states of West Africa might also have some potential to emerge as survivor states behaviorally, although this is unlikely, given the odds against internal unity, their poverty, and the bankruptcy of their cultures. Even so, we cannot judge the degree to which a survivor mentality, in some local mutation, may linger in Africa in the wake of its particularly severe colonial experience—this remains a great question mark on that undecided continent.

The volatility of survivor states and the dangers they pose must be obvious to anyone who simply reads the list of names above. But, again, plotting them on the map shows a clear concentration of these dangerous entities in the monotheist zone, especially where its internal cultures and the divergent branches of its civilization(s) collide. There is an almost uninterrupted belt of these survivor states stretching from Croatia around the eastern rim of the Mediterranean to Gaza and northeastward to the Caucasus.

Watch this space.

Perhaps the greatest error well-intentioned diplomats and analysts make regarding the Middle East is to assume that the creation of a Palestinian state side-by-side with Israel might bring peace. The chances of two such embittered, bloodied survivor states getting along peaceably, while differing in religion and culture, and forced to live side by side, are close to zero.

Even where an uneasy peace prevails, between Armenia and Turkey, or between Turkey and Greece, the situation remains fragile and dangerous—even though the rest of the world sees clearly that the mundane cultures and even the cuisines are nearly identical, and that cooperation—"burying the hatchet"—would profit everyone. The notion that states act rationally in their own self interest is a liberal fantasy. It would be entirely in the practical self-interest of each of these states to cooperate, however grudgingly, with one another. But they will not do so, and they continue to dream of burying the hatchet in each other's heads.

States may, as noted above, display more than one identity at the same time, as in serving as both bridges and barriers. Likewise, bridge states, such as Turkey, may also interpret themselves as survivor states, and historical barrier states, such as Croatia or Armenia, are classic survivor states (their roles as barriers eventually caught up to them). But the most explosive combination of all is that of survivor state and pioneer state, which will be described below.


*Sleepwalker States* are those which, either content with or clinging to traditional beliefs and rigid structures of social organization, miss out on one of humankind's social or technical leaps forward. When the future arrives, as it inevitably does, they react with graphic, but ineffectual violence that consistently fails to maintain the existing order, but which excites the aggressor or intruder state to even more ferocious violence in response, creating a crisis of confidence and the collapse of the governing order (a precise description of the war against al Qa'eda and the Taliban in Afghanistan). While sleepwalker states existed at least as long ago as the declining Hittite empire, and include historical examples as diverse as the Aztec empire and the late Mughal states of India, the most instructive state for us, historically, is China, while the obvious current sleepwalker states are—without exception—Islamic. Even Burma/Myanmar has realized it must open itself to outside influences and investments, although it remains uncertain how to proceed.

China, vast and populous, with its own powerful culture, was content for millennia to live within its own world. Border conquests and even the rare fleet sent on a voyage of discovery were only ephemeral events. China's interests remained more exclusively internal than that of any other such power or state in history. Although a few technologies crept in, the arrival of Western gunboats on Chinese rivers awakened a remarkably introverted culture from a very deep slumber. Chinese responses to the appearance of technologically and organizationally superior intruders included, most spectacularly, waves of anti-foreign violence, from the disastrous Opium Wars, through local rebellions, to the messianic fervor of the Boxer Rebellion. Perhaps a longer historical perspective will allow us to see that Chinese Communism, too, was a millenarian phenomenon, messianic without a formal messiah (until Mao's later elevation), and a fervent collective response to the failure of the old order to defend or redeem China—a religion without god. Now, with the decay of Communism to an empty shell, another wave of collective fervor may be in the cards. This may not happen soon—or at all—but the rise of a new, galvanizing, intoxicating religious movement in China would be the scenario most likely to turn China to aggression.

The immediate problem, however, arises from the sleep-walker states of Middle Eastern Islam, extended at least as far as the Indus River in the east. The rise of fundamentalist terrorism against the West and its influences are the Muslim version—on a far grander scale—of the Boxer Rebellion, a movement born not of confidence, but of frustration and inchoate rage. The siege of the foreign legations in Peking, nowadays Beijing, prefigured the terrorist attacks on foreign bases and embassies in the Middle East and Africa. What all millenarian, messianic movements have in common is that, although they speak of inaugurating a golden age, they all desire to recapture the past, to return their societies to an imagined purity rid of foreign influences. And it simply cannot be done.

The windfall of oil wealth, and the subsequent Arab-internal aid, long allowed Muslim countries between North Africa and the Hindu Kush to drowse as much of the rest of the world, especially the West and the dynamos of East Asia, took off, developing new methods of social organization, of wealth distribution, of technological innovation and, above all, of greater human efficiency. Now, these Muslim states, and especially most Arab states, are so far behind developmentally—especially in the realm of human efficiency—that it is impossible for this author to see how they could begin to catch up and compete with societies that have raced generations, if not centuries, beyond them. A missionary, monotheist culture spanning continents has been thrust onto the defensive (through its own failures, we must repeat). And these sleep-walker states, as they begin to awaken to their true condition, exhibit some of the worst survivor-state behaviors. We may be witnessing the development of the world's first survivor civilization, in the negative sense of the survivor state characteristics described above, but without their virtues. The states of the Arab Islamic world are already caught in a no man's land: They are strong enough to hate, but too weak to reform. It is a prescription for continued failure.

Whether we speak of awakened China in the nineteenth and twentieth centuries, or of Islam today, sleepwalker states awake from their dreams of stasis to sudden disorientation, broad failure, and external influences. Violence is their natural response.

*Pioneer States* are the natural antagonists of sleepwalker states. Pioneer states lead human social, technical, and organizational progress. In their developing phases and at their apogees, these states or cultures are open to new ideas, experimentation, and change to a degree uncharacteristic of humankind (cultures tend to be conservative and closed, once developed). Pioneer states may arise at any time, but are most apt to appear and triumph during times of upheaval or decay in neighboring states and cultures. Pioneer states can be global or near-global in their reach (the Roman Empire; the Ottoman Empire for about two hundred years, down to the death of Suleiman the Magnificent; the British Empire; and today's United States), or regional in their impact (Israel, Singapore—which is also a bridge state, as noted above—and, perhaps in the out years, Indonesia, Iran, and Australia/New Zealand, each of which possesses highly eccentric characteristics that could lead to innovative social orders).

In considering history's most influential pioneer states, it is all too easy to see them first as military powers; however, with the exception of the Ottoman Empire, each of the global or near-global players mentioned above maintained peacetime military establishments that, while technologically advanced, superbly trained, and disciplined, were quite small in comparison to their far-ranging responsibilities. The real power of pioneer states is their development of new formulae for maximizing the potential of their populations, their openness to new possibilities, their extraordinary ambition, and their capacity for internal debate among the governing elites (the lack of the latter crippled the Ottoman Empire early on). Of note, when Rome lost its taste for internal dialog and began to rely more heavily on its military for the maintenance of metropolitan order, it began to decay. In their heydays, too, Rome, the British Empire, and even the Ottoman Empire, as well as today's United States, were open to talent from within or without, to new ideas, and to open regimes for determining the status of the individual. In today's America, of course, we can recreate ourselves several times in a lifetime, whether we use as examples Madonna's various career incarnations, actors turned politicians, military retirees turned investment bankers, or the person who gains a college degree and a new profession in midlife. Our picture of the British empire's class system tends to be skewed badly by novels and films, and we forget the relatively humble, or frankly disadvantaged, births of many of the great men of empire, from Robert Clive, conqueror of so much of India, to Benjamin Disraeli, Victorian-era Prime Minister and best-selling novelist, whose family lineage was Jewish. Certainly, there was snobbery and bigotry a-plenty in the British Empire, but, especially on the empire's frontiers, there never was a dearth of self-made men. Even the Ottoman Empire, in its centuries of blazing greatness, employed Jews, Christians, and just about any other talent that could be drawn to the Ottoman standard. The greatest mosques built by the Ottomans in Constantinople, Edirne and elsewhere were designed by Sinan, born an Armenian Christian. Openness to the greater world—the bane of sleepwalker states—is the oxygen of pioneer states.

The Spanish empire is a great and obvious exception. Although rough men of relatively humble origins, from an Italian sailor to Hernando Cortez, explored and conquered the empire, the repressive, bigoted genius of Philip II closed the door to further innovation and the influences of post-Renaissance culture, and quickly ran down his state bureaucracy until it functioned without creativity or integrity. A man of extreme religious self-righteousness whose character resembled that of Osama bin Laden (Friedrich Schiller's description of Philip II could be applied directly to OBL), Philip II personally destroyed the hope of competitive progress in Spain's dominions. While the empire nonetheless lasted four hundred years, Philip II's forcible transformation of Spain from nascent pioneer state (and empire) to one of the great sleepwalker states of history, meant that Spain's dominions abroad existed in a near-hermetic time-capsule, corrupt, priest-haunted and decrepit, and that the home country, in the early twentieth century, was less industrialized than Japan. Of course, the tale of Spanish cultural, economic, and military failure is more complex than can be described here, but the salient feature for our purposes is that Philip II and his emulative successors were inflexible—and committed to preserving their order, their empire, and their faith, rather than developing these things. It is, perhaps, no mere coincidence that, after frontier Catholicism, the greatest influence that shaped the Spanish states was the long Moorish occupation of the Peninsula, during which, despite intermittent cultural flowerings, Islamic fundamentalist movements repeatedly crushed attempts at social and spiritual development. Imperial Spain thus had before it two prime examples of how to rule: the ferocity of its embattled faith, multiplied by the fervor of the Counter-Reformation, and the example of its Moorish enemies, in which more liberal, open regimes consistently fell prey to fundamentalist conquerors—who were the great nemeses of the Spanish knights (when the Spanish were not fighting as mercenaries in Moorish pay). A state born in war and expanded through war, and confined within a fundamentalist religion, Spain never learned to value anything more than an uncompromising faith and a merciless sword.

It is also characteristic of pioneer states that, while they make war ferociously when they must, they consistently operate under a code of humane laws, written or customary. For example, our image of the Ottoman Empire is skewed by a sense of its Islamic otherness, and by its long, pathetic decline. But, in its heyday, it was the most open, dynamic, and tolerant of empires. The Jews driven from Spain found a refuge in Constantinople, where their descendents still live quietly. And when the "liberating" Christian armies of the Habsburgs retook Budapest at the end of the seventeenth century, the first thing the soldiers did was to massacre the Jews in the city's thriving ghetto. Islam, once the most tolerant and dynamic monotheist faith, has simply traded places with yesterday's Christians.

*Collectible frontiers* are a commodity requiring discussion in association with pioneer states. Monotheist civilizations and cultures are inherently expansive, missionary, proselytizing. They require frontiers that can be "collected" into the faith or the ideological fold. A particular reason for Islam's calcification and violent dismay—in addition to its systemic failures—is that it is now blocked in and cannot "collect" any additional territory or populations. While we hear a great deal about Islamic expansion in places such as the Philippines or Indonesia, the fact is that Islam's expansion reached its farthest extent centuries ago and, since then, has been battling either to hold the line or for incremental, local gains. No religion in recorded history expanded more swiftly than did Islam in its first few centuries. It possessed a stunning force, both ideologically and militarily. But, today, Islam's only serious gains are internal—demographic increases which are anything but positive, as they produce ever more unemployed or under-employed young males in societies with insufficient resources to appease them.

Middle Eastern Islam feels enclosed, surrounded, and stunned by the success of Western pioneer states, especially the United States. And Arab governments are forced to divide up shrinking pies among ever more hungry mouths. Despite the frantic calls for Jihad, Islam isn't going anywhere beyond its present borders—except in the forms of immigration or terrorism.

European and North American powers also have deep expansionist urges, so obviously manifested during the age of European colonialism. We now see Europe—and the U.S.—as averse to the old-fashioned conquest of others. In fact, we have simply developed new, more successful means for conquest, on the cultural and economic fronts. As I have noted in other writings, military conquest is ultimately expensive—sometimes, as in the Spanish case, to the point of bankrupting the conqueror. Physical occupation simply does not pay in the long run. To their enormous advantage, today's Europeans and Americans have figured out the art of looting without shooting.

It would be a grave mistake not to take the mullahs and Islamic commentators seriously when *they* insist that Islam and the Judeo-Christian cultures are at war. They recognize more clearly than do we that we are engaged in a new form of conquest, infiltrating their societies with seductive technologies, customs and behaviors that subvert the standing order. Islamic resistance is violent and vocal, so we foolishly imagine it is powerful. But, the events of September 11, 2001, notwithstanding, Islam's impact on the West in our lifetimes has been negligible, while our impact on the Islamic states has been profound, disruptive, and shaming.

For the United States, much of the world remains a collectible frontier, though in terms of economic advantage, cultural infiltration, and strategic influence, not religious conversion or physical occupation. And our efforts to spread our preferred behaviors do, indeed, amount to a crusade, if a well-intentioned and only intermittently-violent one. We fail to see that our entire mindset vis-à-vis the rest of the world is shaped by our religious traditions, every bit as much as are the less-successful prejudices of the Islamic world. Even the atheists among us are the children of Godfrey of Bouillon and Richard the Lionhearted . . . or of St. Francis Xavier and David Livingstone. Kentucky Fried Chicken, Nikes, and pop stars may not seem much like aggressive missionary gospels to us, but to the most reactionary portions of the Islamic world, they are nothing less.

The media, with exuberant irresponsibility, repeatedly tell us of some young man in Houston converting to Islam, scaremongering with the suggestion that Islam is taking over the world. In fact, the most rapidly-expanding religion in the world, in terms of converts and geographic spread, is not only Christianity, but specifically evangelical Protestant Christianity, with its injunction to believers to "spread the Good News." While the devout Christians among us may applaud this development, the strategists among us should be on high alert. As a number of articles and even a recent book have suggested, the spread of evangelical Christianity may prove an even greater source of instability and violence in the out years than the decay of Islamic cultures.

**The Three Strategic Zones**
North America, from Mexico City to Barrow, Alaska, constitutes a region apart—the home territories of human innovation in our time and the pioneer region containing the ultimate pioneer state, the United States. While some analysts may discount the inclusion of northern Mexico in this zone, it is this writer's belief that, while formal sovereignty and official borders will remain in place between successful states, the coming generations will see more innovation and relative progress on our southern border than on our northern border, and there will be greater integration across both borders. This does not suggest than Canada will lag, only that Canada is already highly-developed, with less margin for innovation and development, and that Canada will inevitably follow developments in the United States, complaining all the way. Mexico, with its greater problems, also has greater potential for innovative change and the pursuit of alternative solutions to social dilemmas. Per capita income in Mexico will continue to lag incomes to the north, but a richer, symbiotic relationship across our borders will develop than has been the case in the past. Far from overwhelming the U.S. with illegal immigrants, as some American ideologues suggest, Mexico will become ever more dependent upon and integrated with the United States, economically, structurally, socially—and organization-

ally and ideologically. Mexico is only now casting off the crippling shell of its colonial legacy. The process will not be entirely smooth as it struggles toward new freedoms. But I personally have moved from pessimism on Mexico a decade ago to wary optimism.

Mexicans and Americans have gone much farther, much faster in overcoming old, bitter legacies than any of us might have thought possible a generation ago. Today, despite serious, enduring problems, Mexico looks increasingly like an extremely useful neighbor, whose human power will help sustain U.S. development. It also serves as a key bridge state to Latin America.

In any case, the United States will continue, for the foreseeable future, to be the world's leading pioneer state, breaking down ever more barriers, while possessing wealth and power without precedent in history.

Want some salsa with that?

### The Monotheist Zone

The frontiers of the Monotheist Zone, where Judaism, Christianity and Islam were born, matured, and continue to dominate the cultural landscape, have shifted back and forth over the centuries. On the eastern, Islamic frontier, the border has been pushed back across northern India toward the Indus River—after centuries of Islamic Mughal rule and the British interval. Although over 130 million Muslims still live in India, Hindu culture dominates today. On the Monotheist Zone's southern border, too, Islam has reached its limit and may begin to recede. In southern Sudan, where the borderlands shift into a syncretic Christianity, tracing east into Ethiopia and west through Nigeria (where Muslims still attempt to push their frontier southward) the most dynamic, if not always the

most politically-powerful, faith is that of the "African Christ."
The hybrid, localized Christianity of black Africa—in the postcolonial zone—is unfinished and vivid, with a dynamism lacking in the sub-Saharan extremes of Islam. But this does not yet
equal an extension of the Monotheist Zone. African Christianity is very much a work in progress, where the religion evolves
almost daily, incorporating local traditions, beliefs and behaviors. It is not monolithic—and may not even turn out to be
monotheist in the traditional sense. African Christianity,
despite the advent of African cardinals and recognized
churches, may develop into a unique, third-path Christianity,
the tenets of which would be dramatically different from those
of Catholicism or Protestantism, sub-Saharan Africa's two par-
ent forms of monotheism. In any case, the traditional
Monotheist Zone ends where African Christianity begins.

In the northeast, where Russia has spent centuries engaging in missionary conquest, first extending Orthodox Christianity, then Leninist Communism, the expansive phase clearly
is over and the best Russians can do is to attempt to hold a
slowly shriveling line. Given demographic disparities, it is difficult to see how Moscow will maintain its control over the eastern provinces of the Russian Federation across our new
century. The only frontiers on which the Monotheist Zone is
not shrinking are the largely postreligious states of Europe
(although monotheist mentalities and behaviors persist, and
likely will for centuries to come). While recent events make
the Islamic states of the Monotheist Zone appear far more
powerful and threatening than they in fact are, pundits and
analysts insist that Europe has lost its way and its will. Yet,
Europe retains great wealth and residual power. If we have
seen no major wars in Europe since 1945 (although there have
been adventures enough beyond Europe, though nothing on

the scale of the colonial era), it is because Europeans have not been galvanized by significant threats. We must beware making the same mistake the Japanese made before Pearl Harbor (and that Osama bin Laden made) in judging Americans, who were deemed morally weak and unwilling to fight or sacrifice. Given the right threat, Europe—or key parts of Europe—may prove every bit as ferocious as in past centuries. Certainly, it is hard to imagine this today. But it is always difficult to foresee the sudden changes that keep human history so painfully interesting.

While the aging of populations in Europe appears to be leading to states that lack the manpower to defend themselves, with lurid images of masses of immigrants, legal or illegal, swamping Italy, or France, or Spain, or Germany, it is every bit as possible that demographic threats from beyond could appear sufficiently threatening to trigger the rise of new, exclusive regimes in Europe that, while preserving democratic forms for their citizens, behave brutally on and beyond their borders. Difficult as this may be to imagine, it is far less difficult than imagining the Somme or Verdun was for Europeans in 1900. History doesn't really march—it lurches, staggers, plunges, and smashes.

In the meantime, Muslim states in this zone will continue to struggle with issues of identity and modernity, and few give cause for optimism. The likeliest scenario isn't a single colossal confrontation between Islam and the West, but decades of intermittent terrorism, state breakdown, stalling on reforms, occasional revolutions, lesser wars, and punitive expeditions— and, sometimes, progress.

Most European states remain pioneer states to some degree, open, however reluctantly, to innovation and reform—though certainly not on the scale to which the

United States embraces change. But every Muslim country in the Monotheist Zone has behaved as some variety of sleep-walker state—obviously, Saudi Arabia, Egypt, Yemen, and their ilk, but also the Gulf States, where petrodollar lollipops cannot sweeten a failed history forever.

Even Turkey forever disappoints on the development front. Hard-luck Turkey has much of the corruption of nearby Arab states but, fortunately, its self-image is not as utterly disconnected from reality. Among the few strategically-crucial states in the Monotheist Zone, Turkey is the single remaining bridge state in the Middle East. The Turks will never be as successful as we might wish, but never as hopeless as their Arab neighbors.

The dark horse, developmentally and strategically, is Iran. Despite sensational headlines and tactical reverses, Iran is decades ahead of other Middle Eastern states that have not yet undergone their experiments with religious rule. The Iranian people have tried theocracy, and it has not worked for them. Like alcoholics who need to hit bottom before they can reform and begin building new lives, Iran has bottomed out and may be the first (hopefully not the only) Muslim-populated state to forge its way to a working compromise with the demands of the modern and postmodern worlds. Despite its flares of extremism, Iran—the population of which is overwhelmingly Persian, Kurdish, and Azeri Turk, with few Arabs—has never practiced a form of Islam as repressive and inhumane as the Saudi variant. Partly this has to do with Shi'ism and Sufi influences (and a lingering flame of Zoroastrianism, which no regime has ever been able to exterminate from the culture), but it also has to do with the Persian confidence that comes from thousands of years of cultural achievement. Iran may prove the first successful market democracy in the Islamic portion of the Monotheist Zone, if events in Iraq do not surprise us. If so, Teheran may have a fight on its hands, again, with its Arab neighbors. In essence, Iran has been a sleepwalker, but may develop into Middle Asia's first pioneer state—while its neighbors continue to stumble backward.

Afghanistan long has been a frontier state, and its natural border is farther east, along the Indus River, which has been the natural dividing line between Middle Asia and the Indian subcontinent since Alexander crossed it. While we may wish Afghanistan well and hope for the best, its society is so conservative, so backward and physically shattered, that the best result we can get may be a more peaceful, somewhat more equitable and just state that does not soon revert to overt oppression and terrorism. Certainly, efforts expended on Afghanistan are not wasted, since the region desperately needs a success story—but that success story is likeliest to come next door, in Iran (or in Iraq), where a new model of Islamic society may emerge across the next generation. It is only a matter of time before the United States and Iran are again strategic partners, and, while we now rely on the badly-failed state of Pakistan as our urgent proxy, the out-years may see Iran as our partner and local policeman once again. At present, we are needlessly in contention with Iran over the future of Afghanistan and other matters, but that is a function more of the bad will among an aging generation of leaders on both sides than it is a reflection of the future or genuine interests. Like India, Iran has no friends among its neighbors and must come, ultimately, to an accommodation with the United States.

Then comes Israel. Simultaneously a survivor state and a pioneer state—the most dynamic, aggressive combination—Israel is surround on three sides by sleepwalker states. As noted above, should a Palestinian state come into an independent existence, it, too, would perceive itself as a survivor state, virtually guaranteeing continued friction. But the danger is even greater (although, on moral grounds, the Palestinians are ultimately entitled to a state): First, the Palestinians are the most creative and innovative of the Arab peoples, a fact obscured by the public and media-enhanced roles of the old guard of terrorists and corrupt power brokers. In fact, the Palestinians are (relatively) highly educated, comparatively secular, and scattered in their own global diaspora. A Palestinian state that could shake off the corruption and authoritarianism of the Arafat model would attract a great deal of money from Palestinians abroad and a return to the homelands of many highly-skilled workers. This Palestinian state, too, could become something of a pioneer state. But no one in the region—especially the other Arab states—wants that to happen. Second, a Palestinian state with a survivor state mentality (and especially if it began to become a pioneer state, as well) would exert tremendous pressure on Jordan. Given the high proportion of Palestinians among Jordan's population, the Palestinian state might make its next priority "reunion" with Jordan, but a form of reunion that would not include the Hashemite dynasty.

Israel truly is a model pioneer society, even in the most literal sense of having pioneered the land and made it fertile. But it is the social, intellectual, and organizational innovations that finally make it intolerable to the sleepwalker states surrounding it. Monotheist religions are very good haters, yet Israel's best chance for peaceful relations with its neighbors would be if it were a traditional, closed, hierarchical society, rather than the open society it has been since its inception. Even Israel's stunning success would be more tolerable to its neighbors if Israel oppressed its women, censored its media, and mandated religious observance for all.

The only chance for peace in the long term in the ancient, Eastern Mediterranean homelands of the Monotheist Zone would be extraordinary upheavals in the short term that shattered regional hierarchies. It is extremely unlikely that this could occur without a great deal of bloodshed. And Arab Islam may be so trapped in its myths and regressive beliefs that change proves impossible.

The Monotheist Zone will continue to be both a cockpit of violence and an exporter of violence. While we Americans must focus on the troubled situation in the zone's Islamic states, the more interesting and surprising future may come in the zone's European region, which has been the greatest exporter of violence over the past five hundred years. While dire warnings are not (yet) warranted, Europe may remain steelier and more vengeful than we sense, resembling the United States on the eve of December 7, 1941. Major terrorist incidents may be Europe's Pearl Harbor. In the long term, it may be some utterly unforeseen event, rather than the anticipated results of aging populations and the determination to maintain its wealth, that returns Europe to its tradition of violent solutions to practical frustrations.

**The Sino-Vedic Zone**

In using the term Vedic (of the Vedas, India's ancient holy texts) instead of Hindu, I intentionally have chosen a term with ancient roots. We Americans, with our habit of obsessing on the crisis of the moment, often fail to identify root causes because we make no efforts to place events in a historical context. The Vedic period in India occurred roughly between 1500 and 500 B.C.E. After three thousand years, the same cultural river continues to flow through the subcontinent. Similarly, in China, enduring historical patterns—which Communism did *not* destroy—date to a similar period.

When we view contemporary India as shifty and truculent, or speak worriedly of Chinese missiles, we express immediate concerns but miss the salient factors behind India's noisome behavior and China's quest for arms.

Compared to the wars of conquest fought, endlessly, within the Monotheist Zone and then beyond it by monotheist powers, China and India appear almost miraculous in their lack of aggression toward each other or toward the greater world. While they certainly fought frequent wars internally, within their own cultures, or on disputed borders, these vast countries, during periods of relative unity, had the capacity to amass tremendous wealth and power for state purposes—despite the poverty of their general populations. Yet, neither thought it worthwhile to attempt to build an empire far beyond its cultural borders, and their few wars of conquest were limited to pacifying frontiers. While mountain and jungle barriers played their roles, it remains fascinating that China never tried to conquer India, or vice versa. Their most violent encounters were border skirmishes during the Cold War. Until the Communist reformation, when a foreign philosophy for-mulated in Europe by a monotheist culture was forced upon the Chinese people—China's most aggressive period occurred when Mongol khans ruled old Cathay. India's farthest-reach-ing foreign adventures occurred when it was ruled by the British. While internal violence in both countries was some-times ferocious, neither felt compelled to export Confucian-ism and ancestor worship by the sword or to impose Hinduism on foreign populations through military occupation. Bud-dhism, the closest thing to a missionary religion this zone pro-duced, stressed non-violence and teaching by example. It subsumed and incorporated existing gods, rather than "break-ing the idols."

Certainly, the peoples of Southeast Asia fought wars of aggression against one another, yet these were ethnic, not

religious, conflicts. Local "empires," whether Khmer, Viet-
namese, Siamese, Burman, Javanese, or any other, all sought
security and wealth—power—but not to impose lifestyles or
modes of belief. The territories that became Indonesia produced lengthy, bloody dynastic struggles, savage pirates, and
bitter resistance to colonial conquest, but the existing cultural
conditions were so deeply embedded that even the arrival of
Islam turned few into crusaders for the faith. Today, Muslim
monotheism may be the cause of, or the excuse for, a good bit
of violence in the Indonesian archipelago, but independent
Indonesia's foreign wars since independence were fought
over disputed territory, not religion. Indonesia has become
something of a bellwether country, in which the world will
see what modern Islam can make of itself, but, for now, the
most impressive thing about this "Muslim" state is how secular
it remains.

Indeed, India's worst problems with invaders and border
aggressors over the past thousand years consistently have been
attacks from the West by monotheist warriors. First, Afghan
and Central Asian Muslims established empires in Northern
India, which were then superceded by the Islamic Mughals,
who reigned, ever more feebly, until those other insatiable,
self-righteous, and fierce monotheists, the British, arrived.
Today, India faces terrorist attacks and subversion in Kashmir
from rigorously, intolerantly monotheist Pakistan.

China, in the modern era, also suffered partial conquest
and successive humiliations at the hands of monotheist cultures from Europe (and the emperor-worshipping Japanese).
The Chinese embrace of Communism has been read in many
different ways, but it may also be viewed as an attempt to wield
an equally powerful, intolerant "monotheist" belief system
against China's harassers.

Having fought the Chinese in Korea and experienced their mischief in Vietnam—while listening to swords rattling over Taiwan—we view the Chinese as aggressive. And the Chinese clearly do intend to control a regional sphere of influence, if they can. But what should astonish us is how narrow, how local, Chinese interests are. Chinese ships are not standing ready off America's coast (or Australia's or Indonesia's coasts, for that matter), and China's brief Cold War flirtation with exporting military elements—primarily advisers—to distant lands has largely withered. The Chinese are certainly glad to export arms, primarily for money, partly for influence. But, contrary to the nightmares of the 1950s, there is no indication that the Chinese have global aspirations—if anything, their desire for hegemony has shrunk markedly since its Communist apogee some decades ago. The Chinese want security and whatever useful authority they can gain over their neighbors, but we have no serious indications of greater aspirations on Beijing's part. While we must remain wary of Chinese threats to our interests and allies, we also must remember that, while we see our own interests on China's borders, the reverse is not true.

The greatest danger of eventual war between India and China will arise if China continues its quest for port facilities on the approaches to the Indian Ocean. Chinese involvement in Burma—in multiple spheres, from business to intelligence-gathering—has belatedly attracted India's attention. China, facing a de facto strategic blockade to the east, where U.S. allies and U.S. ships stand just off its coast, has been seeking alternative routes to the world to even the odds. Beijing sees the path south as the only useful direction in which China can move to extend its influence and lifelines without directly confronting U.S. military power, interests, and allies. While China may, indeed, turn more aggressive than it has been historically—countries and cultures can and do change—for now, at least, China's slow-motion Burmese adventure looks more like an attempt to establish a back-up lifeline and to secure its flanks than like the beginning of a quest to dominate India's traditional sphere of influence.

As for Chinese "fifth columns" among the populations of Southeast Asia, the "overseas" Chinese residents are hated in Indonesia, integrated in Thailand (except for the old Kuomintang colonies in the north), distrusted—though valued—in Malaysia, and masters in Singapore—but Singapore, a monument to the genius of the Chinese character once freed of China's grip, certainly wants nothing to do with the regime in Beijing. Despite some nostalgia, the Chinese residents of Southeast Asia recognize that Beijing wishes to use them but does not trust or truly support them. And the Chinese are entirely unwelcome in today's Vietnam.

China's most successful "conquests" consist of long-established business communities with only tenuous political ties to the old homeland. While Chinese culture is one of the strongest on earth, enduring, at times, for centuries in émigré communities, there is a great deal of suspicion among "overseas" Chinese about the Beijing government. Any scenario that includes a Chinese takeover of Southeast Asia, abetted by local Chinese residents, is nonsense.

Indeed, despite the forces of globalization, China may be entering another troubled, introverted period in which domestic challenges, discontents, and requirements take precedence over foreign policy issues so decisively that China's armed forces will receive an ever-smaller percentage of GDP— perhaps even a great deal less in real terms—than they have in the past. China is proud, and frustrated at our presence so near to its borders, but its ambitions—except for trade—are entirely local. Forty years ago, the Chinese strategic presence abroad reached as far as the Congo. Today, military advisers have been replaced with cheap exports, and China's Communism amounts to no more than an old whore's insistence on her virginity.

We can have a war with China, if we want one. But we must recognize that both China and India were dealt losing hands historically, despite their contentment within their own borders, and were traumatized by contact with the Monotheist Zone—and, in China's case, by the Japanese, as well, whose imperialism mimicked, in the most brutal fashion possible, the conquests of the Western powers in the past. China and India have been struggling to find their balance again, to adjust to the relatively recent shocks of external power exerted against them, and to absorb the lessons and technologies they must if they are to compete in the twenty-first century. For Americans, the 1989 massacre of Chinese students in Beijing is already ancient history. For the Chinese, the opium wars of the 1840s are yesterday.

Despite its greater poverty and slower progress on the economic front, India has long been absorptive, accepting foreign influences from successive waves of invaders and apostles, then Indian-izing them. In a sense, China faces a more difficult time of it psychologically, because it lacks the tradition of openness to foreign ideas and methods, and made a dogma of its cultural superiority for centuries—indeed, for millennia. China, despite its impressive gains in power since the Communist victory, still perceives itself as weak, wounded, and threatened. Beijing's most militant statements are little more than the barking of a nervous dog. And now, after the latest series of displays of American military capabilities, the Chinese absolutely do not want to fight the United States. Nor could they afford to, given their economy's desperate reliance on

China's trade surplus with the U.S. (and others). The Chinese economy is far more fragile than outsiders credit, essentially an automobile that keeps running with a nearly-empty tank, relying on the driver to keep adding another pint of gas just in time.

If we stand back just slightly, it becomes clear that every major war of conquest in Asia, at least since the strange eruption of the Mongols, was either initiated by or the result of actions by Monotheist Zone powers. From the Muslims sweeping into northern India over half a millennium ago, through the Western colonial phase, to Japan's imitation of Western imperialism, to the Communist takeover of China, every great war that reached across major cultural borders was either begun by Monotheist Zone powers or their actions, or inspired by Western ideologies and practices transplanted to Asia. Even during the Cold War, border fights resulted primarily from the often-arbitrary boundaries imposed by the old colonial powers and left behind for newly-independent states to manage. Both modern nationalism and Communism were Western creations. Today, we view Asia as the world's most dangerous powder-keg. If it is—and I do not believe that to be the case—it is because we filled it with powder. More importantly, this is a region that, while violent enough in local wars, never generated anything like the wars of conquest that took European empires around the globe—or even anything like the globe-spanning interests that steer U.S. Navy carriers through the waters off Taiwan.

Japan, particularly, is misunderstood—because of the horrific aberration of the Greater East Asia Co-Prosperity Sphere and Japanese wartime atrocities. In the West, we speak glibly of samurai and admire the battle ballets in Kurosawa's films. But traditional Japanese warfare, within Japan, appears to have resembled the ritual, rules-laden battles of pre-Columbian

America more closely than it did the fluid, merciless warfare pioneered in monotheist domains. In both China and Japan, ritual, in many spheres, became substance in and of itself, defusing or dissipating aggressive tendencies and preserving social order. Japan went wild because it misread the lessons of Western colonialism, perceiving an absence of rules where the rules were only very complex and profoundly different from those prevailing locally.

When speaking of the "inhumanity of the East," we would do well to recall that China's greatest military classic, Sun Tzu's *Art of War*, is startlingly humane in its admonitions, while the West's dominant work of military theory, Clausewitz's *On War*, constructed a theoretical model of wars of annihilation that soon enough became real. The fundamental difference in temperament between Clausewitz and Sun Tzu is that the Chinese author never forgot his sense of humanity, while Clausewitz saw humanity's foibles as an impediment to ideal war-making. We know of no Chinese general setting out to conquer the world. There never was a far-flung Chinese empire that spanned oceans and foreign continents. No Napoleon. No Hitler. No Philip II. No Umayyad or Abassid caliphs. Not even a Mussolini.

We are reading our own history onto the Chinese.

**Yes, But . . .**
Of course, we cannot know the future with certainty. Population pressures, crises of various descriptions, unexpected cataclysms . . . many things could turn the Sino-Vedic Zone outward, making would-be conquerors out of history's homebodies. But we must beware relying only upon our most recent experiences for indications of what the future holds. Even our own Indochina wars were fought against indigenous enemies

inspired by European philosophical systems—Communism, nationalism, or an amalgam of both. And we went there, they didn't come here.

The Sino-Vedic Zone has long held the greatest concentration of sleepwalker states—in benign form—in history. In the nineteenth and twentieth centuries, those states began to awaken. But the Sino-Vedic Zone's sleepwalker states rarely behaved as violently as those of the Monotheist Zone, and when they did it was to cast off foreign occupations. This zone has not generated any global terrorist threats—except for the participation of the zone's Muslims, to a limited degree, in terrorist schemes that originated elsewhere. And, of course, Islam is as much an import, if an older one, to the region as is Communism. Japanese extremists are imitative and overwhelmingly focused on Japan. Where enduring civil strife exists in this zone, it is consistently either between monotheist and old-religion factions, as in India, or between two imported monotheist faiths, Christianity and Islam, as in the Philippines and Indonesia. Naturally, when we look at Asia, we see the technologies we have "given" them. But, if we are honest about everything else we have exported to them—the colonial experience, monotheism, nationalism, Communism...it doesn't look as if the Sino-Vedic Zone has gotten a very good deal.

In classifying the region's states, a sample gives the flavor of the whole. China, of course, has served for thousands of years as a barrier state, blocking foreign influences from its own population and, for many a century, isolating Korea and Japan as well. Today, the rulers in Beijing wish to maintain their old barriers but cannot. The greatest dangers that could appear in China are the rise of a galvanizing, messianic cult religion to replace Communism, or the continued trend in China to perceive itself as a survivor state, harmed in the past and threatened in the present. A virulent explosion of Chinese nationalism, fortified by a new, dynamic religious cult, would be much more worthy of our fear than the shabby, phony Communism preached but no longer really practiced.

India is so complex it defies easy categorization, but in one curious—and hopeful—respect it resembles the United States more than it does any major Asian country: India is absorptive, able to ingest, transmute, and use an endless stream of foreign concepts and ideas. The plague of nationalism, which excited an uncharacteristic, postcolonial xenophobia, damaged this tradition in the twentieth century, but there are hopeful signs that, in the new century, India (or parts of India) may make much greater progress than in the past. India might be categorized as a bridge state—but it is and always has been—a bridge from the world to itself.

Overwhelmingly, the Sino-Vedic Zone is an area in which the violence attempts to resolve local issues. Except for a still-limited amount of Islamic terrorism, it does not export violence to the rest of the world. That remains the job of the Monotheist Zone, in which militant Islam is the current multinational consortium of aggression.

Australia and New Zealand are, geographically but not culturally, part of the Sino-Vedic Zone. Curiously, these two former colonies of a great monotheist power have altered their hereditary identities and have no interests in conquest or the export of violence (except the violence employed, reluctantly, by peacemakers and peacekeepers). In both cases, plentiful territory and small populations are certainly factors in the nation's contentment, as are the unique colonial experiences of both. But if they are unlikely to wage aggressive wars (New Zealand, at least for now, has no capacity to do so), they also need not fear military aggression from neighboring states—

although they will continue to have plentiful problems with neighboring populations, immigrants, etc., and regional states are glad to look the other way if they can export their own problems to their neighbors. But the searing experience of Japanese aggression, as noted above, was a historical anomaly. Nothing is certain, given humankind's capacity for mischief, but colossal wars in Asia in the twenty-first century are unlikely to develop *within* the Sino-Vedic Zone—and much likelier to develop *between* zones. As I write, India and Pakistan, two border countries at the eastern and western ends of the Monotheist and Sino-Vedic Zones are in danger of a nuclear exchange. Samuel Huntington's thesis regarding the clash of civilizations may have been dead right (no pun intended) in theory, but he drew the lines in the wrong places.

The twenty-first century may (or may not) be a Pacific Century, but it is unlikely to be a Pacific Military Century. The portion of the globe which so focuses the attention of American strategists today may prove to be the least threatening in coming decades. The key variable isn't China's external ambitions, but its internal condition.

**The Postcolonial Zone**
This zone includes sub-Saharan Africa and Latin America as far north as Cuba and Mexico's southernmost states (Chiapas, Oaxaca, etc.). This is the zone to which U.S. strategists, planners, and analysts pay the least attention, since it appears to offer no serious threats to our security. Yet, this is an area of tremendous unrecognized potential. If it is largely poor and frequently appears chaotic (which we automatically ascribe, in whispers, to "backwardness"), it is because the Postcolonial Zone is an area still struggling to find a healthy form after centuries of occupation. It cannot go back, but it is unsure how to

go forward. Crises as diverse as the current economic chaos in "developed" Argentina and the recent butchery in Sierra Leone are parts of the same puzzle: How do these countries resolve their internal contradictions and move forward after long periods of European domination—or even their creation and population by European immigrants? Despite the age of some of its societies, especially in Africa, the Postcolonial Zone remains unshaped clay in the strategic sense. It is humankind's last great laboratory, where alternative futures are under development. And it is the last great collectible frontier.

I term this zone "Postcolonial" simply because, from Peru to Tanzania, its societies are still struggling, sometimes desperately, to make sense of themselves in the aftermath of the age of European colonialism. They have fundamental problems of identity, although for very different reasons in Africa and Latin America. This is where colonialism hit hardest, or created the most profound disruptions to indigenous cultures (when it did not simply annihilate them). While colonialism certainly was active elsewhere, it had less impact: China was humiliated, but never fully occupied, and Chinese culture is so robust it never lost its sense of identity; likewise, India, though occupied, never much doubted its Indian-ness or the quality and value of its traditions. Sino-Vedic Zone populations simply wanted the colonial powers to go. Even Indonesia, with its old, complex, layered culture, changed less under colonial rule than the states of the Postcolonial zone. Africa and Latin America, however, are still fighting—sometimes literally—to overcome their colonial legacies. There is no end in sight to this struggle, but there are a number of reasons to hope.

**THE UNDECIDED FUTURE**

For sub-Saharan Africa, colonialism was almost entirely a tragedy, crushing fragile societies and creating artificial identities, whether social hierarchies foreign to the indigenous systems or simply the entire notion of Western-style states. Africa continues to suffer recurrent bouts of bloodshed because of the colonial legacy of dysfunctional borders that either force tribes together that do not want to be together, or divide tribes and peoples between multiple states, although they believe they belong together. The European-drawn map of Africa simply doesn't work as designed, and the old colonial powers left those borders intact as a curse; meanwhile, Africa's independent, artificial states are struggling to function the way the Western model insists they should. But Western states—and old states elsewhere—grew organically, over long centuries, and developed their identities slowly. . . or, more correctly put, their identities slowly congealed. At independence, virtually every African state was nothing but a pretense, with unprepared locals occupying the offices just vacated by Europeans, but without a deep grasp of what those offices must do. Understandably, the new rulers concentrated on the outward forms, which they could more easily emulate, and neglected the inner substance of government, with which they had little or no experience. Newly-independent Africa never had a chance. Now, painfully, Africans are trying to create chances, against daunting odds. Not every country will survive, and we must expect a great deal of turmoil as this region attempts to fix itself after being massively damaged by external forces.

Certainly, Africa has had—and continues to have—more than its share of horror stories—massacres, man-made famines, pointless wars. But given the brutality of the European colonialists in so many of the states, the lack of preparation of an educated local class suited for government, the foreign nature of the rules of statehood and the practices of the world community, and the real or relative poverty of so much of the continent, perhaps we should be less shocked than we affect to be. While we must not paint pre-colonial Africa in false, romantic colors as an ideal society (wars, slaving, conquest, and massacres are old African traditions—just as they are old human traditions just about everywhere else as well), we will never know how the region might have developed—or failed to develop—left to its own devices. When we see country X's strongman abuse his own subordinates and treat his people callously, he simply is behaving as Europeans did before him when dealing with the native population. This is the way the powerful man believes "real" leaders behave, that showing disdain for inferiors is simply the way things are done. This is beginning to change, as the generation of leaders who knew the European governors and bureaucracies first-hand leaves the stage. But the question of identity remains—not the old leftist silliness about what it means to be black and African, but the more meaningful, if less gratifying, question of what it means to be a citizen of a state. Africa's dilemmas have less to do with what color makes of a man than with what states make of their constitutions. To suggest otherwise is nothing but leftist racism and paternalism.

Viewed objectively, the current struggles we see in Africa—the near or complete anarchy in shattered West African states; the inner formlessness and sputtering warfare of Congo; the furious disappointment of Zimbabwe; the ethnic and religious divisions, as well as the crippling corruption, in Nigeria; the recent slaughters in Rwanda and Burundi—amount to a continent trying to find its way out of a swamp into which others led it. Countries of more immediate promise, such as South Africa and Senegal, have plentiful issues of their own to resolve, and no country is fully safe from the temptations of factionalism and selfishness. But just as we may suspect that Africa's internal strife will not end overnight, we also may fairly assume that it will not last forever. The fundamental question, despite the obscurant horrors of AIDS, dictatorship, and violent atrocity, is: What might come out of all this? What might the Africa of the future look like? Or will it be Africas, in the plural, perhaps with social progress and the development of regional power in South Africa and in East Africa, with regressive social and government structures (or the lack thereof) elsewhere? Will we see a rich Africa and a poor one? What will the region's deep cultural differences bring about? Which qualities will prove strongest, blood ties, belief, or allegiance to the state? At present, the trend is for African states to differentiate themselves from one another as regards progress, but the events of a decade are fragile indicators of the long-term future. Will Africa force the world to redefine success, on lower but far broader terms?

The safest bet is, indeed, that Africa's future will not be uniform, that the process of differentiation between successful states and the failed will continue. Perhaps no continent faces so many negative factors, or has so many variables at work. But when Africa begins to wake from its often-nightmarish sleep to look for alternative bonds of community, it will not look north, where it is bounded by implacable, age-old enemies who simply have put on velvet gloves. Nor can it look east, where it faces the most ferocious prejudices. When Africa finally turns its face to the world, it will look across the Atlantic, to the Americas.

**The Three Non-Amigos**
Latin America, the other half of the postcolonial zone, presents three distinct cultures to the world, none of which has integrated deeply with the others. Some countries, such as Peru or Brazil, exhibit two competing cultures within their

borders, while others, such as Argentina or Chile, are dominated by a single culture. Bolivia contains two parallel, but weirdly-separate cultures (and a number of odd subcultures). A very few countries, most notably Cuba, have moved toward a genuine fusion culture (in this regard, Mexico is promising over the long term). But for most Latin American countries of varied ethnic and cultural composition, integration is often superficial—constitutionally enshrined, but disregarded in practice—and more about socio-political claims than about genuine fusion (most obviously, in Brazil). Latin America remains a region of "soft apartheid."

The three basic cultures of Latin American are:
- Latin (European in origin)
- African
- Indian (indigenous)

None of these cultures are "pure" today. Each has mutated over the centuries (or, in the case of Iberian populations transplanted to Latin American, failed to develop psychologically from a colonial mentality). Today's ethnic Europeans are not only profoundly different from the contemporary populations of their ancestral countries, behind which they lag in terms of social development, but differ widely within the region. African culture, too, incorporated local influences. Perhaps the least changed are the indigenous populations, wherever they have survived in sufficient density to maintain autonomous cultures—as in Bolivia and much of Peru, but even in remote areas of Mexico, Venezuela, or in upper-Amazon Brazil (although eco-tourism likely will destroy the integrity of local tribes in ways that European conquerors failed to do).

Unable to blend constructively over the centuries, each culture has stagnated. While we may admire the music or dance of Brazil or Argentina, with their fusion of influences, sambas and tangos do not build healthy postmodern societies by themselves.

Yet, there is more cause for hope today than there ever has been for Latin America. While the current cliché of the triumph of democracy, does, indeed, have its positive aspects, the most important factor changing Latin America is the rise of a new generation of leaders, largely educated in the United States, who are not content with the bad habits of centuries. Democracy doesn't make men, men make democracy—although some Washington pundits imagine democracy as some sort of political miracle of loaves and fishes of which men and women are but the passive recipients. The second most important factor is the rise of a global information culture. Though it has yet to affect the lower classes and the underclass to a meaningful degree, it is making a tremendous difference in the awareness, ambitions, and attitudes of the middle classes and skilled members of the working class. The third factor is demographic growth, which is forcing change by itself. Finally, the wild card is the spread (as in Africa) of charismatic Protestant Christianity, which, while empowering to individuals and entire classes, may have the capacity, in the long term, to release uncontrollable social energies. While the world watches Asia, the most innovative and surprising futures—and, potentially, the unexpected dangers—may be brewing up slowly in the Postcolonial Zone of Latin America and sub-Saharan Africa.

This largely-ignored region has the greatest capacity for building alternative futures of any portion of the globe.

**Equality? In Principle, of Course . . .**
Most of Latin America maintains a soft apartheid system in which ethnic Europeans continue to dominate the political,

economic, cultural, and social scene. In countries such as Argentina, where the indigenous population was virtually exterminated (quite late, in the nineteenth century, from the southern pampas to Patagonia) and slaves were few, this hardly matters—the population is Latin, primarily ethnic Italian, then Spanish, with a broad monotheist admixture below those two primary groups (from Welsh to Lebanese). Argentina is something of a dream country for leftists to study, since its fundamental structural problem is its class system, with an extravagant, shamelessly corrupt ruling class, a servile middle class (servile at least until now), and a yearning, politically-vigorous proletariat that historically has been susceptible to demagogues, from Rosas through Peron to Menem, the latter a man who could sell you the same bottle of snake oil several times over.

Yet Argentina has proved that leftist, statist solutions do not work, foundering on simple greed. Today's Argentina, with its aspirations to first-world status, has simply been living beyond its means far too long. It is the state equivalent of an individual who grabbed every credit card offer that ever arrived in the mail, then maxed out the cards immediately. Even before its current financial crisis, Argentina had the highest rate of citizens undergoing psychoanalysis in the world, as well as a high suicide rate (just listen to a few good tangos—they're suicide soundtracks). If Argentina were a single human being, we would recognize the personality type immediately: The sort who always looks for the easy way out, the angle, the quick fix, the high-liver who doesn't worry about paying his bills. Today, there is an especially-sharp edge to the social divisions in Argentina, with the population divided anew into those few who could hoard dollars off-shore and the majority of the population, which relied on its salaries and passbook savings to survive. The fact that a majority of the population is suffering to some degree would make Argentina ripe for another round of authoritarianism, were it not for the fecklessness of the political class and the overall sense of being defeated.

Argentines know they need serious reforms, but they do not want them to interfere with their lifestyles. The country looks played out. Of course, so did Germany in 1932. I do not suggest that the rise of an extreme right-wing movement is on the horizon—another round of empty populism is more likely—but that no one yet knows which path Argentina will follow as it tries to marshal its energies to move forward again. What does a relatively-developed (and almost-hysterically vain) country do when its leaders have bankrupted it and there are no appealing options left?

The Postcolonial Zone truly is humankind's biggest laboratory.

In Brazil, a country of profound ethnic complexity, national propaganda has long held that society is integrated— yet, with few exceptions, the rich are white, mixed-race citizens are in the middle, the blacks are the poorest of the poor, and the Indians of the interior are regarded as curiosities beyond the pale—as pet Martians valued by space travelers from Europe and North America. Yet, in a disconnect of the sort that isn't supposed to happen, according to development theory, Brazil's popular culture is perhaps the best-integrated and most mature in the entire zone: The music is African combined with Portuguese to create a distinctive new form that is as light and flirty as the best Argentine music is brooding and self-dramatizing (although I must confess I prefer the Argentine tangos of Piazzolla—real wrist-slasher, it's-been-raining-for-a-month-and-my-baby's-long-gone stuff). Likewise, Brazilian social mores are unique and, if anything, behaviorally anti-Catholic (whereas, in Mexico, the local hybrid of Catholicism, an admixture of Spanish medievalism and Indian traditions, remains extraordinarily powerful, despite decades of ruthless government attempts to destroy organized religion in the wake of the Mexican Revolution). An academic analyst looking only at the statistics of poverty, exclusion, and inequity, but not knowing the name of the country, would predict that Brazil was over-ripe for a revolution. But national character trumps theory. Brazil, despite intervals of authoritarianism, has been remarkably stable by comparison with many of its neighbors. Brazil is an extremely violent country, but the violence is personal, not collective or purposeful.

In Peru, recent elections constituted a genuine upheaval, with Alejandro Toledo, an ethnic Indian (albeit with a North American wife), elected to the presidency. In the Latin American context, this is a far greater jolt than the election of an American of African ancestry to the Presidency would be in the United States. While I am not espousing Marxist solutions to anything (because they just don't work), analysis of the class system remains the best initial approach to understanding Latin America's persistent problems—and that class system is based primarily upon race, secondarily upon wealth and culture.

There are a few hopeful exceptions: Mexico, where genuine and powerful changes are underway at last, despite deep remaining problems; Chile, where a modern society appears to be solidifying itself, though ultra-conservative elements remain influential; and Cuba, whose government we may despise, but whose genuine integration and limited meritocracy (restricted by political, not social barriers), provides one of the few inspiring models for a workable fusion of society in Latin America. In the post-Castro years, Cuba has a very good chance at becoming a model democratic, market-economy state, without significant racial divisions—but it will not become a "model" for others (talk of Cuban models—except the sort who walk down a runway—will die with Castro). Social models don't work. Countries do not imitate when it comes to social systems. They may imitate forms of government or economy, but populations grow into their own organic forms of social organization. Attempts to force deep and broad social changes on a population never succeed, no matter how many are killed to clear the way, as the last century proved all too painfully. You can, in a successful, rule-of-law state, force through one reasoned change at a time, as the United States did with court-ordered school integration. But you cannot force human beings of different ethnic, religious, and cultural backgrounds to harmonize until they are ready.

The current turmoil in Venezuela, too, is essentially an ethnically-based class struggle, pitting the least-successful mixed-race citizens and Indians, led by their savior of the moment, President Hugo Chavez, against a white and pale-mestizo traditional ruling class. Colonial rule is gone, but colonial class distinctions persist to an astonishing degree. While leftist revolutionaries, from Guevara to Allende, had no workable solutions, we must admit that they were correct that Latin American societies were—and remain—brutally unfair. And race continues to trump every other factor, even in (or especially in) countries where the overwhelming majority of the population are non-white. Even in the most promising countries, when any family has a blue-eyed, blond-haired male child, that child will be treated as the family's great hope and may expect social deference.

Except for countries with high levels of ethnic homogeneity, such as Chile, the most hopeful countries in Latin America

are the northernmost—Mexico and Cuba—adjacent to the
U.S. and subject to its magnetic pull. They are not the richest
countries (especially not Cuba), but their emerging social
orders are setting them up for future success, whereas we
should worry about potential stagnation in Argentina and
even Brazil, countries which so often have looked so irre-
sistibly inviting to so many analysts and investors. Whether
modern (and postmodern) values can triumph over the *prevailing feudalism* of Latin American society in the coming
decades is the primary issue confronting the vast region
between Tierra del Fuego and the Rio Grande.

**The Last Preserve of Feudalism**
I term this region—Africa and Latin America—the Postcolonial Zone because it is that portion of the earth where, even
two hundred years after independence (in Latin America's
case), the pernicious legacies of colonialism endure most powerfully. We tend to think of colonialism as a formal mechanism, such as the rule of a given territory by a distant state
imposed in order to extract benefits from the colony. But colonialism is also a matter of culture and mentality. In this regard,
Latin America is still very much a collection of colonies. Two
centuries after Bolivar, O'Higgins, and San Martin, the spirit
of the *conquistadores* of five centuries ago, their public behavior
and social values, persists, from the barrios of Los Angeles to
the Rio de la Plata.

An in-depth study of the formation of sixteenth-century
Spanish culture and its export is far beyond the scope of this
paper (although this is a topic of immediate relevance to
understanding today's Latin America), and what follows is
only a very short summary of influences and connections that
usually go ignored by strategists or theorists of international

diplomacy. And all this is predicated upon the conviction, based upon extensive first-hand observation of the world, that you cannot get close to meaningful insights unless you are willing to examine current problems in a deep historical context. Just as a psychologist will ask about a troubled human being's childhood, we must ask about the troubled childhood of nations, if we wish to understand them.

The first thing any student of Latin America must grasp is the origin of today's Latin American male values and the lingering ideal of the strong-man, or *caudillo,* with his dual nature of tyrant and dispenser of gifts—even where he is officially gone from the political scene (President Menem of Argentina was nothing more than a modernized "big man," one who ruled with bribes rather than bullets). The real origin of the Latin American strong-man, obsessed with public honor and personal authority, goes even beyond the Spain of the early sixteenth century, with its ruthless knights, so mighty of sword arm, but utterly lacking in personal restraint . . . all the way back to the Moorish occupation of Spain. The political strong-man, but also the dominant family head in a Brazilian *favela* or a shack across the river from El Paso, the brutal drug-lord, and the teenage assassin who kills from greed and vanity, can each be traced to the intolerant Islamic culture of North Africa— which gutted the rich, creative culture of Iberian Islam centuries before the end of the Spanish *reconquista* in 1492 made a formal end of the Muslim presence.

In late-medieval Spain, the two dominant monotheist forces of the age, Islam and Catholicism, did battle. The fanaticism on one side inspired greater fanaticism on the other, inspiring, in turn, yet more fanaticism (the Spanish Inquisition, which we associate with hunting witches, had far more to do with uncovering false conversions among Muslims and Jews, and with maintaining religious militancy). Despite the attempts of revisionist historians to paint late Moorish Spain as something of a dreamy Atlantis destroyed by nasty Christians, by the closing centuries of the Moorish presence both sides had hardened ideologically. Yes, Christian knights sometimes fought as mercenaries under Muslim banners—not least Rodrigo Diaz, "El Cid," whose nickname has Islamic origins: *al sayyid,* the big man, chief or lord—and feudal states crossed religious lines for their advantage. But, ultimately, this became a bitter struggle between two aggressive, expansionist faiths. At first, Christianity was on the defensive, then Islam found itself on the ropes— across eight centuries of struggle, a period of turbulence that could not help but shape the Spanish character.

Indeed, both sides learned from one another—with the Christians getting the advantage of the lingering traces of Islamic scholarship and thought left over from the true golden centuries of Muslim Cordoban culture toward the close of the first millennium. But the *conquistadores* who came to the New World, men such as Cortez and Pizarro, were an amalgam of European feudal knights and Islamic warriors, combining, along with their exemplary bravery, the most callous, intoler-ant and brutal qualities of both cultures. A true man despised the importance of life, although he generally preferred to illustrate the principle on others. And the centuries of reli-gious warfare in Spain had taught even men for whom reli-gion was a mere formality to regard their enemies as less than human. Slaughtering Aztecs or Incas came naturally to these conquerors, especially when local practices appeared repellent and opaque to Spanish logic. The persistent Latin male values of personal honor requiring the respect of others; physical prowess (or, at least, the ability to enforce physical domina-tion); empowering wealth as the ultimate worldly attainment and the association of land, or at least turf, with wealth; control of females and an emphasis on female "virtue" within the family, but on the "conquest" of females without; the low priority assigned to education; the lack of personal self-restraint; the sudden lurches into piety; and the emphasis on building, through largesse and favors, a web of personal allegiances and obligations, are each fundamentally anti-modern qualities. It is only a slight exaggeration to claim that, behaviorally, Latin males are medieval Muslims crossed with a Spanish Catholic knight of the waning Middle Ages.

Another related contribution to the persistence of feudal social forms, even in the face of liberal constitutions, is the emphasis on the extended family as society's organizing principle in Latin America. This obviously inhibits the development of a meritocracy, but it also tends to consolidate assets in land and foreign accounts, starving societies of investment capital—and of the psychological investment necessary for development and a sense of civic responsibility. Colombia, today, remains very much a feudal society, where no one much wants to fight for the state (we may hope that this will change), but where families will do all they can to maintain their own power. A rich Colombian will readily pay a kidnapper's ransom demands, but will go to great lengths to avoid paying his taxes.

The United States had many advantages in its cultural development, but two are of immediate consequence: The U.S. attracted a wide range of immigrants from different cultures, and, from the beginning, multiple interpretations of religious faith existed—and thrived. Citizens of the thirteen colonies and then the United States had to build cooperative relationships across familial, national-origin, and religious lines. Latin America, on the other hand, suffered from an iron uniformity from the beginning, and family-centered, rather than corporate, behavior became the fundamental organizing principle of both society and politics. We find it unthinkable that a modern politician would provide plum jobs for all of his relatives, but the traditional Latin American politician would find it incomprehensible not to do so. This has begun to change at the top, but, in building a modern society, the local level is decisive.

When you study the political alignments in most of Latin America, the U.S. political system is a guide of little value. Study the factions of fifteenth-century Spain and how allegiances were built—or, better still, the history plays of Shakespeare—all the Henry plays, and Richard II, Richard III, and King John. Coalitions are still built upon families, secondarily upon ideologies or laws. Latin America is still very much a medieval society—with skyscrapers, corporate jets, and Mercedes limos.

Like Islam, Latin America skipped the Renaissance.

**The Hermetically-Sealed Empire**
If you lived in Buenos Aires in the eighteenth century and wished to order a book from Europe—and if the book was not forbidden by church or crown—your position on a great river feeding into the Atlantic Ocean was irrelevant. Because Spain maintained careful control over trade and movement, long employing only a few approved ports (all in the Caribbean) for an entire continent's trade with the world, your order traveled by mule westward over the Andes to Lima, Peru. Then your order sailed north to Panama, crossed the isthmus on another mule, and boarded a ship for Spain. The book then retraced the same route to your hands (I am resisting jokes about the original Amazon.com).

This mercantile lunacy had several effects, none of them good. First, it sealed a continent from external influences, which Spain judged wise, but which meant that ecclesiastical painting in eighteenth-century South America looked like sixteenth-century painting in Europe. Societies were closed, inbred, ordered closely by church and state, and isolated. Lacking exposure to wave after wave of European intellectual and social dynamism (by the end of the seventeenth century, Spain itself had become a backwater, so Latin America was the distant backwater of a backwater), societies followed a different developmental path, preserving social structures, strictures, and patterns of behavior that elsewhere had died away. By the nineteenth century, the duel over a point of honor was outlawed in most European states, but it still occurs in the Latin American world, as far north as Los Angeles—although it is altogether a less formal affair these days.

When the colonial yoke was thrown off by the Spanish colonies in the first decades of the nineteenth century, it made surprisingly little difference. Travel opportunities abroad increased for the upper classes, but internal travel became even more dangerous as rural order broke down. The rich could buy a wider range of products. And taxes, when they could be collected, were stolen locally, instead of in Madrid. But the revolutions, and the near-endless coups and revolutions that followed those revolutions, had something of the nature of wild, bloody parties, a letting off of steam, after which little changed and long hangovers had to be endured. The true believers fared worst, and Simon Bolivar died of a broken heart.

Globalized information is finally having an impact upon Latin America, waking broad swathes of the population to new possibilities and providing foreign comparisons for local conditions. Perhaps the most profound effect of the information explosion in Latin America is that it works against fatalism, suggesting that things do not have to be the way they are now and always have been. We will not know the results for at least a generation—perhaps longer—but the proliferation of citizens' organizations is one hopeful indicator. And it is harder for any leader to tell great lies and have them believed.

These days, the books arrive much more quickly.

**A Note on Mexico**
Personally, I have changed my thinking—if cautiously—on Mexico. The election of Vicente Fox was certainly good news, though not irreversibly good. But the crucial factor that reshaped my thinking was that, finally, in the 1990s, the Mexican establishment began to get over its tradition of defining Mexico in the negative, as the anti-United States. Fewer and fewer Mexican intellectuals blame the U.S. for all of Mexico's problems, and ever more Mexicans are anxious to examine their home-grown ills. The system remains far too closed—and the military remains untouchable, by and large—but Mexico is experiencing a new political maturity . . . as well as a renaissance in the popular arts, from music to film. Far from the sleepy cliché of old films, Mexico may become Latin America's most vibrant, perhaps most successful, large country. The relationship with the United States is key, troubled though it may have been in the past. The famous immigration "problems" have benefited both countries, providing critical labor for the U.S., while providing a safety valve for Mexico's surplus population, providing funds for impoverished small towns and villages through remittances (self-help aid), and, again, showing Mexicans first-hand that there are alternative models. Right-wing extremists in the U.S. rant that Mexican immigrants are

turning our cities into little Mexicos. The truth is that those workers, who travel back and forth across the border (often at great and unreasonable risk), want to turn Mexico's cities into little Americas. The American Dream about which we all have heard so much remains an incredibly powerful, galvanizing model.

And if that model applies to the working classes, it applies even more powerfully to the new generation of the Mexican elite, with its degrees from Stanford, Harvard, and MIT. There is no secret plot to take back the Southwest. But there is a great desire to extend the economic and social successes of the American Southwest still farther to the south.

The United States and Mexico long have had an unacknowledged symbiotic relationship. Every indicator suggests that the relationship is at the beginning of a new take-off phase. For all its problems, Mexico is beginning to look like a country of the future, and NAFTA looks less like a final goal attained and more like a first step in the intensification of relations between our two countries.

### The Mighty Fallen

It is easy to forget that Portugal initiated the age of European colonialism. Not only was tiny Portugal once a great imperial power, but its empire quietly lingered on long after others had faded away. This "Lusitanian Empire" once stretched from Brazil, along the African coast, to Goa in India, and beyond to East Timor. And that empire, though impoverished and threadbare, ended less than three decades ago. It was the longest-lasting European empire. When the last Portuguese troops left Mozambique and Angola, and the Indonesians grabbed East Timor, it marked the end of five hundred years of foreign adventures for Lisbon. As with the influence of eight hundred years of Moorish Islamic occupation on Spain, so Portugal influenced much of the world far more than we realize today. And the empire continues to strike back. Mariza, one of the two greatest fado singers of our time (fado is the haunting, ravishing national style of song in Portugal) is black, with roots in Mozambique, and Cesaria Evora, a Cape Verdean who sings in Portuguese, has become a world-music star. Of course, Brazilian music is sung in Portuguese as well, as is a surprising amount of new music from Africa. Ms. Evora is especially interesting, because her music, from her island home set well off the West African coast, blends African, Brazilian, and Portuguese strains until they are something new and inseparable. Perhaps she is simply a singer among many—but I wonder if she is a cultural harbinger of a re-ordered world.

There are two important influences we miss in assessing Latin America. The first is the Portuguese influence, which ties that continent-within-a-continent, Brazil, not only to Europe (a fading tie), but to so much of Africa. Slavery only ended in Brazil a few years after the American Civil War (and de facto slavery lingered much longer). Integration within Brazilian society, though professed, is in many ways less accomplished than it is in the United States. Yet, the influence of Africa on Brazilian society is profound, and Brazil, with its historical, cultural, ethnic, and linguistic ties, could function as an important bridge country to Africa in the future. Because of the way we compartmentalize, we overlook the existence of a centuries-old tie between Africa and Latin America.

Nor is that tie limited to Portuguese-speaking countries. Spanish-language countries of the slave belt, from Brazil northward through the Guyanas, Venezuela, and lowland Colombia into Panama, then across so much of the Caribbean, all have cultures that, to greater or lesser degrees, have digested African influences, brought by slaves. Even English- and French-speaking islands, from Haiti to Jamaica, bind Africa to the New World—and the New World to Africa. "Afro-American" culture isn't something limited to our own black citizens. It is one way of describing our entire culture.

While there is one important difference between the former Portuguese and Spanish colonies—Portuguese influence crossed the Atlantic in both directions, while Spanish influence was largely a one-way affair, making Brazil's ties to Africa much richer in their potential—the African influence on Latin America, and the search for common ground between these two elements of the Postcolonial Zone could prove a very productive line of inquiry.

Of course, this writer is not the first to notice that Africa's influence upon Latin America could be turned around into Latin American influence on Africa. As soon as the Portuguese left Angola, Fidel Castro dispatched Cuban troops to assist in the "liberation struggle." We saw it as World Communism on the march. But it was really a canny recognition of natural affinities. Ultimately, the Cubans lacked the resources to hang on in Africa (although the parties they backed won, and ours lost, more often than not). But the United States has almost inexhaustible resources. Should we be clever enough to learn from Castro's failed vision?

Consider the strategic neglect of the entire Postcolonial Zone. Europe sends aid to Africa, but even the French presence is much diminished. There is little current sense of the continent's potential, only of its liabilities. In Latin America, some countries have complex European ties, from the tragicomic Argentine love for things British (despite the Falklands War) to Madrid's attempts to keep a trans-Atlantic political bridge in reasonably good repair. But Latin America has long been a graveyard for European ambitions (and empires), and the neglect with which it is regarded as a strategic factor is curious, amounting to a surrender to the Monroe Doctrine in an expanded form and to U.S. hegemony. The only missing piece is that the U.S. doesn't bother to be much of a hegemon.

Are we looking in the wrong places for strategic advantage? Or at least not looking in enough different places?

## Unexpected Opportunities

Certainly, we will need to pay attention to the Islamic world for many years to come. And China is far too great to ignore, whatever behavior we expect from Beijing. But consider just a few ways in which the traditional wisdom—or just plain habit—might be turned on its head. This extended essay finally comes down to three alternative lines of strategic thought:

• We see Europe as safe and benign, assuming it will always remain so. Yet, if attacked or sufficiently threatened, Europe may turn again to the export of violence. The United States need not worry overmuch, but other states sharing the Monotheist Zone with Europe had best be careful—especially Islamic states whose citizens might initiate campaigns of terror against Europe, imagining Europeans to be weak-willed.

• We see Asia as the region of the greatest future potential when, in fact, North America is the area of the greatest continuing potential. Asia, while it may grow wealthier, is less likely to innovate new social and governmental forms. Asian development will be evolutionary, not revolutionary, and some countries may stagnate for decades in a cultural strait-jacket, as Japan is in danger of doing. For alternative futures, we must look to areas we have ignored.

- When we look at Africa and, to a lesser degree, Latin America, we see only problems. Given the unfinished nature of these societies, this may be the last human frontier, the zone in which the twenty-first century will see the most dramatic—and perhaps positive—changes. We are foolish if we refuse even to consider the potential in front of us, especially since Africa's and Latin America's natural strategic partner is North America. Ours is the society with cultural ties to both continents, we have done them the least harm, and we provide the most attractive model for the future. We have an appeal as irresistible as our wealth and power are great. Natural affinities are there, right in front of our faces, but our attention is fixed elsewhere. With exclusive, competitive societies in Asia and introverted societies in Europe, our natural sphere of influence lies southward. Africa, especially, may not seem very appealing to American strategic thinkers at present, but that is because we think in short stretches when we think about the future—we run strategic sprints when the greatest power in history is a natural for the marathon. If we truly were adept, the twenty-first century might end with a cultural and economic triangle (and, frankly, a new, benign form of American empire) encompassing North America, Latin America, and much of Africa. Latin America and sub-Saharan Africa may be our last "collectible frontiers." If you want to expand your power and influence, "go where they ain't."

What if the twenty-first century turns out to be an Atlantic, not a Pacific century, based on a huge Afro-Latino-American triangle of strategic power and resources, with aging Fortress Europe looking on?

The future likely will turn out far differently than any of us can imagine, but that does not mean we can afford not to imagine it.

**In Conclusion**

This is, of course, a brief and superficial overview of the strategic environment. To some, it may appear marginally relevant, at best, given the immediacy of our struggle with terrorism. But that is a struggle we are bound to win, although we likely will suffer painful wounds along the way. I argue, instead, that this is exactly the time to devote at least a fraction of our attention and resources to the out years, to alternatives, to both threats *and* opportunities.

The twentieth century conditioned us to think about the threats. Thus, we may be missing some of the greatest opportunities in history. Beyond all the speculation here about the effects of different forms of religion, the power of culture, the patterns of history, and issues of wealth and might, we may, without embarrassment, acknowledge that the United States has one distinguishing gift that sets it apart: We are able to see the potential in others. The vast Postcolonial Zone, spanning two continents, is waiting for us to notice its potential.

This is not necessarily an argument for more aid (although, in the case of Africa, effectively targeted, stringently controlled aid might work wonders) or for a flood of investment (a bucket poured well, here and there, might be preferable). And it is certainly not a recommendation for military exploits or political bullying. In the end, I only suggest that those who live in poverty and powerlessness in disordered societies today need not always be poor and weak. How might we make today's victims tomorrow's allies?

Cuba sent arms to Africa, but it also sent doctors. Castro's vision failed, but he *had* a vision, for exactly those continents under discussion here. He saw the hidden unities. Surely, the United States can do better than that old, failed cigar-chomper in Havana. If he could see the potential a quarter century ago, how on earth can we continue to miss it?

# PART II

## Our Wars

# How Saddam Won this Round

## Newsweek

*November 30, 1998*

The aborted military strike against Iraq may say more about the future of war than any combat encounter of the past decade. In today's Pentagon, where buzzwords substitute for ideas, phrases currently in vogue include "asymmetrical warfare" and "information warfare." Often discussed, they have never been adequately defined or tested. Until now. Saddam Hussein, a low-tech, medieval-minded opponent, used both concepts to neutralize the quarter-of-a-trillion-dollar-a-year military of the United States. The United States may yet be forced to strike, if Iraq doesn't resume full cooperation with U.N. inspectors, including turning over documents that they have demanded. But—at least so far—Saddam has beaten the Pentagon at its own games.

Let's start with asymmetrical warfare. Simply put, that's when a weaker enemy manages to defeat his stronger opponent by coming up with an innovative and affordable strategy. This can be done by developing an unexpected weapon or by rendering the enemy's advantages meaningless. When it tested the asymmetrical thesis in war games, the U.S. military assumed that America would face sophisticated electronic attacks against the national infrastructure by computer hackers. That was a classic case of mirror imaging: the Pentagon convinced itself that America's enemies would do what Americans might do in their position.

Saddam's approach was more incisive. Recognizing America's overwhelming offensive strength and ability to strike any target, he moved the targets into populated areas. Saddam knew that Bill Clinton not only feared risking the lives of his own service members, but dreaded the negative publicity that Iraqi civilian casualties might bring. The Iraqi leader was right: when Saddam appeared to be offering an olive branch, President Clinton seized the move as an excuse to call off an attack that was already in the air, hence avoiding world reaction to the 10,000 Iraqi casualties predicted by the Pentagon.

This hidden weakness of even the smartest weapons and all the myths of precision strikes and bloodless war were instantly exposed. Saddam judged Clinton more clearly than Clinton judged Saddam. And another billion-dollar-plus deployment ground to a halt. Ironically, it was Saddam, not the United States, who won the first bloodless military victory of our time.

Information warfare, the second Pentagon hobbyhorse, has been used as an excuse to spend billions of dollars on digital technology. In its strategizing, the United States again took a narrow view. Military planners assumed that this new form of warfare would rely on dueling computer networks and exotic technologies. The victor would control the opponent's perceptions through "information dominance"—yet another hot phrase in the Pentagon. It was a wonkish vision of war that was more convincing to defense contractors than to America's enemies.

Saddam instead waged old-fashioned, low-tech information warfare against the United States. In a brilliant (if crude) seven year campaign, Saddam managed to shift part of the focus from himself to the harm done to the Iraqi people by U.N. sanctions "dictated by the United States." Facts were irrelevant—image and repetition were all. Over and over again, the world saw video footage of hungry Iraqi children, of Baghdad hospitals without medicine and of Iraqis forced to sell their last possessions to survive. The Clinton administration—and the U.S. military—shrugged all this off as unconvincing propaganda. But much of the world is perfectly willing to believe the worst about the United States—even as countless individuals hunger for America's freedoms and pleasures. Ultimately, the effectiveness of the Iraqi propaganda effort reached even the White House. Without realizing it, the president, too, succumbed to those images of suffering Iraqis when he called off the U.S. attack.

The most open nation on earth, its society and economy powered by information, just lost a strategic campaign to a computer-illiterate society that drastically restricts the circulation of data. This matters. Iraq's strategies would have crumpled under a display of will by Clinton and a determined attack by the U.S. military. But the president lacked the will, and the military missed the opportunity. Ask a general or admiral about it, and you'll be told, "We could've kicked their butts." As North Vietnam's Gen. Vo Nguyen Giap, victor of another asymmetrical conflict, observed about American military prowess, "That is irrelevant."

Iraq just taught the world how to put the most powerful military in history on a leash: plant your vulnerable assets in cities, broadcast the misery of your people and convince America's leadership that political defeat will be the price of military victory. It's an ingenious variation on the old threat to shoot yourself if you don't get your way. There will be countless future versions of this strategy, but all will focus on avoiding rather than confronting America's military strengths. The finest military in the world is meaningless if America can't—or won't—use it.

The United States may yet be forced by circumstance to attack Iraq. But the lessons of America's recent failure of nerve will not be lost on future opponents who lack its wealth, but possess the strength of will to fight with unconventional means.

# This Time, Strike Without Flinching

## The Washington Post

*September 23, 2001*

After the terrorists themselves, America's greatest enemy in its new war may be traditional wisdom. In the military and diplomatic spheres, the rules we have struggled to honor have failed us. Yet in the wake of the atrocities of September 11, the media have been crowded with armchair strategists prescribing the same discredited twentieth-century solutions and warning that any bold response will lead to frightful repercussions. In his address to the nation last Thursday, President Bush rejected the counsels of the timid and defeatist. Yet dangerous myths remain.

The president made it clear that we are at war, that the war will not be short, and that it cannot be waged on the cheap. Certainly, our enemies regard it as war. But this is a new variety of war, without an illuminating precedent, and we will have to learn much as we go. We face enemies whose fundamental beliefs and chosen behaviors cannot coexist with our own, no matter how we attempt to explain away their cruelty. After sleepwalking through the past decade, as we did in the 1930s, we have awakened in our own blood. We can, and will, prevail. But before we can fight well, we must think clearly.

All eyes are focused upon Afghanistan as our likely target, although our strikes may range far afield, simultaneously punishing other states known to sponsor terrorism or host terrorists. Already, we have been subjected to solemn warnings that the British could not conquer Afghanistan in the nineteenth century, the Russians could not subdue it in the twentieth, and therefore America will fail in the twenty-first.

We have heard these warnings before. During the buildup to Desert Storm, the pundits warned us that the Iraqi military was "battle-hardened," and that tens of thousands of American soldiers would come home in body bags. When our success disarmed them, the deep thinkers next warned that the Serbs were born guerrillas (although most were overweight bullies) for whom young Americans were no match. Now we are told that the Taliban warriors are ten feet tall. But I have stood in the Khyber Pass, unlike so many experts, and, if necessary, I would pit our soldiers and Marines against the best fighters the Taliban has to offer. Their rank and file are often brave, but they are war-weary and under assault by their own countrymen, who, although religiously conservative themselves, do not share the extreme views of these "warriors of god." Despite their defiant rhetoric, we would do well not to underestimate the underlying fear our enemies have of our power.

Nor do we want to conquer or occupy Afghanistan, as earlier armies sought to do. We are hunting specific men and groups of their supporters, whom we must kill before they strike us again. Certainly, geography and logistical issues complicate operations against targets in Afghanistan, but all military operations involve risk. We have armed forces of immense skill, capable of raiding a darkened room or destroying entire armies.

We also have been warned that we dare not kill terrorists, thus making martyrs of them. This is absolutely wrong. The surest way to make an effective martyr of a terrorist is to put him in prison, inspiring his followers to commit hijackings, kidnappings, and other acts of terror in an attempt to set him free. We have seen that scenario played out by Germany's Red Army Faction and Colombian narco-terrorists, by Palestinian, Indonesian, Filipino, Peruvian, and even Russian czarist-era terrorists. Osama bin Laden himself has suggested that the United States must be punished for imprisoning his comrades.

Nor is it a matter of jailing a handful of these men. There are thousands of terrorists now, and we may face tens of thousands across the years and decades. In which jails shall we keep them? They are our enemies, in a war. And they are fanatical in the extreme sense of the word. Only by killing them and striking the governments that succor them may we deter their weaker supporters and deny them a place of refuge. The humanitarianism we cherish is regarded as a sign of impotence by such opponents. Theirs is the mentality of the schoolyard bully writ very large, and you cannot appease them anymore than you could a Hitler. Deadly bullies must be beaten down, and those who cheer them on must be chastened as well. If we are unwilling to instill fear in our enemies, we must be content to live in fear ourselves.

The use of special operations forces is much discussed. But they are only one tool in our strategic box, if a superb one. The myth of the surgical strike is as dangerous as it is seductive. We will not be able to reach all of the necessary targets cleanly, nor should we try to economize on the use of our power, which is our great strength. The military is a killing instrument; if we want finesse we should hire a ballet company. Above all, we must seize the initiative, wherever we can, and never ease the pressure in any sphere, military or otherwise.

Crisis drives innovation, and military or security techniques barely imaginable today will seem timid and clumsy in ten years. Our military, though strong and well-trained, is far from perfectly structured for the task before us, but we are in far better shape than we were in 1941. We have large, well-trained, and well-equipped standing forces, and we will not have to expand hastily from a small, resource-starved military to the ten million man establishment we required for World War II. But we will have to change many of our practices and priorities. In the near- to mid-term, we should cancel expensive, irrelevant systems such as the F-22 fighter and buy more transport. Except for the Marines, with their expeditionary tradition, our forces are in the early phases of a transition to less ponderous structures that can reach distant trouble spots more swiftly with sufficient power. The pace of change will have to be accelerated, and it is only lamentable that it took a catastrophe to make the need for more responsive forces seem urgent.

Much remains unknown, as it always does at the beginning of a war. We do not even know where we will fight with certainty. Though Afghanistan has our attention at the moment, there appear to be more terrorist-related targets on the territory of our provisional ally Pakistan than there are in the Afghan mountains and valleys. Iraq supports terrorism, despite pronouncements from specialists that Saddam Hussein fears fundamentalist extremists. In reality, Saddam appears to have tried to use terrorists to his own ends, while placating them with support. There is already compelling evidence that our pursuit of terrorists and their supporters will lead deep into Saudi Arabia and the Persian Gulf states, and that their networks are embedded from Algeria to Canada. Nor do we know who our ultimate allies will be. In future years, we may again align with Iran, our natural strategic ally in the region.

At least in geographic scope, this unsettling new struggle truly is a world war.

A last, well-meant, but pernicious warning has been that, if we adopt ferocious means of fighting back against our enemies, we will become just like them. This is nonsense. In World War II, we responded to Japanese and German savagery with indescribable brutality of our own. We firebombed the cities of our enemies and ended the war by dropping atomic bombs. On the bitterly contested islands of the Pacific, our GIs did not read Japanese soldiers their rights before burning them to death with flamethrowers. Yet the men and women of the "Greatest Generation" did not come home to stage a military coup. They came back, gladly, to peace, liberal democracy, and the GI Bill.

We must recognize that this is a new age, with new rules and new requirements. We cannot prevail with the failed wisdom of a failed century.

# In Praise of Instability

## The Wall Street Journal

*November 1, 2001*

The greatest allies Islamic extremists have in the West are America's strategists. Still unable to move beyond Cold War models of geopolitics and subject to the diplomatic group-think that cuts across party lines in Washington, those who would pass as sages warn us that we must restrict our actions in Afghanistan so that we do not destabilize Pakistan and other countries in the region. But stability is a false god, and on September 11 we paid dearly for worshipping it above all others.

The Cold War deformed our strategic thinking beyond moral recognition. We supported monstrous dictators and demagogues—many in the Islamic world—because they were "ours." After the collapse of the Soviet empire, the world changed. But our thinking did not. Across the past decade, the supreme goal of American foreign policy was global stability. In an age of breakdown and devolution, we have struggled to stop history in its tracks.

Even as the Soviet Union was dissolving, the first Bush administration, incredibly, tried to persuade its components to remain together. We squandered our victory in Desert Storm by not deposing Saddam Hussein because we feared a power vacuum. The price of an imaginary stability was the slaughter of the Shiites in the south and the Kurds in the north, with the remainder of Iraq's people deprived and oppressed unto this day—while Saddam supports terrorism and nurses weapons of mass destruction. In shrinking Yugoslavia, first the Bush then the Clinton administration wasted their efforts on attempts to preserve the fiction of unity and intact borders, instead of recognizing the popular will. Even in Somalia, we pretended a state existed where tribes ruled.

Now the usual suspects warn us of the threat of instability in the middle of Asia. But what if the world needs more instability, not less? What if change is both overdue and inevitable? In any case, how much blood and treasure are we willing to expend to prop up more decayed or dying regimes?

Certainly, civil conflict in a state such as Pakistan is a serious matter, but such reckonings cannot be postponed forever. We must look beyond the red-herring issue of Pakistan's nuclear weapons, which could be neutralized, and ask ourselves if lines drawn hastily on a map by retreating empires still serve adequately in the twenty-first century. The greatest geostrategic con-game going is the threat of self-indulgent states to collapse if we fail to support them. Might not re-drawn borders better serve the people of both Pakistan and Afghanistan? And, later, the citizens of Iraq?

Instead of focusing exclusively on short-term problems, we should be thinking many moves, and years, ahead. Rather than fighting a losing battle to maintain a false, imposed stability, we should ask ourselves how we might best influence and shape instabilities to our long-term advantage. The model of stability at all costs has failed us. This is an age of transition between old, decrepit regimes and new forms of political organization. It is time for our strategic thinking to move on.

We also need to maintain our resolve. We need to destroy all terrorist networks in Afghanistan (and, later, elsewhere) and eliminate the Taliban government that supported terror. But we have already gotten bogged down in nonsensical debates about whether or not the Northern Alliance should be allowed to take Kabul, given Pakistani sensibilities. We owe Pakistan nothing. Pakistan, which has supported both the Taliban and the terrorists, is in our debt—at best, Pakistan should be on very strict probation, with no veto power over our reckoning with our enemies.

The Taliban and their Arab religious-mercenaries have done exactly what military thinkers predicted such enemies would do. Confronted with American military technology, they hid among the population in urban warrens or took to remote hide-outs invisible to our sensors. Common sense says it would be better to let the Northern Alliance do the initial dirty work of trying to root the Taliban out of Kabul and other cities, rather than using U.S. troops in the bloody initial phases (they still might be necessary for the endgame). But common sense gets lost in National Security Council meetings. Thus we have only belatedly begun to give the Northern Alliance the logistical and air support needed for an offensive.

Worse, we continue to let Saudi Arabia bully us. My own greatest worry is that the Bush administration will be unable to rise above its oil-field roots. We have allowed the Saudis to convince us that we need them, when the opposite is true. Without the oil revenue to bribe its own population (including terrorists) and its neighbors, the House of Saud would collapse. The Saudis have the blood of September 11 all over themselves. We owe them less than we owe the Pakistanis, and it is time to call their bluff.

Imagine if the Saudi oil fields were confiscated, administered in trust, and the revenue used to develop public health, sanitation, and education systems throughout the Islamic world, instead of funding the degenerate excesses of royalty on vacation in the West. Of course, we would hear initial threats and complaints from other Arab states—even as they calculated how best to grab their share of the financial spoils. The Saudis are hated at least as deeply as we are, and the crocodile tears shed for them would barely mask the underlying grins.

If such a scenario seems extreme today, let the reader wait five years and look back. September 11 truly did inaugurate a new age. The global ramifications have barely begun to be felt. While the domestic lives of Americans will, in fact, be the least affected in all this, much of the Islamic world will be bitterly challenged and dramatically reshaped.

It is their moment of truth, not ours, the hour when Islamic governments must decide whether to embrace a comforting, medieval interpretation of religion that excuses failure and blames others, or to begin the much more difficult effort to build more modern, tolerant, decent societies. Many will make the easy and wrong choice. But this decade likely will see the most profound geo-strategic changes since the 1940s.

Washington, for its part, must stop relying on old answers to deadly new questions. Our obsession with an often illusory, and always transient, stability, and our corollary insistence that even the worst borders must not change and that even the most despotic regimes may fairly claim sovereignty, is ultimately more dangerous than Osama bin Laden or any other terrorist.

# The Saudi Threat

## The Wall Street Journal

*January 4, 2002*

The Bush administration has done a remarkable job, thus far, of counterattacking terrorists physically and psychologically. Pundits complain of imperfections, as they always will, but the administration has succeeded magnificently in a challenging military environment, while cutting through a great deal of diplomatic nonsense and received wisdom that paralyzed America during the Clinton years.

President Bush has reinvigorated America's strategic will and made a useful display of our might. He and his secretary of defense out-generaled our own generals, who had become timid when not defeatist. But all of this administration's admirable successes to date fall short of addressing the obvious source of fundamentalist terrorism, subversion, and hatred: Saudi Arabia.

This is an oilman's administration, and long affiliation with energy affairs appears to have blinded an otherwise superb strategic team to the abundant, well-documented evidence. Far from examining Saudi Arabia's deep and extensive complicity in supporting terror and undermining secular regimes throughout the Muslim world and beyond, the administration reflexively defends the Saudis. I do not believe the administration is intentionally dishonest—only that ties to the oil business and a half-century's assumptions prevent it from facing up to Saudi Arabia's support for, and funding of, the cruelest, most benighted and hate-filled version of one of the world's great religions.

A few months ago, I suggested on this page that the U.S. must overcome its Cold War–era obsession with stability and open itself to the possibilities of creative instability in a world that still has far too many dictators and corrupt, oppressive regimes. When it comes to Saudi Arabia, we get the worst of both stability and instability. While we automatically support the Saudis, no matter how high-handedly they treat us, and insist that they are the foundation of regional stability in the Middle East, the Saudis themselves have engaged in a decades-long campaign to destabilize secular and relatively tolerant regimes throughout the Muslim world.

Instead of an instability that opens the door to freedom, the Saudis foment instability that leads to still-greater oppression, backwardness, and bigotry. By funding religious extremists from Michigan to Mindanao, the Saudis have done their best to destroy democracies, turn back the clock on human rights, and deny religious freedom to Islamic and other populations—while the United States guarantees Saudi security. It is the most preposterous and wrongheaded policy in American history since the defense of slavery.

Consider, concretely, what the Saudis have done. While the average American newspaper reader knows that the majority of the September 11 hijackers were Saudis, that Osama bin Laden is a Saudi, and that Saudi money funded the attacks on the U.S., this is only a small fraction of Riyadh's misdeeds.

In Indonesia, a state whose only hope for survival rests on religious tolerance, the Saudis have funded and encouraged the most extreme Muslim groups. The syncretic, easygoing version of Islam that long prevailed in most of Indonesia is anathema to the Saudi Wahhabi vision of religion, and the Saudis have tried to undermine social rights, to suppress other religions, to poison the educational system—and even to determine the architecture of mosques. As a result, Indonesia is under externally induced stresses that exacerbate the state's home-grown problems. What might have been an example of how Islam can adapt to the future threatens to become yet another example of how Islam drags a country backward.

Pakistan, seduced by Saudi money, has sown the wind and is reaping the whirlwind. Saudi religious schools, mosques, and bribes encouraged fundamentalist movements that have supported terror against the U.S., India, and the more liberal elements in Pakistani society. The Saudi vision of anti-Western, crusading Islam essentially took over Pakistan's intelligence services and infiltrated the military, with the result that Pakistani support not only for the Taliban, but for al Qa'eda, plunged the world toward September 11. Finally the Saudis were essential sponsors of Pakistan's push to develop "Islamic" nuclear weapons, although the U.S. government ignored the evidence.

Saudi citizens and Saudi funds supported the Taliban's reign of terror in Afghanistan, enabling al Qa'eda to become a state within a state. Saudi funds bankroll the fiercest anti-peace terrorist groups in the Middle East and pay the bills for ultra-extremist mosques and Islamic schools from Europe to South America.

Yet our nation's leaders insist the Saudis are not only our allies, but our friends—even as Saudis and Saudi money kill Americans and the Saudis refuse to arrest or even freeze the bank accounts of their implicated citizens. Meanwhile, we cannot use the air bases from which our forces are supposed to protect Saudi Arabia to protect ourselves, our female service personnel must go about in Islamic dress when they leave the quarantine of those bases, and religious hatred of the West is the national diet of information—and Saudi Arabia's only meaningful export other than oil. Our blithe acceptance of this is madness.

Since September 11, the Saudis have mounted a well-funded campaign to convince Americans that they bear no blame for anything. But they're worried. It long has been a Saudi assumption that they could buy whatever influence they needed in America, and they have, indeed, had many an influential American on their payroll, from lawyers and lobbyists to businessmen and out-of-work politicians. They joke about us as they would about prostitutes, and regard us as no better, if more enduringly useful. Their strategy worked as long as the rest of America slept. But the Saudis learned, after the attacks on New York and Washington, that the American people as a whole cannot be bought. Not even with cheap oil.

The same voices that cautioned us to do nothing meaningful against terrorism now warn that any alternative to the current Saudi regime might be even worse. That is a coward's argument. The Saudi cancer will continue to metastasize if we shy away from treating it, and any new government on the Arabian peninsula is likelier to be scrutinized and contained than the checkbook terrorists of the royal family. Why not give change a chance, instead of supporting the most repressive and vicious monarchy remaining on this earth?

We must begin by confronting the Saudis and giving them the clear choice President Bush offered the rest of the world: Either you are with us in the fight against terror, or you are against us. There can be no middle ground—especially not for terrorism's most enduring sponsors.

We must work against the Saudis' campaign of religious hatred and subversion around the world. And we must begin looking for other regional partners, from a liberated Iraq to a future Iran. Finally, we must be prepared to seize the Saudi oil fields and administer them for the greater good. Imagine if, instead of funding corruption and intolerance, those oil revenues built clinics, secular schools, and sewage systems throughout the Middle East. Far from being indispensable to our security, the Saudis are a greater menace to it than any other state, including China.

Terrorism is not going to disappear, no matter how successful our military, diplomatic, and economic efforts. Those efforts can, however, greatly reduce the appeal of terrorism to prospective acolytes and diminish dramatically its power and reach, while denying hard-core terrorists safe havens.

Our efforts are off to a superb beginning, and there is much reason for optimism, so long as the strength of will of this and future administrations does not waver. But we will not get close to the heart of the matter until we face up to the hateful, medieval, murderous nature of the Saudi vision of Islam. Anti-women, anti-meritocracy, anti-democracy, anti-education in any meaningful, liberating sense, racist, and profoundly anti-freedom. Saudi-sponsored religious extremism, funded by all the drivers of those over-sized SUVs on American roads, is the most destructive vision in the world today.

# In War, Soldiers Die

## The Wall Street Journal

*March 5, 2002*

To be an effective critic, you must also know when to praise. In the five short months since the beginning of combat action in Afghanistan by U.S. forces, our military has shown a remarkable ability to learn as it fights. The broadcast media, by comparison, has fought the opportunity to learn. As I write, various television and radio networks are trumpeting reports of half a dozen or so American combat deaths in tones reserved for catastrophes. The reportage is naive, irresponsible—and just plain wrong.

I have been a soldier. My most cherished friends still wear Army uniforms. Several are in Afghanistan or Pakistan at this moment, and a man I love as a brother is in an extremely dangerous position. I can assure the reader that my feelings regarding American losses are serious. But let me be blunt: While every American life matters, in war good guys get killed as well as bad guys. Soldiers know this when they volunteer. And nine or ten—or a hundred—U.S. combat deaths do not indicate defeat or even a meaningful tactical setback, depending on the scale of the operation. (By the way, did the hundreds of firefighter deaths in the World Trade Towers mean the New York Fire Department had failed?). Combat deaths indicate that we are serious about destroying the enemy, that we are willing to do whatever it takes. I would be far more distrustful of a campaign without casualties.

Consider how far we have come in a very short time. Immediately after September 11, the great majority of commentators and pundits warned that any U.S. military intervention in Afghanistan was doomed. Of course, most of those talking heads had never served in uniform, had never been in the region, and had only the most superficial grasp of history. All they had were opinions—but their defeatism was delicious to the media. To its enduring credit, the Bush administration ignored the think-tank cranks and soft-bellied columnists, with their taste for mediocre prose and imitation thought.

Our military, admittedly still suffering a residual infection from the cowardice of the Clinton years, moved timidly at first. Then the generals and admirals seem to have gotten the message that our national leadership was serious this time. The lights went on, and they were green ones. Our military embarked on an extraordinarily impressive program of learning-by-doing in wartime. When our Kosovo-style, stand-off bombing cued by strategic sensors didn't work, we quickly put special operations forces on the ground to identify targets. The effectiveness of our airstrikes soared. Despite more "expert" advice and handwringing from the punditocracy, we realized soon enough that the Northern Alliance was the horse to back.

When bombing fixed targets failed to have the desired effect, we turned to bombing the Taliban's frontline troops—and watched them collapse. The war went even faster than a handful of optimists believed it could. According to our doctrine, our combination of the use of the most sophisticated strategic resources and old-fashioned boots on the ground (with satellite communications) was not the way such a campaign was supposed to work. But it was the way things did work. Given that the military is, above all, a bureaucracy, we were able to adjust to the new rules with astonishing speed.

In the Tora Bora operation, which was a powerful military success by any standard, we did get some things wrong. We expected too much of our Afghan surrogates, and, as a result, more of the Taliban and al Qa'eda fighters escaped than we would have liked. But Tora Bora was an important milestone in getting over the no-ground-forces nonsense of the Clinton years—it proved irrefutably that there are times when our troops must go in and do the job themselves.

That is what we are seeing now. Larger numbers of special operations forces and infantrymen are engaged in the current operations south of Gardez simply because that is what it takes. The Tora Bora operation was staged in haste, amidst the confusion of a fast-moving war and a collapsed state. This time, there has been a careful intelligence build-up, coordination with Pakistani forces on the border and with our allies, a build-up of innovative munitions for our aircraft, training, and equipment for at least some of the Afghans fighting alongside of us—and a detailed plan of operations. We timed the operation carefully, so the enemy would still be obstructed by winter conditions. Even security was better than it had been in the past, despite the scale of the effort. Our enemies were not allowed the time and the means to escape. Many, if not all, of them are surrounded now. Should we be surprised if encircled fanatics fight doggedly?

There likely will be more American casualties. Perhaps many more. We may see some American elements ambushed and even wiped out. That's war, folks. You suck it up and keep on marching. War is, ultimately, a contest of wills. And our war with terrorism is a knife-fight to the bone. When Americans die, the sole correct response is to hit back even harder.

Even the best-planned combat operations by the best-trained, best-equipped troops can go awry. Combat is disorienting, confusing, and indescribably dangerous. Your enemy is intent on killing you and surviving, just as you are intent on destroying him. Our combat losses, though we feel each one, are understandable and, to a painful extent, inevitable. We have done an astonishing and commendable job of limiting our casualties. But soldiers die in war.

My sole fear is that some elements within our government, responding to the broadcast media's alarmist whining, will argue for interrupting the operation. That would be entirely wrong. We cannot afford any more Mogadishus, where U.S. victories convince our leaders to cut and run. The least wavering merely encourages our enemies and costs us far more casualties down the line—as the last administration's failure to take serious action against terrorism led directly to September 11. I don't think the Bush administration will follow such a course—but we must not flinch for even an instant. Not even if the casualty figures soar. The best way to honor our dead is to defeat the enemy.

# What Terror Wrought

New York Post

*March 11, 2002*

In the opening days of our new world war against a global evil, mortified critics attacked President Bush for calling our effort a crusade. Of course, we must be sensitive to the feelings of mass murderers and religious fanatics everywhere—especially in the hate-swept Arab world—but the truth is that our president had chosen exactly the right word. This war is a crusade.

It is not a crusade against a religion, but against the perversion of religion by human monsters. It does not aim at occupying a Jerusalem new or old, but at providing safety from terror for decent and law-abiding people everywhere.

It has nothing to do with minor campaigns in the Middle East a millennium ago, but it has a great deal to do with the Middle East's self-inflicted wounds, pervasive bigotry, and relentless oppression in the more recent past.

Our crusade against terror pits a better future against the tenacious grip of past hatreds, and tests our hard-won freedoms against the power of the fist, the bomb, and the assassin. This is not a religious war—unless it is a war *for* Islam and

151

against those who have poisoned a great religion with blasphemy, bloodshed, and tyranny.

This is, truly, a war against evil.

We, the American people, in our powerful, peerless diversity, may be unreservedly proud of our government's resolve and our military's performance in the six swift months since September 11.

Although this struggle will last for many more years—likely for decades—and though its focus will shift from one tormented scrap of the globe to another, we have made a remarkable beginning.

Those who believed that a handful of vicious attacks might terrorize America into submission now must live in terror themselves—if, indeed, they are still alive.

The world is learning yet again that, although America does not seek wars, the American people know how to fight when the fight matters.

With unprecedented speed, we toppled one of the world's most oppressive governments, imprinting our power upon a wild land.

Legions of pundits, at home and abroad, said that it could not be done. But we did it.

Our military has burnished old skills and mastered new ones, startling even our closest allies with our capabilities.

We have taken the offensive against terror, seizing the initiative from those who would rewrite history in the blood of the innocent, and we are pursuing those terrorists not only in the mountains of Central Asia, but in the Caucasus, in the Far East, and in the backcountry of the Arabian peninsula.

Less publicly, our soldiers, diplomats, and law enforcement officials are at work on every continent except Antarctica—and if the last al Qa'eda members try to hide out among the penguins, our Navy SEALs will track them down. Perhaps the most hopeless and frustrated human being on earth today is a terrorist trying to qualify for a life insurance policy.

Despite our successes, the future will bring setbacks. This is inevitable in so mighty a struggle. Human genius is not always used to good ends, and the powers of jealousy and hatred alive in this world are seldom understood by Americans.

We are not hated because we are evil. We are hated because we are good, and successful, and free. A society where power flows from the bottom upward, from the citizen to the state, a society in which men and women of every race deal with each other simply as fellow human beings, and a society in which men and women do not need to guard their speech from government spies and religious tyrants is a society that terrifies dictators, demagogues, and street-corner bullies everywhere.

We compose the society that says an emphatic "Yes!" to human aspirations. And we are at war with those who believe the answer to human hopes and desires should always be "No!"

We will suffer more terror attacks in the coming years, despite our best efforts at defense. But our enemies will never destroy, nor deter, nor even discourage us.

And we will be relentless in our pursuit of them. We will suffer casualties. But our military will make certain that our enemies suffer far more.

Our true strength, though, lies not in weaponry, though arms are necessary in this troubled world. America's strength resides in every citizen reading these words on a March morning, in all those who will go on to do their daily parts to make our country prosper, in those who will work, think, teach, learn, sweat, dream, and love as part of history's greatest experiment in human freedom.

We are six months into a great crusade. It may last beyond our lifetimes. But the outcome is not in doubt.

# A Case for Killing

New York Post

*April 2, 2002*

It's about who dies. Therein lies the most profound difference between Palestinian terror and the Israeli response.

The masters of terror employ unstable young Palestinians as human bombs to slaughter the innocent. Israel responds with disciplined military force that attempts to target the cynics and cowards behind the campaign of terror.

In Israel's wars and conflicts, a disproportionate number of leaders die, for Israeli officers lead from the front. The men who pull the bloody strings in Palestine hide, sending children to do the dying for them.

Without question, the young suicide bombers are guilty of horrendous crimes. But theirs is the guilt of the fool, the patsy, the mere accomplice. Where is the outcry from human-rights organizations against the Palestinians—and other Arabs—who carefully identify, seduce, brainwash, and murder, through the missions assigned them, eighteen-year-old girls and twenty-year-old young men?

If martyrdom for the cause is so glorious, why are there so few middle-aged Palestinian martyrs from the terrorist leadership? Why do the masterminds of the bombing campaigns go to extraordinary lengths to survive themselves? For the people? For the Palestinians whose misfortunes terror has only worsened?

The truth is that the cowards are calling the shots in the West Bank and Gaza—or from their hide-outs in nearby Arab states.

Although I believe that the founding of Israel was one of the few great moral acts of the twentieth century, I long saw the injustice in the Palestinian situation. Nor did I overlook Israel's errors and self-defeating arrogance. But the Palestinians have blown away their pretense at being the wronged party. Even their most legitimate claims have withered with the long campaign of targeting Israeli civilians.

There are many hallmarks that make a human society worthwhile. One is courage. That particular quality may be out of fashion in Paris or Berlin, but it is back on the strategic runway in Washington—and it was never out of vogue with the American people beyond the Beltway. A society that behaves with forthright courage, that fights as a body to defend itself, deserves our admiration and support.

And Israel's people serve, whether their parents are rich or poor. (In Palestine, the poor die while the powerful steal from them.) Risks are shared in Israel. A vigorous, even raucous, democracy, Israel is a rule-of-law state that offers hope to its citizens. It does not slaughter its sons and daughters wantonly, but values human life.

The hypocrites and demagogues behind the "Second Intifada" demonstrate many qualities—greed, cruelty, vanity, cynicism—but courage is not one of them. They hide, and fatten, and send the young to die for them.

Were they to laud their young martyrs less, and to carry the bombs themselves, we might have some grudging sympathy. But the men in the shadows have no intention of dying for their cause—especially since their cause is personal power, not very useful in the grave.

The old men behind the young bombers intend to live, to lord it over feudal Palestinian fiefdoms in a bigoted kleptocracy. The corruption and rigged elections of Arafat's government were nothing compared to what the really good haters heading the terrorist movements would bring to pass.

And Yasser Arafat is a terrorist. It's a shame the Israelis did not have the audacity to kill him on the first day of their recent counter-offensive. Arafat's "Who me?" response to every new terrorist incident is absurd. He knows. And even the Europeans know he knows. Yet now the U.S. government, braking Israel yet again, has guaranteed Arafat's survival (unless a minor miracle occurs in that Ramallah compound).

But, ultimately, Arafat is an over-the-hill con man, not a lion or a leader any longer. As long as Israel does not shrink from the task at hand, as long as Israel's armed forces and intelligence arm go after the worst terrorist leaders and their organizations—wherever they hide—the Palestinian threat can be diminished to a bearable level.

That threat will not disappear. But the Palestinian sponsors of terror, even within Arafat's own organization, must be hunted down and killed.

No matter the outcry from Arabs who talk but won't fight, or from third parties whose credibility is even lower than their capabilities. Success will be forgiven.

But Israel can no longer bow even to grotesquely misguided American pressure to give in to terror at home, while America takes the offensive against terror everywhere else to defend our own people.

Terror is terror—and Palestinian terror is arguably the worst in the world today: The terrorists want to see Israel destroyed and its people annihilated. The Palestinian vision isn't one of freedom, but of the Holocaust Part Two, in slow motion.

The United States and Israel must present a united front against the butchers of the world. And that means accepting the fact that the major Arab states are not now, and never will be, our allies. They are our enemies.

If America continues to argue—essentially—that suicide bombers must be rewarded with concessions and that Israel should display forbearance, make no mistake: The apostles of terror around the world will learn the lesson well that suicide bombing works.

If only a fraction of the horrendous bombings Israel has endured had occurred on American soil, our response would have been ferocious. We cannot impose a double standard on Israel—for our own sakes.

We are in this together, even if our State Department thinks terrorists are just misguided souls who need understanding. Terrorists need to be killed. Wherever we—or the Israelis—find them.

There is no moral equivalence in this conflict. None. The formally recognized Palestinian authorities, as well as the dark men behind the scenes, are evil.

The word may be unpopular with anemic scholars or with European governments—most notably that of France, which remains permeated with anti-Semitism—but President Bush used the correct word in describing terrorists and the governments behind them elsewhere in the world: Evil.

Now he needs to apply it to the Palestinian terrorists.

# The Real War Crime

New York Post

*May 3, 2002*

A terrible war crime has been committed in the West Bank. It will have far-reaching and heartbreaking consequences. But it has nothing to do with lies about an imaginary massacre in Jenin. The war crime—committed brazenly before a global audience—is the occupation of the Church of the Nativity, in Bethlehem, by Palestinian terrorists.

Where is the outcry? International law forbids the parties to armed conflict from using churches, as well as hospitals, museums, and monuments, for military activities. The Laws of Land Warfare are even stricter.

The United Nations, which is ever quick to condemn Israel, has been silent about this violation, even though the Palestinian actions violate the U.N.'s own rules. The church is even under UNESCO designation as a protected site.

Even the ancient tradition of murderers, thieves, and other criminals seeking sanctuary on holy ground denies them the right to take weapons into the sacred precincts. Under every single applicable code of law, as well as the custom of nations, every Palestinian who carried a gun into the Church of the Nativity, turning it into a fortress, is a war criminal.

Not one voice has been raised to condemn them.

Why? The fact is that, beyond Europe's reflexive anti-Semitism, liberal racism plays a role. Despite widespread criticism of Israel as inhumane, the world holds Israel to a much higher standard than it does any of Israel's mortal enemies.

Bluntly put, this is just a left-wing version of the pathetic old notion that "our little brown brothers" aren't really as capable or as responsible as "we" are. The motivations of Israel's critics are as disgraceful as their one-sided condemnations are unjust.

The Palestinians did not decide spontaneously, by telepathy, to gather in the Church of the Nativity as the Israelis approached. The action was planned well in advance, as any veteran would recognize. The church had been predesignated as a rallying point for hard-core terrorists and others who feared Israeli retaliation—doubtless with Yasser Arafat's blessing.

The immediate and well-organized occupation of one of Christianity's holiest shrines was an illegal, cynical gambit.

The Palestinians knew they could count on several things:

• First, the Israelis *do* observe international law, and they respect religious and cultural monuments. Unless savagely provoked, they would not even fire in the direction of the church, so the terrorists were safe from immediate capture.

• Second, despite the level of provocation from inside, any Israeli action could be portrayed as an attack on a Christian shrine.

• Third, any damage to that shrine would be blamed on the Israelis, on their tanks and firepower, by those portions of the world anxious to paint Israel as a land of devilish aggressors. In that regard, we should be prepared for an orgy of destruction on the part of the church's occupiers.

The Palestinians stole a lesson from, of all people, Gandhi, though they corrupted it hideously. Despite his litany of complaints about British inhumanity, Gandhi knew the British courts in India would never hang him, and he turned London's sense of decency and fair play—as well as the rule of law—against the British themselves. So, too, the Palestinian terrorists count on Israel's sense of decency and morality, as well as its laws, to save them from the justice they deserve.

Why does this matter to us? Apart from our emotional and spiritual ties to the site, if we are Christians? And our respect for the sanctity of the shrine, no matter our religion?

It matters because the Palestinian terrorists in Bethlehem just set a precedent. They broke *all* the laws and rules—and got away with it. Instead of condemning them, the world community has shown a tragic, nearsighted tolerance for their deed. By turning the Church of the Nativity into a gangsters' hide-out, the Palestinians placed themselves on the same level as the Taliban savages who destroyed the Bamiyan Buddhas. Instead of expressing its outrage, this time the world showered the criminals with sympathy.

The result will be future occupations of churches and synagogues, the military use of hospitals, the betrayal of symbols such as the red cross and red crescent, and the inevitable destruction of cultural monuments in the name of one deluded cause or murderous movement after another. The Church of the Nativity has just been turned into the Golgotha of the remaining rules of armed conflict.

Welcome to war in the twenty-first century.

# Their Monument is America

## New York Post

*Memorial Day, 2002*

Never let anyone tell you that freedom is priceless. As you read these words, miniature flags adorn countless graves across America. In the cemeteries where our nation's veterans lie buried, the price lies there for all of us to see.

From Arlington to small Midwestern towns, aging veterans listen in silence to the firing of salutes, honoring comrades who did not come home from the fields of France, or the hills of Korea, or the jungles of Vietnam. Or from Somalia or Afghanistan.

To commemorate the sacrifices of those who died far from home—or who returned from war to die years later—we hold parades and listen as politicians speak from the steps of monuments of granite, marble, and bronze.

But no one remembers our war dead the way the veterans do. They go about it more quietly, many recalling other mornings when they did not know if they would live to see the night.

They recall the friendships cut short by death, the loneliness that even buddies cannot penetrate, the misery of being wet or cold for weeks on end, the counting of the days, the doubts, the hopes and fears . . . and feelings not of triumph but of relief, when word came of the enemy's surrender, or when they boarded a ship or plane for home.

Beyond all the marching bands and well-meant accolades, there is something else, too . . . a mix of pride and sorrow, an identity that sets apart the soldier who survived his nation's wars, or even the dangers and dislocations of peace. When those who have worn a uniform look into one another's eyes, there is a shared knowledge that no words can communicate to others.

Of course, soldiers, young or old, are honored by holidays and the tributes of their fellow citizens. But they know, too, that the fuss goes only so far.

Valued, too, are the "lasting" memorials—from the monument at the edge of Central Park honoring the Fighting 69th, to the solemnity of Gettysburg and Shiloh, to the vast cemeteries in Belgium, France, and Luxembourg.

But the real memorial to our vets isn't a pillar, plaque, or statue. Their great, shared monument is our country itself.

Look beyond yourself and the concerns of the moment. Look at this blessed, prospering, remarkably humane and decent nation, this homeland of simple fairness without precedent in history, this triumph against the odds, where so many cultures, religions, and races merged and continue to merge to our common good.

Look at your fellow citizens, in all their wonderful, aggravating, entertaining, nearly impossible diversity, all of them Americans.

Being American is something utterly new in human history.

In an age of reborn fears and old doubts resurrected, when even Europe is wracked again with hatred and so much of the world is ravaged by antique bigotries, Americans have built a living monument of what humankind can become when we reach out to our neighbors with open hands, instead of with fists, and when the law stands not for what is forbidden, but for what is possible.

I have seen firsthand how easily it can be otherwise. I have seen it in country after country, from impoverished refugee camps in the Caucasus, to wantonly ruined towns in the Balkans, to societies afraid of a simple conversation in the street . . . to lands where armed men face each other across a fragile border, determined to kill because their ancestors killed each other hundreds of years before.

As a writer, I respect the power of words and am cautious of their misuse. But I do not hesitate to use the word "miracle" to describe the United States of America.

I realize that we, too, have known hatreds in the past. But we have not reveled in them or celebrated them. Americans look forward to all that can be . . . while too many in this troubled world look only backward, without mercy or forgiveness.

While millions of men and women around the world cannot escape from old nightmares, we Americans are humanity's great dreamers. Nor are we idle dreamers. We dream great dreams, and then we make them real.

And of those who would become Americans, we ask only that they share the dream, that they, too, leave old allegiances and hatreds behind, and join us in this peerless, unfinished project called the United States of America, where no man or woman need bow down because of the accident of birth, where every peaceful path to God is valid, and where the children of old enemies can become friends, partners, and even husband and wife.

What greater monument could there be to any soldier's sacrifice?

One day each year we honor our military veterans. But we do not honor war. We Americans regard war as a failure, as a desperate necessity and last resort. We seek peace, not conquest.

But, as we were reminded so brutally last September, this world remains a troubled, hate-filled place. Saints may walk among us, but devils trail in their shadows. Evil is a very real presence in this world, and madness stalks the earth in human form.

We know that we would all be better off if the pacifists were right and we could outlaw war. But it is the outlaws who make war, who kill the unsuspecting and the innocent, then deem it good.

It is a story as old as humankind, and it is, sadly, a story that will continue to be told. We will continue to need good soldiers, Marines, airmen, and sailors to protect this shining, incomparably decent nation. It is a human tragedy that we need a military, but it is a human reality that we need a strong one.

Now let us go forward, on this holiday, to enjoy the nation our veterans have given us.

# A Mob Hit in Kabul

## The Wall Street Journal

*July 9, 2002*

One of the finest military officers I know recently returned from six months in Afghanistan. He describes the warlords and their followings as "the five mob families" from America's past, each with its turf, feuds, and occasional taste for cooperation with one of the other mobs. Last Saturday, the mob hit one of Afghanistan's vice presidents.

My friend, who is an officer of great experience as well as a man of conscience, believes we should deal with and through the warlords, since that is the most effective way to make things happen. I believe he is tactically right, but strategically wrong.

Americans want quick results. But if we expect quick results in Afghanistan, we might as well pack up our gear and come home now. Worthwhile results will require long-term engagement. The process will be endlessly frustrating and it will not be cheap. Yet, even if such engagement ultimately fails, it will be less expensive than the alternative. The Muslim world does not need another country run by the mob.

We may find it useful to work with the warlords now and then. But we must beware our tendency to do what is easy today, though destructive tomorrow. During the Cold War, we fell into the habit of supporting dictators and strongmen who made things easy for us. It would be all too simple to do that in Afghanistan. And the mob can be very seductive.

Certainly, the rule of the warlords and the relative autonomy of their tribes or clans has been the way things worked in Afghanistan for centuries. But our goal should not be to reclaim the country's past. We need to help the Afghans develop a moderately more humane, somewhat more tolerant, slightly more promising future. And even our most realistic expectations are apt to be frustrated in the short term.

More government officials will be assassinated. Various factions will seek to undercut our influence even as they attempt to exploit us and turn America's might against their local adversaries. We must not expect to discover virtues among Afghan politicians that we cannot find among our own. Positive results may require a generation to take root.

None of this is what our country or the Bush administration wants to hear. Washington would be only too glad to hand off the Afghan tar-baby to European ditherers and to allow Kabul to turn into yet another vacation home for the salaried tourists of the world's nongovernmental organizations. But, instead of seeing Afghanistan only as a liability, we should regard it as a crucial opportunity.

The Islamic world between Cairo and Karachi badly needs a success story. One of the most powerful sources of Muslim hatred toward the U.S. is simply Islam's failure to generate a single healthy state. Muslims are, indeed, humiliated, and it little matters that they have humiliated themselves. The region desperately needs a model of success.

At first glance, Afghanistan doesn't look promising. Broken by generations of war, diseased, impoverished, and under-educated, with less infrastructure in its provinces than Europe possessed a thousand years ago, it seems a doomed country. But the paradox is that Afghanistan has fallen so far it has hit bottom. War hasn't worked. The religious rule of extremists failed and embittered much (though not all) of the population. And there is a large émigré population in the West that has experienced alternatives.

Certainly, Afghanistan is not going to turn into Orange County overnight. But in a land so devastated, incremental improvements can make a tremendous difference. America's continued engagement, with an adequate number of troops, reasonable funding and, above all, a long-range plan could have a profound impact—a return far in excess of our investment. For too long, we have given extremists and reactionaries free rein in the Muslim world. We surrendered the battlefield to our enemies in advance.

If we could help Afghanistan progress, however haltingly, toward the rule of law, rather than accepting continued domination by those "mob families," if we could further human rights, assist in building a rudimentary system for secular education, and support the rebuilding of the nation's basic infrastructure, we might finally be seen as a positive force by at least some in the region. Instead of being viewed as a country that only bombs Muslims, we might be seen, at last, as a country that builds, too.

The keys to success in Afghanistan will be commitment, patience, and reasonable expectations—all difficult qualities for our ebullient democracy. But even a moderate success would prove that the Muslim world possesses forward gears and isn't stuck hopelessly in reverse. Progress in a poor country such as Afghanistan might even embarrass those Arab states possessed of oil wealth into conceding a few human and political rights to their own populations.

In our own country, people turned to the mob because they needed help or protection the government did not provide, because they felt defenseless—or because they had tangible needs that went unanswered. Ethnic ties and the bonds of kinship were strong, and prejudice played into the hands of the gangsters. On a much grander, deadlier scale, that is a description of the situation in Afghanistan today.

We must not choose the easy path, embracing the notion that the warlords embody some magical "tradition" we dare not violate. Respect for local values does not mean surrender to local blackmail, and our worst enemies will be the diplomats and advisers who warn us that "that's the way it's always been done in Afghanistan." Furthermore, we cannot listen to the defeatists—the same voices who warned us last autumn that Afghans could not be defeated by our "pampered" military. We must know the past, but only fools and anthropologists adore it. Afghanistan has more history than it needs. It is time for us to help that country focus on the future.

# Iraq Too Tough?

## New York Post

*August 29, 2002*

If you predict disaster constantly, you may be right eventually. But the track record of America's pundits on military matters looks laughably shabby for now.

For the past dozen years, self-appointed experts have told us, over and over again, that American troops are inferior to our enemies of the moment. Wrong every time, the library lefties and bow-tied wise guys aren't going to give up now. Always rooting for America to lose and imagining spectacular virtues for our enemies, they despise trivial qualities such as dedication, skill, self-sacrifice, and courage.

Tell it to the Marines.

At present, all the pop-up geeks with eyeglasses wider than their shoulders, as well as a parade of yesterday's failed "statesmen," warn us, oh-so-solemnly, that a military campaign to destroy Saddam and his regime would be too tough for our troops, suggesting intolerable casualty levels and near-certain defeat.

Does this sound familiar to anyone?

When Saddam invaded Kuwait, the armchair generals assured us that the Iraqi military was battle-hardened, that our own forces were soft and untested and that tens of thousands of American soldiers would come home in body bags if we intervened.

Well, our troops went through Saddam's sad-sacks faster than Lizzie Grubman can drive an SUV through a Hamptons party.

Remember those ten-foot-tall Serbs in the wreckage of Yugoslavia? The guys who were "natural-born guerrillas"? They were going to eat GI Joe alive, according to the pundits.

Today, Milosevic is on trial and all those Serb hard boys are hustling black-market cigarettes for a living.

The Somalis, too, were supposed to be unbeatable tribal warriors. Despite being denied the arms for which their commanders had asked, U.S. troops under attack killed more bad guys in Mogadishu than anybody could count, performing magnificently. Only the world-class cowardice of a president who modeled his patriotism on the leaders of Vichy France brought us a declaration of defeat in the wake of a battlefield victory.

Finally, last autumn, countless talking heads assured us that Afghanistan had never been conquered and that our troops were no match for warriors who had been fighting for more than twenty years. Our defeat was inevitable.

Where are they now, all those "informed sources" who warned us that we were bound to fail in Afghanistan? They're back in print and on the airwaves, insisting that a campaign against the Iraqi regime will end in a strategic disaster.

This time out, the prophets of doom have been reinforced by a self-righteous squad of former Washington insiders who left nothing but problems behind when they left government to peddle their reputations. It's a sad day when we have former secretaries of state who sound like they're on the Saudi payroll.

Certainly, there are genuine challenges and dangers attendant to a war to end what our previous war against Iraq left unfinished.

• Saddam is unlikely to refrain from using weapons of mass destruction, against us and against his own people, if he can manage it.

• While the bulk of the Iraqi army will not fight—except to fight to be the first to become POWs—the SS wannabes surrounding Saddam may resist.

• The specter of a vast urban battle for Baghdad must be considered, but, frankly, the likelier scenario is the fall of Kabul (or Paris).

• And the logistics problems of supporting an all-out war are formidable (though not insuperable), thanks to the refusal of our Arab "friends" to support any efforts to bring justice and democracy to their disgracefully bigoted neighborhood.

As a former soldier, I certainly do not take the prospect of any war lightly, and I dearly wish that one of Saddam's inner circle would help us all out with a couple of 9mm rounds. I am willing, even now, to listen to arguments as to why we should not attempt to depose Saddam. But I will not listen to the chairborne commandos who tell me that our military cannot defeat the Iraqi regime.

If we go, there are three things we need to make clear up front, to help out our troops (instead of constantly belittling those who risk their lives for our country):

• The Bush administration needs to announce, publicly, that any use of weapons of mass destruction against our forces or our allies will bring a disproportionate response with our own weapons of mass destruction. No second chances.

• The administration should announce, just as publicly, that we will grant a blanket amnesty to every other Iraqi general and official—*if* they eliminate Saddam and his inner circle themselves. As a minimum, this would make Saddam even more untrusting and apt to purge the very men he needs for his survival struggle.

• We need to stop yapping about elegant solutions and low-cost operations. If someone manages a clever way to bring down Saddam, great. But we cannot count on it, and we cannot afford a defeat or even a temporary setback. We must not move against Iraq without sufficient forces in theater to finish the job.

Give our troops the backing they need, practical and political, and they will always give us victory. Listen to the pundits and the self-serving revisionists, and we'll spend our lives waiting for 9/11 Part Two (and Parts Three and Four, etc.).

We must always question, honestly and searchingly, the wisdom of any war. Healthy skepticism is a vital part of our national character. Just don't tell me America's men and women in uniform can't win.

# Cowards' Counsel

New York Post

*October 11, 2002*

There are few things more repugnant to a soldier than a coward who claims to speak on his behalf. At present, there seems no end of politicians and pundits claiming we dare not strike Saddam because of the danger of friendly casualties. Self-appointed voices of conscience warn of tens of thousands of American dead.

That's nonsense. And when those who despise the men and women in uniform invoke the welfare of our troops to further their failing agendas, they transcend the commonplace cynicism of Washington. This is hypocrisy as a moral disease.

Our soldiers do not fear Saddam. I do not know a single man or woman in uniform who believes that our military will fail or suffer badly, should we go to war with Iraq. The best-informed insist we will hit the Iraqi regime with such overwhelming, unexpected fury that the world will be shocked by our effectiveness.

And that is what Saddam's defenders fear, whether they are in the Middle East or in the middle of their congressional terms. This debate is about dogma, as philosophical derelicts attempt to salvage their homegrown anti-Americanism. The liberation of Iraq would discredit their outdated doctrines of Leftist liberation (Hey, our GIs wear berets now, just like Che! We've even stolen their costumes).

Make no mistake: The anti-war voices long for us to lose any war they cannot prevent.

How many casualties might America's military really suffer? Not the many thousands of which the benchwarmers warn. Even if Saddam were able to employ his weapons of mass destruction effectively, and if, simultaneously, everything possible were to go wrong for our troops, the worst-case number of casualties would be in the low thousands.

But losses that high are unlikely, even with the use of chemical or biological weapons. And even that level of casualties would be better than the eventual deaths of hundreds of thousands of American civilians at the hands of Iraq-backed terrorists.

In the face of the awesome power we are going to bring to bear from every conceivable angle and with the speed of revelation, the Iraqi regime's weapons of mass destruction would be little more than suicide kits. Saddam may be willing to go down mean, but if his generals are, they're fools. And men who have been clever enough to survive under Saddam's reign of terror are not stupid when it comes to self-preservation.

My own worst fear would be Saddam's use of chemical or biological weapons on his own people, killings many thousands of Arabs, just to kill some hundreds of Americans.

Our greatest vulnerability is right now, during the buildup phase, before our forces are in place and our preparations completed. The relatively static targets offered prior to hostilities are the best Saddam will ever see. Once we attack, we become much harder to engage—and we'll be beating on the Iraqis like Tony Soprano on top of a one-armed burglar.

Our military is aware of the present danger, and they're on their guard. That does not mean Saddam can't pull off a surprise strike of some sort. But it does mean it would be hard to pull off a meaningful, coordinated series of pre-emptive strikes. And Saddam knows very well that one missile launched across his borders will bring ferocious retaliation. He would have given us the very excuse he's desperate to avoid.

Instead of reveling in their fears, the domestic opponents of our just war should try to envision the panic among Saddam's cronies these days. I guarantee you that, this minute, Saddam is so jumpy he's purging the very men he needs to make war. And his underlings are calculating the odds. His generals do not want to die for Saddam. Their goal is to outlive him.

A few elite Iraqi units may fight. And those brief combats will provide our troops with the world's best target practice. This time, let us hope that cowardice at the top does not force a premature cease fire on our troops. Any Iraqi military unit that resists us should be annihilated as an object lesson to their comrades who have not yet had the sense to surrender. And to the world.

As for the ludicrous claims that Baghdad will turn into another Stalingrad, consuming U.S. troops by the tens of thousands, well, that's the biggest lie since Bill Clinton said, "I did not have sexual relations with that woman."

The Iraqis aren't the Red Army of WWII. We aren't Nazis. Nor is this Russians-versus-Chechens in Grozny Revisited. Our troops are the best-prepared in the world, and we've made great strides in urban warfare training. And, frankly, we're likely to bypass any pockets of resistance, isolating them for later destruction. We'll face snipers and end-of-the-line terrorists, not masses of bitterly determined troops.

There's a much better chance that our entry into Baghdad will look like the liberation of Kabul—or Paris—than the bloody siege of which the amateurs warn.

As for the risk of increased terrorism if we attack Iraq, that's just bull. The terrorists are going to do their best to hit us, no matter what we do. Why leave them a huge safe haven, where weapons of mass destruction are brewing up?

That would be absolute folly, if not premeditated suicide. Saddam has, indeed, supported terrorists over the years and continues to support them today. The Iraqi regime and the terrorists have differences, but they're unified in their hatred of America.

I do not underestimate the dangers or horrors of war. I value every American soldier's life. Even a few hundred casualties means a terrible burden of heartbreak for many an American family.

I do not suggest the campaign against Iraq will be easy—war is never easy. But we can do the hard stuff better than anyone else. And no one else has the will or the moral force to do it.

# The Gloves Come Off

## New York Post

*December 12, 2002*

America's military posture toward terrorists and tyrants finally escaped the Clinton legacy of cowardice and wishful thinking. In a distinctly un-Washingtonian display of common sense, President Bush told the world that the United States will not let bullies throw the first punch any longer, and that those who fight dirty will die an even dirtier death.

The new strategy makes two critical points. First, the United States will not feel obliged to grant the initiative to mass murderers. If our enemies pose a credible, substantive threat to the security of America's citizens, we will not hesitate to hit them before they can hit us. Simply put: If someone points a gun at our heads, we won't feel compelled to let them pull the trigger before we draw on them.

Second, attacks with weapons of mass destruction against our forces or citizens will be avenged with the weaponry we find appropriate, even if that means nukes. This finally ends the Clinton-era folly of telling our enemies in advance that, no matter how savagely they behave, we won't even use ground troops against them.

We are the most powerful nation in history. But power is only effective if your enemies understand you are willing to employ it. President Bush just gave our enemies notice. Lefties will refuse to acknowledge it, but a strong posture is more apt to preserve the peace and save lives than timidity or appeasement.

Terrorists and dictators are like dogs (at the risk of being unfair to our canine friends): They sense fear. Weakness excites them. The Clinton administration's dread of fighting seriously for any cause, ever, together with its Max Factor approach to warfare (cosmetic strikes only), accelerated the expansion of global terrorism dramatically. Clinton was al Qa'eda's best recruiting agent.

A nation that will not take a stand in its own defense soon finds itself on its knees. President Bush may not understand much about protecting the environment, but he does understand how to protect Americans.

And when those dreary Eurocrats call us Hollywood cowboys, we should be proud, not apologetic. Is it really better to be Jean-Paul Sartre than Jimmy Stewart? Well, let me just start that fan letter to Comrade Stalin while Simone de Boudoir takes her annual bath . . .

Why should we be ashamed to let the world know that Gary Cooper just stepped into the street with his six-guns strapped on? Indeed, the film *High Noon* may be the most symbolically relevant work of art for our time. Our cause *is* just, and our fight *is* virtuous.

Instead of mumbling apologies, we should grab Pierre and Hans by their limp wrists and ask them if America's lone-gun, frontier-sheriff tradition isn't preferable to the European tradition of "teamwork" that gave the world Auschwitz, the Gulag, and Gerhard Schroeder.

Well, we need not take the French or German seriously, with their anti-American racism and cultural bigotry (man, I can't wait to watch another evening of Belgian television—how about you?). But we do need to take our domestic left seriously, though in a manner different from that for which it hopes. The problem isn't the power of American liberals but their self-satisfied powerlessness.

The inanity, disarray, and blind conformity among American lefties wounds our political system and our society. In order for conservatives to remain intellectually sharp and avoid stagnation, we need a vibrant, new-ideas Left. Monopolies are no healthier for political systems than they are for economies or religions.

If conservatives really believe that competition improves human systems, they should stop gloating and pray for liberals to move beyond the stillness of the Nancy Pelosi school of antiquated non-solutions to a re-engagement with the core issues of our time.

The self-imposed exile of our liberals into a crippled, whining opposition that can only criticize, not create, serves every American badly. The Democratic Party needs to trade in rhetoric for responsibility.

Certainly, the left wing's attitude toward things military is as utterly untouched by logic as it is by experience. Liberals will wring their two left hands with dismay over the president's new strategy. But they have proposed no coherent strategy of their own, only a policy of eyes-closed, pants-down, hand-the-mugger-your-wallet.

The truth is that neither the Democrats nor the Republicans have new ideas. The Republicans simply lucked out because their old ideas work reasonably well in the twenty-first century, while Democratic true-believers can't see past the old glorious successes of the collectivization of Cuban agriculture. We need both parties to escape the grip of old dogmas and formulate new policies relevant to our contemporary challenges.

America's diversity really is its strength—that isn't just a cliché. Wouldn't it be a wonderful thing if, instead of automatically rejecting President Bush's new military strategy, the Democrats would engage in a positive critique that improved it and provided an even stronger defense of our nation and its citizens?

Don't hold your breath. During the recent shouting match over the Department of Homeland Security, Democrats couldn't see beyond outdated union issues, as if Tom Joad were still picking the grapes of wrath, and we lived in a nation of breadlines.

Come on, Dems. Any volunteers in your ranks to propose an effective military strategy that can go beyond President Bush's latest step in logic, effectiveness, and courage? Or are you going to continue to play your pathetic starring role in *al Jazeera West?*

President Bush took a great and courageous step Tuesday, telling America's mortal enemies that we will make the rules, not them. But in order to become a truly great president, he needs a great domestic opposition to challenge him constructively and demand excellence of him. The position is currently vacant, and our national security is all the weaker for it.

# The Sovereignty Con

New York Post

*February 3, 2003*

When you appear in the broadcast media, amid the snarls and wails, self-control helps you sell your ideas. Yet I do not regret the time I lost my temper on the air.

During the Kosovo fuss, I appeared on a talk show with the editor of a lefty journal whose motto should be, "The truth is irrelevant." The editor blathered on about American aggression and how Milosevic's Yugoslavia was a sovereign state in which the United States had no right to intervene, no matter what was done inside its borders.

I blew up. Unlike left-wing extremists, I'm not very good at finding excuses for genocide, mass rape, and torture. I pointed out that, by her standards, Hitler would have been just fine if he had limited himself to killing German Jews.

For perhaps the first time in history, a left-wing scribbler found herself at a loss for words.

At the beginning of a new century, the United States needs to revolutionize international relations. The Bush administration has already begun to do this on a practical level by pursuing terrorists around the world, bringing down the Taliban regime in Afghanistan and preparing to depose Saddam Hussein. Still, we need to move beyond our current piecemeal approach, to forge a new American doctrine on sovereignty.

Today, claims of territorial sovereignty by dictators and illegitimate regimes amount to the biggest con in history. No matter how unfairly borders are drawn, no matter how monstrously tyrants behave toward their populations, no matter how ruthlessly a strongman seizes power, the world pretends that those who hold the reins in the capital city are entitled to do whatever they want on their own territory.

The current system is the greatest collective violation of human rights in our time. The United States must shatter this antiquated scam designed by kings and princes to protect their personal fiefdoms. In the twenty-first century, a government must *earn* its right to claim sovereignty.

How? By working for the benefit of its citizens, not just for the privileges of a small, armed elite. By respecting the dignity of its people, including its minorities. By providing for its citizens, instead of stealing from them. By allowing them to speak freely and to live without fear of their own government. Above all, a state must earn its right to sovereign borders by adhering to universal standards of human rights.

And don't try to tell me that human rights are relative. We all know better. We may argue about the morality of the death penalty, but we can all agree that mass murder is unacceptable. Torture is not a cultural tradition, nor is mass rape merely a social construct. Yes, there are nuances. But on the level that matters internationally, we all know human-rights violations when we encounter them.

Leftists, clinging to their memories of protests past, will object that America has no right to judge others, that we violate human rights ourselves. That's nonsense, and we all know it.

Next, the lefties will warn of "slippery slopes" and American imperialism. That's nonsense, too. Deposing Saddam does not lead inexorably to the invasion of Sweden.

To the left's horror, today's international revolutionaries are on the political right. The left wing represents the *ancien regime:* old slogans, old prejudices, and badly failed approaches to security and human rights. American "conservatives" are the driving force behind overdue global reforms.

And we are led by a president who appears to have recognized an obvious truth resisted by the left: The human rights of one dictator are not more important than the human rights of the tens of millions of citizens he oppresses.

What could say more about the intellectual and moral bankruptcy of the left, here and abroad, than its defense of Saddam, of the Taliban, of international terrorists, and of every thug who wins a game of capture-the-flag in the developing world?

The Bush administration has a chance to pioneer an international system of *tiered sovereignties* that would strip tyrants and their apologists of their current, horribly unjust diplomatic defenses.

It should work like this:

*Level One:* Every government, from Mexico to India, that respects the will of its people through democratic institutions, works for the betterment of its citizens, demonstrates progress toward respect for human rights, and strives toward the rule of law deserves continued recognition of its full, legal sovereignty.

*Level Two:* States that cannot control their own territory, that lack the ability to protect their own citizens or to prevent international terrorists and other criminals from using their territory as a refuge, would be able to claim only partial sovereignty. More capable, rule-of-law states would have the right to intervene for limited purposes to bring killers and other criminals to justice. In every other respect, these weak but well-intentioned states would enjoy the traditional privileges and protections of sovereignty.

*Level Three:* Regimes that refuse to enforce the rule of law inside their borders, that knowingly harbor terrorists and criminals, that behave aggressively toward their neighbors, or that abuse their own citizens would forfeit their territorial sovereignty and their right to govern. Period.

Of course, dozens of United Nations members would howl, given their own governmental inadequacies, their addiction to corruption, and their present ability to get away with murder in the most literal sense. But we must recognize that the majority of the voices in the United Nations do not represent the majority of their own populations. The United Nations has become a travesty, a talkathon for tyrants. We must forge ahead, regardless of criticism.

If President Bush has the vision to see through the sovereignty con and to begin to dismantle the diplomatic defenses that coddle dictators, we just might live to see the day when a majority of the world's states will accept the self-evident truth that every government should be of the people, by the people, and for the people.

# Crocodile Tears

## New York Post

*March 10, 2003*

I spent last month in Africa, pausing for a respectful visit to Robben Island, the former prison that confined Nelson Mandela for two decades. It was a physically beautiful setting spoiled by humankind's past intolerance and by the crocodile tears of European tourists.

Young and old, the German, French, and Dutch visitors deplored what had been done to one of the great men of the last century—who remains a powerful, if aging and erratic, voice in the cause of freedom. I certainly shared their regret at the suffering imposed on Mr. Mandela and his comrades.

But I wanted to smack the lot of them and yell, "What about the Iraqis? Don't they matter, you smug, little hypocrites?"

As deplorable as conditions were on Robben Island during the imprisonment of South Africa's champions of freedom, they were civilized compared to the treatment of uncounted thousands of Iraqis at the hands of Saddam and his henchmen.

I do not underestimate the crimes of the apartheid regime. Yet, despicable though that government was, it didn't use nerve gas on thousands of men, women, and children, torture children in front of their parents, rape wives in front of their husbands, exterminate entire families and clans on a whim, or slaughter minority populations.

Those Euro-trash tourists were right to mourn what had been done. But why on earth didn't they care about the *present* sufferings of their fellow human beings?

The sorry truth is that Europeans love to cry over corpses, but won't lift a finger to prevent the killing in the first place. They shake their heads over the Holocaust, though their parents were happy enough to pack the local Jews off to Auschwitz.

The French grudgingly accept that their intellectuals defended Stalin long after evidence of his crimes came to light, but they avoid the issue of how many of their thinkers and artists admired Hitler and profited from the Occupation (French cafés and cabarets boomed under the Nazis).

Was there ever an African dictator the French didn't adore? The Dutch criticize America's military as trigger-happy, but their own troops didn't fire a shot in defense of the Muslims of Srebrenica, who they had been tasked to protect and whose slaughter was the worst single massacre on European soil since the end of the Second World War.

When I served in Europe in the '70s, Chairman Mao prefigured Viagra in his effect upon the European Left. Of course, the Soviet Union remained noble and virtuous until the end, its failure to construct heaven on earth explained away by American scheming and malevolence. Today, Europeans dismiss their historical guilt toward Jews by insisting that Israel is as bad as Nazi Germany—a Big Lie worthy of Hitler and Goebbels—while cheering on Israel's genocidal enemies.

What can we do in the face of such a profound lack of honesty, morality, or even decency? How can we work constructively with those for whom evidence only matters when it supports their prejudices?

What shall we make of those who would let millions die at the hands of tyrants while accusing America of aggression for opposing the killers?

The short answer is: Not much. In the longer term, though, we must accept the fact that states such as France and Germany have declined to the mentality of yesteryear's Mexico, blaming the United States for all their failures and defining themselves not in positive terms, but merely as the anti-America.

We must accept, from today onward, that America shall often need to act alone or with a handful of courageous allies. Increasingly, we will need to do that which we recognize as strategically and morally necessary, disregarding those states, in Europe and elsewhere, that weep so readily for the dead while caring so little for the living.

We must accept the world's jealousy as a given and must not become distracted by attempts to placate European racists who refuse to set high standards for governance in developing states. Indeed, nothing so abets tyranny and oppression today as French and German condescension toward black, brown, or yellow populations—and their unspoken conviction that nonwhites remain inferior.

When Robert Mugabe, the Stalin of Zimbabwe, is welcome in Paris, while the French government takes pains to insult Colin Powell, you have a very clear illustration of the ethics of French diplomacy. The current wave of jokes about the French are ill-judged only in the sense that the French impulse toward racial totalitarianism is no laughing matter. Ask the populations of Ivory Coast or Rwanda. Or Algeria. Or of the brown and black suburbs of Paris.

Of course, sincere allies will always be welcome in this new century of struggle between postmodern freedoms and the bankrupt sur-realpolitik of Paris and Berlin. And we must distinguish, of course, between Europe's freedom-loving frontier states, either on the Atlantic periphery or in the east, and the twilight states of "Old Europe."

Our natural allies are those who either have pioneered democracy, such as Britain, or who have struggled long and hard for their freedom—Poland, Hungary, Spain, and so many others who suffered under Communism or fascism.

Saddam looks very different to a Romanian or Latvian than he does to a German or a Frenchman. The Frenchman sees a tantalizing business proposition, while, as a friend of mine serving in the Gulf remarked, "The Germans can't help loving Saddam. He's a dictator with a mustache . . ."

Beyond Europe, America's efforts to face down tyrants are resisted by—surprise!—tyrants. The United Nations never had the strategic relevance its partisans insist Washington's liberation of Iraq will destroy. We should not seek to harm the U.N., but we cannot prevent it from slashing its own wrists.

We Americans can expect neither gratitude, understanding, nor support from the baroque regimes of France, Germany, and their fellow travelers. Chancellor Schroeder? Bill Clinton without the moral fiber. President Chirac? The mouth of de Gaulle, the soul of Petain, and the morals of a pimp. Humanitarian Belgium? Yeah, just ask the Congolese. The European anti-war movement? Necrophiliacs licking the corpse of Josef Stalin.

Europeans will always be willing to weep over the dead. The United States must take a stand for the living. In Iraq. And beyond.

# Dead Americans

## New York Post

*March 12, 2003*

The government of France is fighting an undeclared war with the United States. The result will be the needless deaths of American soldiers in the Gulf. And the more Americans Saddam manages to kill, the greater President Chirac's satisfaction will be.

The French pride themselves on their rationality. But the rabid anti-Americanism that has gripped the Parisian elite is a form of collective madness, spawned by jealousy, wounded pride, and astonishing delusions about French power. To embarrass America, the French government is willing to destroy no end of international organizations and alliances. The real cowboys in this conflict are galloping along the banks of the Seine.

In the end, the greatest loser will be France, since French power is as crumbly as Roquefort cheese. Paris isn't a "third force," but a third farce. French behavior in the current crisis is obsessive, not reasoned, and ultimately self-defeating.

In the short term, though, the bill-payers for the Gallic tantrum will be the additional American soldiers—as well as

Iraqi soldiers and civilians—who will die because Paris has encouraged Saddam to believe the international community, led by France, will protect him even after a war begins.

Thanks to Jacques Chirac, Saddam Hussein and his generals now see hope where there is none. At least some of those who would have surrendered readily will now fight. Saddam will pull every possible trick to excite world opinion against the United States, including staged atrocities. And our troops will have to kill men who otherwise would have surrendered. Some of our own fighting men and women will die in the process, all because France has led the Iraqi regime down the garden path.

Of course, France will abandon Saddam in the end. But we must make no mistake about French culpability for the ultimate casualty figures. This is not a mere diplomatic tiff. At the highest levels of government, the French know what they are doing, at least tactically (their strategy is a dangerous, pathetic muddle). We cannot allow a French betrayal in so important a matter to go unpunished. If there are no consequences for French complicity in the deaths of young Americans, there will be no future for American diplomacy in Europe.

Too smart for their own good, the French have upset Carl von Clausewitz's old dictum that "War is a simple continuation of politics by other means." For Chirac and for Foreign Minister Dominique de Villepin, international politics is now a form of war. And their war is not against terrorism, or tyrants, or injustice. Their war is against the United States of America.

The French would love to prevent the war in the Gulf, thus setting themselves up as the champions of tyrants everywhere and of Arab tyrants in particular. But Paris realizes there is really very little chance of deflecting Washington. So their essential goal is to complicate matters, to vilify America and to make the United States pay the highest possible price for any success it achieves, while remaining ready to capitalize on any American failures.

When the war in Iraq ends with a decisive American victory, Chirac will put on his little *C'est la vie* smile and insist that our differences were nothing but a disagreement between old friends, something one must expect in our complex world. Meanwhile, he and his closest advisers yearn for a bloody American defeat.

Nothing would please Chirac more than thousands of dead American soldiers inside the borders of Iraq, with Saddam alive and defiant. If this war goes badly, Chirac could have more American blood on his hands than does Osama bin Laden.

Consider the practical effects of French cheerleading for Saddam:

• Saddam should feel hopeless by now; instead, he has been led to believe that, even if war cannot be averted, he has a real chance of defeating the United States diplomatically by fighting our troops to a bloody stalemate. He believes—thanks to the French—that the more blood he sheds, the likelier he and his regime are to survive.

• Saddam will be even more inclined to employ weapons of mass destruction on as wide a scale as possible, certain that France and his other supporters will excuse his behavior as an inevitable response to American aggression, not proof that he possessed such weapons all along.

• The war is delayed, day after day, giving Saddam ever more time to strengthen his defenses, while American troops sit in the desert, watching Saddam wire his oil fields with explosives, dig in his troops and prepare a massive defense of Baghdad. Our troops are ready *now*, and each delay only weakens our readiness compared to that of our adversary.

- The French support for Saddam encourages terrorists, Iraqi-sponsored or otherwise, to believe that wartime actions against the United States could have a decisive effect, given the opposition to American policy even among Washington's traditional "friends."

The last point is easy to undervalue. Terrorists—and Saddam himself—do not live in our world of abundant, competitive information. Rather, they live in worlds of enthusiastic self-delusion and megalomania. The ruthless French defense of Saddam—an unspeakable dictator—has played into the fantasies of tyrant and terrorist alike, convincing them that they are stronger than they really are, that they are not alone, and that it is America which is evil and vulnerable.

Readers may note that I have not even raised the issue of recent reports that French firms continued to help Iraq improve its armaments into the early weeks of this year. Although one of the many reasons the French do not want us in Baghdad is that they don't want us going through Iraqi archives and uncovering the extent of their complicity in Saddam's defiance of sanctions, the material aid French firms may have provided to Iraq is a trivial issue compared to the moral and diplomatic encouragement Paris has given Baghdad.

Ultimately, this grotesque resurgence of French "diplomacy" will fail. France is weak, ill-defended, and hated in Africa and much of the Middle East with a quiet hatred that goes far deeper than the topical anti-Americanism so much in evidence. Nor will its attempts to glorify itself at America's expense provide France with any security. The terrorists will not reward France for its pandering; on the contrary, I expect we shall see a major terrorist strike in France in the future. The French do not merely live in a bad neighborhood—the bad neighborhoods live within France. The French are bribing their executioners in the expectation of mercy.

We may hope—and pray—that the war against Iraq will be swift, with low casualties. But every American who dies in this war will have a French diplomatic bullet in his or her body.

# The Limits of Emotion

## New York Post

*March 16, 2003*

If anyone in our domestic antiwar movement offered me a convincing alternative to a war to eliminate Saddam Hussein, I would be the first in line to sign up. But the protesters do not offer serious solutions to the threat of weapons of mass destruction or the agony of the Iraqi people. They merely shout well-intentioned slogans, bond briefly, pat themselves on the back, and go home to their insulated lives.

If platitudes could change the world for the better, I would be out there myself, marching in favor of universal disarmament. I credit the anti-war movement within the United States with sincere emotion. But it is utterly lacking in intellectual integrity. An earnest, if vague, sense that war is bad may inspire undergraduates, but it does not prevent massacres, depose tyrants, or deter terrorists.

Consider the greatest lie that adorns those posters, as our fellow citizens march in the streets: "War doesn't solve anything."

On the contrary, war solves a great deal. Not always for the better, that I grant. But, fortunately, the good guys have won more often than not for the past few hundred years. Do the protesters believe that our Civil War, which ended the institution of slavery in our country, failed to solve anything? Would we be better off had blacks remained in bondage on our soil? It was civil society, after the war, that failed African-Americans. The soldiers did their part and broke the chains.

Shortly before writing this piece, I watched a TV interview with a Parisian woman. A singer by trade, she, too, argued that war never accomplishes anything. I assume she wishes our GIs had not disturbed the love affair between Nazi Germany and the Vichy regime. She could be singing "Lili Marleen" night after night.

As a man with some remaining shreds of conscience, I wish the protesters *were* correct, that war was pointless and useless, and that we could abolish it. But humankind is not made so.

Setting aside the Freudian issues involved when Americans insist their own country is the font of all evil (although few protesters buy retirement homes in North Korea), the indisputable fact is that free and tolerant societies cannot survive under conditions of weakness. Cain will always raise his hand against Abel.

Of course, the protesters would disagree with that view of human nature. But it is easy for Susan Sarandon or Sean Penn to look at things through their rose-colored sunglasses. Less privileged than the stars-who-always-know-best, my military comrades and I spent much of our lives wading through the wreckage of other people's wars, and I may claim with eyewitness authority that we live in a dangerous world, where bullies must be checked and murderers disarmed.

Singing songs, however lovely the voices, will not soften the killer's heart.

If you leave these shores, where you can duck into a cozy Starbucks after an hour or two of protest marching and celebrate your virtue with a latte, the world rapidly takes on a different coloration. How would the protesters feel if they had to live under Saddam's regime for even a few months? Without a decaf or doppio in sight?

I would feel much more sympathetic to the antiwar movement if they would offer me rigorous answers to a few straightforward questions:

1. Do you honestly believe, after twelve years of failure, that U.N. inspections can disarm Saddam Hussein? If your reply is "Yes!" or if you refuse to believe the evidence that Saddam possesses weapons of mass destruction, wants more of them, and intends to use them, proceed to question 2.

2. Should we simply turn our backs on the Iraqi people and allow Saddam to continue to torment and murder them? Should we, thereafter, allow one of his homicidal sons to succeed him? Don't the people of Iraq, who have been gassed, tortured, raped, shot, and starved (while Saddam builds dozens of vast palaces for himself), deserve liberation? Or is freedom only for educated white people and the Botox brigade?

3. What would *you* do, in practical terms, to prevent the spread of weapons of mass destruction and their eventual use by terrorists against us? No generalities, please—specific answers are required.

Until our antiwar activists, with their presumed monopoly on virtue, can answer those questions, I shall remain unconvinced that they know whereof they shout. It is not enough to oppose, if you cannot offer convincing alternatives. Progress and security demand a sense of responsibility. It is always satisfying to complain, but far harder to forge solutions. It is, above all, the dishonesty and the moral capriciousness of the antiwar movement that disappoints me.

I wish the activists had better solutions—genuine alternatives to war. I wish they would engage the rest of us intellectually. Competition is as vital in the marketplace of ideas as it is in any other marketplace. But behind the fashionable poses and quaint campus anger, the closed minds and indestructible prejudices of the antiwar movement are cause for dismay. How can we speak with those who are always shouting?

And those falling stars who never fail to appear before the cameras at the protests? A part of me would like to dismiss them all, yet I recognize that there are sincere celebrities who take their causes seriously and who truly do make a difference: Bono is an admirable, remarkable example, with his crusade against poverty and AIDS in Africa. Audrey Hepburn lived her causes and didn't simply show up for a photo-op once a season.

Celebrity *can* be put to higher purposes. But the celeb has to live the cause, not merely visit it at autograph time.

Now consider those who routinely show up to support Saddam Hussein (for that is what they are doing, no matter their demurrals): The bluntest manifestation of their self-interest came last month, when several members of the Sarandon-Penn Collective worried aloud that, as a result of their protest activities, they might be blacklisted in Hollywood.

Really?

This was a brilliant tactic, the deployment of a self-licking ice-cream cone. The fading celebrities put Hollywood—where ticket-sales and DVD-rentals rule—on notice: If they are not offered future roles, it will have nothing to do with their strings of box-office failures, but will be solely because of their noble anti-war stance. In other words, "If I don't get plum film roles now, you're all fascists."

Brilliant. I wish they would apply that sort of tactical genius to improving the lot of the Iraqi people.

And I wonder how much our sad, silly Hollywood protesters really know about the McCarthy era and blacklisting? If any of them had read even one book on the subject, they would know that, while all of the actors and writers and directors were running for cover and betraying their friends, only the United States Army had the guts to stand up to Tailgunner Joe (a great part for Sean Penn). It was the Army vs. McCarthy hearings, with their insistence on strict constitutionality, that brought the reign of terror to an end.

Just as the United States Army, and the rest of our military, will bring Saddam's reign of terror to an end.

Might be a movie in it.

# Patience

## New York Post

*March 18, 2003*

The American people have been admirably patient with the United Nations' cynical diplomacy and French shenanigans. Now we are on the eve of war. And our troops need, and deserve, the patience of the American public as they fight a war without precedent to remove one of the world's worst dictators and free 20 million of our fellow human beings.

In a perfect world, major combat operations could be over in less than a week. But we do not live in a perfect world. We can count on a host of minor problems—Murphy's Law at work—and our troops may encounter some major challenges, as well.

Any difficulties and delays in the march to Baghdad will not signal a lack of competence, although there will be plenty of media pundits ready to criticize our fighting men and women from the safety of TV studios. The unexpected is the stuff of war, and it always has been.

That said, I'm no pessimist. We're going to fight a brilliant war. And while we all know the old saying about no plan surviving contact with the enemy, it's also fair to say that plenty of our enemies are not going to survive their first contact with our plan.

When glitches occur, we must avoid the impatience of the 24/7 broadcast world and the snap judgments that are so easy to make from half a world away.

If things goes smoothly, we may all thank Providence, GI Joe, and GI Jane. But the American people can also rest assured that our troops and their leaders will be giving their best at all times.

From a distance, it can be very hard to understand how difficult seemingly simple actions are in the vastness and confusion of war—especially in the sort of hyper-velocity war America has prepared to wage. Just remember: We truly do have the best-trained, best-prepared military in the world.

But no unit can be prepared for all eventualities. Training has to focus on a finite set of skills deemed essential, but war breeds the unexpected.

For every fierce combat encounter, there will be countless man-hours of plain hard work. Combat engineers must prepare trails through miles of Iraqi tank ditches and minefields. They're good at it. But it still takes time and a lot of sweat to prepare superhighways in the sand for tens of thousands of military vehicles to pass into enemy territory. And all the while you're doing the work, your enemy is trying to stop you.

Bridges may well be down, forcing us to conduct large-scale river-crossing operations. Saddam's hardcore loyalists will try to strike our forces as they establish bridgeheads—or as they seize airheads deep in Iraqi territory. The great majority of the time, Saddam's forces will fail. But you can never write off an enemy until he's dead or his hands are in the air.

All of this matters profoundly, because the moment a U.S. unit takes casualties—and some units will—a faction of the microphone militia will declare the entire campaign a disaster. Well, soldiers die in war. Sorry, but it's true. Our men and women in uniform will be doing their damnedest to accomplish some very dangerous missions, and they know the risks. If we are only patient, they will bring us victory. But we only insult them if we judge the lives they sacrifice in battle as a symptom of failure.

We cannot say exactly which course the war will take. Our forces plan a swift campaign of "shock and awe." But even if we defeat the Iraqi military on every side, Saddam's inner circle of protectors may be able to shield him successfully from the many Iraqi generals and colonels who would be glad to kill him and put an end to their country's misery. The "big war" should end swiftly, but the end game could drag on for weeks.

Perhaps the greatest impediment to the lightning victory we desire is our decency. Saddam knows we do not wantonly butcher civilians, so he will hide behind them, as will his elite forces. That could impede operations significantly as the campaign approaches its climax. And a slowdown in operations on the edge of Baghdad—if it occurs—will lead to dire pronouncements that we're bogged down in a morass, a new Vietnam.

Disregard all such nonsense. Calm, deliberate action may not provide the drama and instant gratification media gigolos crave, but the old line about "fools rush in" applies in spades.

There are times in military operations when speed is of the essence, when ferocious, stunning strikes are the order of the day. But there are also times when we need to patiently execute a lower-intensity plan, to wear down an opponent, to slowly bring about his collapse at a minimum cost. Whenever the action goes into slo-mo, trust the generals, not the talking heads.

And make no mistake: If we are not lucky enough (and luck matters powerfully in war) to kill Saddam early on, and if he survives the wrath of his own people, we are going to face international calls, led by the French, for a negotiated settlement, for a safe conduct for Saddam and his paladins to a comfortable exile—after Saddam has done his best to ravage his own country in a war he easily could have avoided.

That is when we Americans are going to need to show our steel, the sort of hard resolve we demonstrated after 9/11. In a bitter military end game, the diplomats will always try to interfere, to snatch defeat from the jaws of victory. We must stand resolutely behind our troops and our leadership: Once this war has begun, there can be no end until Saddam and his regime are vanquished.

If things break our way, this admonition to patience may be unnecessary. I hope it is. I hope this will prove to be the most irrelevant column I ever write and that our enemy will collapse before we can even approach Baghdad.

But if there are a few delays along the road to Saddam's citadel, we should remain absolutely confident about the end result.

# The War that Will Change the World

## New York Post

*March 20, 2003*

This present war will not last long, but its effects will echo for decades. And they will be positive effects—for Iraq, for the Middle East, for the world beyond the theater of conflict, and for the United States of America.

This war will be smaller in scale and shorter in duration than many of the conflicts in which we have been engaged over the past half century. It is not without grave risks. But its practical benefits and the message it sends make it the most important "hot" war we have waged since World War II.

President Bush is not the most articulate of the world's heads of state. Elitists who speak artfully, while failing to listen honestly, dismiss him. Yet while the intelligentsia clings to the past, our president has the vision to see that the old patterns of diplomacy have failed us, that the world's health is too grave for yesterday's quack medicines.

He will never write a scholarly tome on strategy that will win the applause of academics and diplomats. But our president is rewriting the strategy itself, in a manner so bold and vital that we have not yet begun to grasp its full import.

The new American policy toward which the times have driven us *is* as radically different as our critics fear. It breaks with a failed and blood-soaked past. We have finally accepted that it is no longer enough to wait for enemies to attack first. We have accepted our unique responsibility to intervene abroad in the cause of global security and human rights.

And we have dispensed with a corrupt sham sustained by our critics: the notion that a dictator, no matter how cruel and illegitimate, is untouchable behind his "sovereign" borders.

It is no accident that the core countries of "Old Europe," France and Germany, oppose us. Between them, they have been responsible for every major European conflict since the Napoleonic era. Those who now accuse us of aggression bear the weight of hundreds of millions of corpses.

President Bush has turned away from the murderous logic of European diplomacy, from mechanisms of statecraft that have led only to unchecked aggression and unchallenged genocide. The essential purpose of European diplomacy has been, and remains, the preservation of the powerful, by the powerful, for the powerful. Wherever in the world we see a dictatorship protected by diplomatic custom and webs of trade, we see an outpost of "Old Europe." Saddam is more European than Tony Blair.

Just as we fought our Civil War to cast off the European legacies of human bondage and political power vested in a landed aristocracy, we are now fighting to cast off an Arab dictator who embodies the European tradition of a tyrant sustained by a bureaucracy of terror. Europeans pioneered the methods. Saddam is merely an imitator.

Our Spanish-American War shattered the inviolable image of European empires. Underestimated in its importance because it was a "small" war, the Spanish-American War was the first time a non-European power reached out to destroy an oppressive European empire. It sparked the century-spanning collapse of European empires that ended with the disintegration of the Soviet incarnation of the empire of the czars, in 1991.

The Europeans will never forgive us for spoiling their party.

Now we have begun a new endeavor. It, too, may last a century. With the old empires gone, we are sending notice to dictators everywhere that the rules formulated by Old Europe no longer apply, that Saddam may be only the first dictator to fall, that the United States will no longer overlook massive violations of human rights, that we shall no longer allow ourselves to be threatened without responding, and that we will no longer heed the voices of those foreign capitals that have failed the world with such devastating consequences.

What shall we say to those who accuse us of violating "time-honored" and "proven" rules of international relations?

None of us would want to be operated upon by a surgeon using a medical text from the nineteenth century. And we cannot address the strategic cancers of the twenty-first century using antique diplomatic etiquette designed to protect the kings, czars, and emperors of bygone Europe.

I do not suggest that our government has a detailed road map to the future. We are learning as we go, improvising and gradually shaping a new strategy to address new challenges. The pace of change is so rapid that we have not even developed the new vocabulary we need.

But Europe is the continent of words; our world is one of action. We are shaping tomorrow, while those who mock us cling to discredited yesterdays. Our instincts are good, our motives are sound, and our standards of behavior are the highest in the history of nations. Who shall lead the way, if we do not?

This is an epochal war, one of those rare events that mark the end of one era and the beginning of another. Much attention has been paid to the new technologies we will bring to bear in this conflict. But our new convictions will leave the greater legacy.

As our aircraft pierce the skies over Baghdad and our tanks roll toward the Tigris and Euphrates—along with those of our like-minded British allies—history has returned to the sands that gave rise both to the world's earliest civilizations and some of the world's most brutal tyrants. Our president's command to our forces to enter Iraq marks a break with an ancient and enduring legacy of cruelty, with ideologies of statehood that have killed rather than protected and with the unacceptable tradition that one man, having seized power, has the right to oppress, torment, and butcher millions.

I do not underestimate the possible costs of this war. Nor will we know its true results for years, until we survey the altered landscape of the Middle East at least a decade hence. But the cost of continuing to subscribe to the great-power politics and corrupt behaviors that constitute the European tradition of diplomacy is far too high for humanity to pay. In a sense, President Jacques Chirac of France did us a great favor in making the choice between the future and the past so stark and clear.

When Saddam ignored our president's ultimatum, he chose the past. We have chosen the future.

# Revolutionary War!

New York Post

*March 21, 2003*

We have entered a genuine revolution in warfare when the casual American TV viewer or newspaper reader has a vastly better picture of the theater of conflict than the enemy's commanders possess. While all attention is on improvements in our weaponry, the most devastating imbalance between the forces of the U.S.-led coalition and those of Iraq lies in the realm of information.

An American sergeant riding into battle as you read these lines has greater "situational awareness," to use the military's term, than does an Iraqi general. As a former intelligence officer, my most important task was to imagine myself in the enemy's place. And I would not want to be in the place of an Iraqi general today.

Consider the terrifying lack of information confronting an Iraqi division or corps commander positioned somewhere between Baghdad and our advancing forces.

He continues to receive extravagant, impossible orders from Baghdad, accompanied by shrill propaganda he knows to be nothing but lies. He is not trusted with meaningful intelligence on the situation—to the limited extent even the top leaders in Baghdad have it. The Iraqi military is blind in this conflict, waiting to be attacked out of the darkness.

Neither will his fellow commanders share information with him, fearing for their own survival should they be revealed as defeatists. His reconnaissance assets can barely see over the next ridge.

He has no idea when a devastating airstrike might obliterate his command post, when attack helicopters might begin the annihilation of his rusting combat vehicles, or even if an American or British tank is rolling up behind him.

He cannot trust the troops below him. He cannot trust the leaders above him. And all the while, a team of secret police, Saddam's Gestapo, follows his every action, waiting to execute him at the first sign he might disobey Baghdad or attempt to surrender.

He has been assaulted by allied broadcasts, leaflets, and unnerving calls on his cell phone warning him that, if he obeys orders to use weapons of mass destruction or destroys oil fields, he will be tried as a war criminal. He also has been warned that, if he tries to resist and fails to surrender, he will face the unfiltered wrath of the U.S. military.

His prime source of intelligence? Rumors. And a shortwave radio he listens to in private, quietly tuned to the BBC Arabic service or the Voice of America.

His enemies, however, possess an almost godlike ability to see across vast distances, through darkness and smoke, and even down into the earth.

Do you think that general will lead his troops to victory?

Meanwhile, our "new" doctrine of shock and awe, of applying physically and psychologically overwhelming force with unprecedented simultaneity, is an impressive step forward in the evolution of military affairs—but it isn't a revolution.

Shocking the enemy into paralytic awe has been a military goal since the days of the Roman legions. The Mongols, while weak on table manners, were brilliant at exciting shock and awe in their enemies. Blitzkrieg was about shock and awe. As was Desert Storm.

But a revolutionary event in military history *did* happen Wednesday night (Thursday morning in Baghdad).

The target-of-opportunity strike on a command-and-control facility suspected of harboring top Iraqi leaders was a stunning break with centuries of warmaking tradition. It was an enormous practical and *moral* leap forward.

Instant analysis focused on whether or not the attack, by stealth aircraft and cruise missiles, succeeded in killing Saddam Hussein or his sons. Certainly, the immediate results matter. But the "experts" missed the greater point.

Regardless of the practical results, that attack was a milestone, marking our rejection of the traditional rules of waging warfare, which insist that we should fight through conscript armies and masses of civilians, while sparing the killers above them. We leapt across the lines and aimed directly at the leaders responsible for the war, at the men with blood on their hands, in an attempt to punish the guilty and spare the innocent.

It was a revolutionary step in making warfare more humane.

Our government spoke of a "decapitation" strike. Reflexive opponents of all we do will use the loaded word "assassination" in speaking of our attack. We still lack satisfactory new terms for a new age of warfare and diplomacy.

But stand back for a moment. Consider how, since time immemorial, kings, sultans, and emperors ordered our powerless ancestors to their deaths in bloody wars of aggression, knowing that they could surrender politely to a fellow ruler when defeated, raising a scented white handkerchief above endless fields of corpses.

Now we have said, "Enough."

Americans will no longer make the enemy's foot soldiers, or even his captains and colonels, our first targets.

We will use all our might, technology, and will to punish the genuinely guilty.

We may or may not succeed in targeting Saddam and his key subordinates in this war. But simply to have made the effort is a great step toward reducing the carnage and horror of warfare.

And the day will come, if not immediately, when we will, indeed, be able to reach beyond the frightened privates to punish the privileged few who endanger humanity.

Imagine the warning such a doctrine sends to tyrants around the world. My fellow Americans, *that* is a revolution.

# Boots on the Ground

New York Post

*March 22, 2003*

With our air campaign of shock and awe pummeling the Iraqi regime with all the technologies America's military can muster, the infantryman remains the indispensable man. Airpower may give us the decisive edge, but ground troops remain the foundation of military victory.

I certainly do not mean to slight our pilots or our technology. While I am not shocked, I certainly am awed by the devastating, yet precisely focused, attacks on our enemies. The ongoing airstrikes are undeniably accelerating our march to victory. And I do not suggest that ground forces alone can win our wars.

Rather, the basic lesson of this war is that we continue to need balanced forces—every one of our armed services—in order to give our country the flexibility and depth to respond to humanity's capacity for deadly mischief.

But our ground forces are now the slighted stepchildren of our military establishment. The requirement for boots on the ground has been dismissed time and again by "visionaries" who insist that one technology or another has finally eliminated the need for massed divisions.

211

Time and again, the theorists have been wrong. But it hasn't deterred them from trying to cut our ground forces to the bone.

This is a critical issue, since there is another very dangerous war behind the war in Iraq. This other fight is underway in the halls of the Pentagon.

Defense Secretary Donald Rumsfeld has been a superb leader in crisis and war, but he remains an ideologue when it comes to the future of our armed forces. And he is as close-minded as a commissar when it comes to his preference for high-tech weapons over adequate numbers of well-trained personnel.

Rumsfeld and his key advisers have argued, ceaselessly, for cutting manpower in the Army in order to underwrite a blank check for the defense industry. Since he entered office, Rumsfeld's staff has undercut the Army's efforts to field more deployable medium-weight forces—of exactly the sort that would have been invaluable in this crisis—in order to force the Army into strategic irrelevance.

The new brigades the Army has fought to field could have been airlifted into Iraq or could have supplemented our hitting power as our forces crossed the Iraqi desert from Kuwait—if only those brigades had been given adequate support and funding.

In order to prove his contention that airpower is the single critical arm in twenty-first century warfare, Secretary Rumsfeld dismissed the advice of his generals over the past several months, delaying the deployment of Army divisions to the Gulf and limiting the number of ground forces finally deployed. He may win his gamble, but he has taken an unnecessary risk.

We had the resources, and our secretary of defense chose not to use them. Just to prove a point.

Certainly, we are going to win this war. But a key planner now serving with our ground forces in the Gulf worries that we have gone into battle without a sufficient reserve in place in the theater of war.

Despite the images on your TV set of tanks sweeping across the desert, our ground forces in Iraq, though powerful, are spread very thin. Things can go wrong, even in the best-planned, high-tech conflict. And we have not taken out much insurance.

We may well get away with this gamble. But it was an unnecessary and callous risk to take simply to force a "proof" that our Army is of diminishing relevance.

As the campaign of shock and awe went on hold in the first days of the war and the Iraqis began to ignite oil fields while launching missiles into Kuwait, it was our ground forces from the Army, Marines, and allied militaries who had to accelerate their plans and thrust into Iraq on an emergency basis.

Airpower is a magnificent tool. But you cannot stop sabotage from 25,000 feet. You cannot convince enemy military formations they are beaten until you demonstrate your presence on their soil. You cannot take prisoners, or protect refugees, or secure crucial facilities and resources from the air. And you certainly cannot stop genocide or ethnic cleansing from the sky.

Ground troops had to seize ports and oil infrastructure targets in Iraq. Tanks had to race across the desert to provide tangible evidence to the Iraqis that the Yanks really *were* coming.

Ground troops will be critical to winning any engagements against units that decide to resist, especially in urban terrain (although we will not be foolish enough to engage in widespread combat in cities). And good, old-fashioned grunts will need to patrol the peace that all of our military arms, working together, will establish.

From Bosnia to Afghanistan, ground forces continue to contribute the bulk of the forces deployed in support of our enduring missions around the globe. And ground forces will need to remain in Iraq long after the stealth bombers have returned to their base in Missouri.

Again, I want to stress that I am *not* elevating the Army and Marines above the Air Force, Navy, or Coast Guard (and yes, I know that the Marines are an arm of the Navy—though they fight on terra firma). But we need to beware attempts to assign our ground forces a *lower* priority than the other services for political purposes or to please civilian theorists who have never served our country in uniform.

After the dazzling effects of the shock-and-awe air campaign have faded, we need to remember that the key to an effective national defense will always be balanced forces. We need all of our services, adequately manned and equipped, to face the daunting range of challenges posed by this troubled world.

The greatest problem, of course, is that, when the posturing in Congress is over, the individual soldier doesn't have many friends on the Hill. But defense contractors, with their campaign contributions and promises of jobs in congressional districts, will always have plenty of elected supporters. And the defense industry always pushes for fewer troops and more expensive technologies.

Appropriate technologies are marvelous tools, but they still are not a substitute for well-trained, motivated troops.

We need both.

As you watch the stunning campaign unfold on television screens and read about our technology-driven successes in the newspapers, always remember that tens of thousands of young Americans in uniform are doing the far less glamorous work of warfare on the ground in Iraq.

I would argue against any fool who derided our technological advantages, but I will always fight the abstract theorists and greedy salesmen who dismiss the enduring importance of GI Joe.

# Cultures in Combat

## New York Post

*March 23, 2003*

Amateurs judge militaries by counting and comparing artillery pieces, tanks, and aircraft. But the system behind the shooters—especially the human system—is far more important to a war's outcome than the number of weapons fielded by either side.

Our combat technologies, from "smart bombs" whose accuracy appears supernatural to the individual equipment of a Navy SEAL, are certainly of great value—impressive to our friends and enemies alike. But even if our forces were equipped with exactly the same types and quantities of tanks and guns as the Iraqis possess, we would still be destined for victory.

Of course, the war would be longer and there would be more casualties. But our military *culture*, our system of seamlessly integrating skilled military personnel and machines into a huge war engine fueled by a constant flow of reliable information, gives us a far greater battlefield advantage than does any weapon.

Traditional military values, from good training and discipline to physical fitness, remain essential. But our greatest strength is simply that our entire military fights as a team. This may sound obvious, but genuine teamwork is rare in military history—and still surprisingly rare today.

In short, we fight like Americans.

Every American service member knows that he or she can count on every other service member during wartime. This, too, sounds like a given. But it isn't.

In Iraq's military, no one can trust anyone else. Allegiances are to blood relations, not to military units or to the government. The army doesn't trust (or train with) the Republican Guards, while the Special Republican Guards do their own thing off to the side. The "Gestapo" that answers to Saddam and his sons watches everyone—exciting fear, but certainly not trust. And the Iraqi air force (what still exists of it) is kept apart from the other services.

All this is done to prevent coup attempts or the development of alternative bases of power. Saddam's system is "divide and rule" at every level. It makes for successful domestic tyranny, but it isn't much good for postmodern warfighting.

America's troops, on the other hand, train together at every level. Oh, there's no lack of friction. We're all human. In peacetime, you'll hear officers and men from one service bitching about the other guys. But once the shooting starts, the sense that we're all Americans and all in the fight together takes over.

That Marine heading north of Basra knows that, if there are no Marine aircraft in the sky when he needs support, he can call on our Air Force—and the enemy positions will erupt in flame as soon as the fast-movers can divert to the target. The trooper from the 7th Cav crossing the Euphrates River and heading for Baghdad knows that, if the Army's attack helicopters are busy elsewhere, any Navy ground-attack aviation in the area is ready to help him out. And a downed pilot knows that *every* service will move heaven and earth to rescue him.

Famously, we even bring back our dead. But the quality of unstinting cooperation between the living keeps our casualties to a minimum.

Naturally, our attention is riveted by battlefield events, by the speed and precision with which our forces are striking. But those successes would be impossible without the enormous support networks in the rear. It's impossible to describe adequately how much skill and effort is required just to "deconflict" the skies, to keep aircraft safe not only from enemy fire but from one another, to keep them out of the fans of our artillery fire, and to insure they know where our troops are moving on the ground—and where special operations teams are active.

And that's just one aspect of an overall effort so complex that it has no like in any other human endeavor.

Armchair generals make fun of the REMFs (sorry, folks—can't explain that acronym in a family newspaper), the support troops behind the tip of the spear, but every tanker wants his fuel to come up on time. Every commander wants his communications to work without interruption. And every soldier wants a reliable MEDEVAC system backing him up.

We cherish the individual hero, but it's the great, cooperative system that brings us victory.

The couch commandos complain about our "tooth-to-tail ratio," the high proportion of support troops to the much-lower number of soldiers actually shooting at the enemy. But it is exactly that powerful system of support and services that enables our combat troops to fight so effectively and with casualty rates that are astonishingly low by historical standards.

You cannot measure our military against any other force in history. We're simply too different for comparisons. You can only judge us by our success.

The way we handle information supercharges all this cooperation. We and the Iraqis agree that information is power. But we enhance that power by sharing information wherever and whenever it's needed. The Iraqi approach is to hoard available information as if sharing it would dissipate its strength.

And our information, from our rates of fuel consumption to the most critical intelligence, is reliable. We are a fact-based society and military, facing an opponent who relies on lies, myths, and rumors.

Our approach enables us to bring precisely the right tools to bear at the right time. In his first briefing of this war, Gen. Tommy Franks stressed how each of the services might appear to lead the effort at different times and how our plans exploit our institutional flexibility. We can react to war's surprises or opportunities in hours or even minutes, while our opponents require days or weeks—if they can react at all.

This openness to innovative solutions goes all the way down to the individual soldier. The initiative of our sergeants and lieutenants on the battlefield is justly famous. But that spirit of initiative also inspires battle staffs, logistics headquarters—and even the young private in the maintenance section repairing a vehicle during our charge across Iraq.

A decade ago, one of our country's most courageous intellectuals, Samuel P. Huntington, wrote a controversial essay called "The Clash of Civilizations," suggesting that some measure of conflict was inevitable between the West and its failed rivals. Many will argue that the current war is a clash of civilizations. Whether or not this is so, we are certainly seeing a contest of military cultures.

And we need not doubt which side will win.

# Winning Big

## New York Post

*March 24, 2003*

In combat, the ideal leader is the man who remains calm and methodical under fire. Today's 24/7 broadcast news demands just the opposite: raised voices, an atmosphere of crisis, and a rush to judgment.

After declaring victory on Friday and Saturday, a number of media outlets all but announced our defeat yesterday, treating the routine events of warfare as if they were disasters.

Nonsense.

We're winning, the Iraqis are losing, and the American people have executive seats for what may prove to be the most successful military campaign in history.

I do recognize that the majority of our journalists are doing their best to cover this war accurately and fairly. But, with a few admirable exceptions, even seasoned reporters lack the perspective needed to judge the war's progress. Few have read military history. Even fewer have served in the military. They simply don't understand what they are seeing.

Every low-level firefight seems a great battle to them. Each pause in the advance is read as a worrisome delay. While they see friendly casualties up close, they rarely witness the devastation inflicted on our enemies. And when isolated groups of Iraqis do stand and fight, the journalists imply it means the Iraqi people are opposed to our intervention.

Let's try to understand what's actually happening.

*Is Iraqi resistance a surprise?* No. And it isn't nearly as strong as some reporting suggests. In a nation of twenty-two million people, one to two million have a stake in Saddam's regime—the officers in "elite" units, corrupt Ba'ath Party officials, secret policemen, and all those who have enjoyed good careers at the expense of the other twenty million of their countrymen—who all want Saddam dead.

Some thousands of Iraqis will fight to the death. Out of twenty-two million.

*But wasn't the war supposed to be a cakewalk?* No responsible official ever said this would be a bloodless war. The pundits who suggested such nonsense never served in uniform themselves. Anyone with the least knowledge of warfare expected some measure of resistance—and friendly casualties.

Were we less humane, of course, this war would have gone even faster. We could have destroyed the Iraqi military in days, killing tens of thousands of their soldiers from the sky. Instead, we have been trying to spare lives by giving our enemies a chance to surrender. Many are doing just that—or simply deserting and going home.

*But what about the Iraqis still resisting in the cities in the south, such as Um Qasr and Basra?* Those are small groups of die-hard regime supporters, thugs from the security forces that answer directly to Saddam's sons. Their fates are tied to Saddam's rule. Many of the men firing at our troops from building or bunkers in the south would be killed by their fellow Iraqis if they laid down their arms.

*Haven't they tricked us?* If they have, the tricks weren't very effective. CENTCOM did confirm that, in several instances, Iraqi elements pretended to surrender, then opened fire on our troops. Others have worn civilian clothes to ambush resupply convoys. These are not regular Iraqi army forces or even members of the Republican Guards. They appear to be from the Fidayeen, gangs of murderous thugs, and from the security services and the Special Republican Guards—the regime's Gestapo and SS.

While they certainly want to kill allied troops, their most important mission is to make it harder for all the thousands of Iraqi soldiers who truly do want to surrender. They want to convince us to fire on white flags. But we won't.

And the perpetrators of these fake surrenders, as well as those using civilian clothes to stage ambushes, are war criminals. Both the traditional laws of war and the Geneva Convention prohibit such actions. If captured, these men could be executed on the spot, with complete legality. But we're too decent to do that—even to them.

In the end, all the Iraqi irregular forces are accomplishing is to make our troops more determined. The latest message I had from a friend serving in the war made it clear that our troops are enraged, not deterred, by Iraqi actions—not least by the possible execution in cold blood of American prisoners and the abuse of other POWs.

*Hey, weren't all those cities in the south supposed to be secure?* No. Even in Um Qasr, our priority was to secure key port facilities, not to occupy neighborhoods. Consistently, allied forces have bypassed major population centers to avoid getting drawn into urban combat and causing needless harm to civilians.

A great deal of potential resistance can simply be left to wither away. Some Iraqis are zealots—for instance, the Sunni

Ba'ath Party enforcers now stranded behind our lines. They will either die or be taken prisoner.

*Isn't that risky, just bypassing entire cities?* Yes. In war, calculated risks are required. Our British allies are fond of saying that "Fortune favors the bold." You don't win wars through timidity. Our lead ground forces were more than two-thirds of the way to Baghdad yesterday. That sort of progress is unprecedented in the annals of warfare. But it does leave some potentially dangerous enemy elements in the rear.

We are relying on speed to operate "inside the Iraqi decision cycle"—to keep the enemy on the ropes, physically and psychologically. We are aiming for a large-scale, operational victory. But the inherent risks mean that there will continue to be sharp tactical encounters—isolated, but deadly—behind our advancing tanks.

*It sounds like there have been big, tough battles all of a sudden.* No. Every fight is tough for the soldiers under fire, of course. But what the broadcast media reported as significant battles consistently have been one-sided tactical encounters, with overwhelming casualties on the Iraqi side.

When our forces pause to destroy enemy forces methodically, that is a sign of professionalism and common sense, not of fear or a reverse. Cameramen might wish our troops would charge wildly into the enemy machine guns, but that's not the American way of war. When faced with a dangerous situation—if the mission allows us the time—we break contact to a distance that allows us to call down a storm of mortar fire, field artillery, and air strikes on the enemy. Whenever possible, we spend shells, not bodies.

Still, there are times when our forces have to get up close and personal with the enemy, as the Marines did in Nasiriyah yesterday. When that happens, we win. Period.

*So you think we can just roll on to Baghdad, huh?* No. We'll get to Baghdad in due time and in good shape. Several Republican Guard divisions may make the mistake of trying to take us on in large-scale battles as we move closer to the city.

If they do, there may be some intense tactical encounters. But those Iraqi divisions will be attacked so ferociously that a key decision for Gen. Tommy Franks will be when to turn off our destructive power and spare the survivors.

*Will they use chemical weapons?* That remains the greatest single risk to our troops and to the Iraqi population. If any weapons of mass destruction are used, it may slow us down for a time—and there could be painful casualties—but any such attacks will only strengthen our resolve, while proving to the world that we were right all along about the threat posed by Saddam.

*But we've taken casualties and American soldiers have been captured—doesn't that mean we're in trouble?* No. I wish it were otherwise, but, in any war—especially one of this magnitude—soldiers die, suffer wounds, or fall into enemy hands. We cherish every service member and mourn every loss. But, to be frank, our losses thus far are remarkably low, given the scale of our enterprise.

We may lose considerably higher numbers of casualties before this war is over. But I can promise you that our military commanders are relieved by the low level of our losses to date.

*Are the Iraqis really trying to lure us deep into their country so they can spring a trap on our forces?* The Iraqis have no choice in the matter. Our troops go where they want to go.

Yes, the Iraqis are probably planning a large military confrontation, an operational-level ambush, close to Baghdad—while forces remaining in our rear area attack our supply lines. They may even have left some of the bridges across the Euphrates standing on purpose.

If so, it was a grave error. If those Republican Guards divisions confront our forces, they simply will not survive. Even if their plan includes the use of chemical weapons.

Thus far, our troops have performed magnificently, seizing an ever-growing list of airfields, bridges, roads, oil fields, and other critical infrastructure, enabling us to maneuver swiftly and freely, while preserving the backbone of Iraq's economy for its people. And we prevented an ecological catastrophe, although those on the left will never credit us for doing so.

Even if the Iraqis have some ambitious master plan they still believe they can spring on us, they never expected to lose so much of their country so quickly. They are reeling; any plan could only be executed piecemeal, at this point.

After less than four days of ground operations, the Iraqis have lost control over half their country, they have lost control over most of their military, and allied forces are closing in on Baghdad.

*But what about the "Battle of Baghdad?" Will it be a bloodbath? Haven't the Iraqis already lured us into urban warfare in the south?* No. The Iraqis haven't lured us into anything. We have consistently imposed our plan and our will upon the enemy. While there have been some incidences of urban combat to date, with friendly casualties, our forces are far better prepared for such encounters than are the Iraqis. The Marine Corps, especially, has been training intensively in urban environments.

We are not going to be lured into a "Stalingrad" in Baghdad. Ignore the prophets of doom, who have been wrong consistently. As this column has steadily maintained, we have time, but Saddam doesn't. If we have to sit in a ring around Baghdad for several weeks while the last resistance is dismantled in innovative ways, then that's what we'll do.

Grave dangers lie ahead. Only a fool would underestimate them. But this war is not being run against a clock. The counsel that we must all be patient and let our troops do their jobs remains the best a former soldier can offer.

As long as the American people keep their perspective—which they will—it really doesn't matter how many journalists lose theirs.

# No "Baghdad Bloodbath"

## New York Post

*March 25, 2003*

The war in Iraq yesterday was a story of the dog—or many dogs—that didn't bark. Iraqi forces remained unable to launch significant counterattacks. Irregular forces failed to mount serious threats to our rear area. Regime officials continued to wave their arms and tell us that now we've *really* made them mad. And allied forces continued to move toward Baghdad.

We lost at least one Apache attack helicopter, probably to an aircraft malfunction. But what no one at home got to see was the destruction our strikes left amidst the Medina Division of the Republican Guards—despite the Iraqis positioning many of their combat vehicles in civilian neighborhoods.

The pilots of that downed Apache appear to have been captured. Their welfare is of paramount concern. But, otherwise, yesterday was another 24 hours of progress on every front, of remarkably low friendly casualties, and of the continued degradation of the regime's capabilities to resist.

A series of fierce armored engagements could erupt as early as Tuesday. Our 3rd Infantry Division is coiling to strike,

227

planning its attack and getting in position to take on the Republican Guards—who are hiding behind civilians.

You may hear some confused, alarmed reporting. We may even suffer our first armored-vehicle losses of this war. But, when the smoke clears, our troops will be rolling on to Baghdad amid the charred hulks of hundreds of Iraqi vehicles and mile after mile of Iraqi bodies.

Despite the steady progress of our troops, we continue to hear dire warnings about an impending bloodbath in Baghdad, once Saddam lures us into the streets of his ultimate fortress, his "Stalingrad" on the Euphrates.

Just a minute there, Herr Professor. Calm down, Dr. Think Tank. I'm just a former career soldier, so I don't understand military operations the way academics and pundits do. Explain something to me, slowly and clearly:

Why on earth would Gen. Tommy Franks do exactly what Saddam *wants*?

We're not stupid—or Russian—for God's sake. We're not going to slug down a couple of bottles of vodka apiece and drive straight into Grozny while Chechens pick off our tanks and troops at their leisure.

*We* are going to make the rules in Baghdad, not Saddam.

I simply cannot understand why anyone outside of Ba'ath Party headquarters imagines we would feel compelled to fight house-to-house in Baghdad, destroying the city, putting civilian lives at risk, and throwing away our soldiers.

Certainly, we'll need to engage in some limited urban combat, for specific objectives—as the Brits are doing on the outskirts of Basra and the Marines have done in Nasiriyah. But there is no iron rule of warfare that says we have to take Baghdad block by block.

Consider a few more sensible options.

Once our forces are ringing Baghdad, Saddam isn't going anywhere. There's no deadline on giving that bad boy the big Indian rub. If necessary—if the regime doesn't implode beforehand—the world is going to witness the first postmodern siege.

Historically, sieges could last over a year, while the population inside the city starved and died of plague. Not our style. We haven't even turned off the lights or shut off the water in Baghdad yet, and we may not do so in the future, except for limited periods and purposes.

Once the last die-hard Saddamites are corralled in Baghdad (and, perhaps, in Saddam's hometown of Tikrit, a city that just brings out the nuclear side of my character), we're going to work 'em like history's biggest cat batting around a blind, three-legged mouse.

And what is Saddam going to do about it? We can even send in food supplies, if the population needs to be fed. Let even our enemies eat as they wait to be killed. Saddam's birthday is coming up in April. I'll pay for the cake and FedEx it myself.

Meanwhile, our national intelligence assets will be focused on one city. Saddam had better renew his subscription to "Bunker Living," because he's not coming out to play stickball. Allied special operations forces—already in Baghdad—will be prowling the hallways and alleys, taking direct action against the regime's remaining supporters, collecting information for precision strikes and working with the growing Iraqi resistance.

When the right opportunities present themselves, our forces will swoop in on pinpoint raids. And no, we're not talking about *Black Hawk Down II*. Anyway, people tend to forget that, in Mogadishu, we actually won the tactical battle overwhelmingly— 20 dead Americans, a thousand dead Somali militiamen.

At the end of that fight, we had thoroughly broken "General" Aideed's forces. Then President Bill Clinton, the most frightened man on earth, declared defeat. The U.S. Army's Rangers were ordered home in humiliation, after winning a tough but enormous victory. President Bush may have his faults, but he ain't going to cut and run on our men and women in uniform.

I'm sick of being told how brilliant our enemies are and how our troops are going to get whupped up on by some Kmart Hitler. Might I pause in my literary endeavors to point out that, while *our* troops are approaching Baghdad, Iraq's Republican Guards are still quite a distance from Washington, D.C.?

Yes, serious dangers remain. It ain't over until the fat Iraqi squeals. There will be some disappointing days. We're going to try some very innovative techniques in Baghdad. Not every one of them will work. And some of our soldiers will die.

I do worry that, grown desperate, Saddam's thugs could begin to slaughter the Shi'as in Baghdad's suburbs, forcing us to intervene on moral grounds. But even if the Iraqis start slaughtering their own people and we *do* push inside the city limits to rescue them, people whose families have just been massacred tend to side with their rescuers, not their abusers.

Human shields would quickly become our best sources of intelligence. We'd have more friends in Baghdad than France has natural-born collaborators.

The final destruction of this regime may take more time than impatient souls would like. But it isn't going to end in a bloodbath of our soldiers.

# Shock, Awe, and Overconfidence

## The Washington Post

*March 25, 2003*

The allied forces on the march in Iraq have performed impressively. Within weeks, major operations will give way to a few months of mopping up. Iraq will be liberated. This will happen despite serious strategic miscalculations by the Office of the Secretary of Defense.

Most wars begin under the spell of prevailing theories that are swept away by the realities of combat. World War I began with a belief that élan and the bayonet still ruled the battlefield. Waves of soldiers fell before machine guns. In World War II, blitzkrieg worked against weak states but failed against those with strategic depth.

Now we are trying to prosecute a war according to another military theory, "shock and awe." Again, bold claims have led to disappointments redeemed only by the skill and determination of our military.

Explained as simply as possible, the shock-and-awe theory proposes that America's arsenal of precision weapons has developed so remarkably that aerial bombardment can shatter an opponent's will to resist. The air strikes are to be so

231

dramatic in sensory effect and so precise in targeting a regime's leadership infrastructure that the enemy's decision-makers see no choice but surrender.

The first waves of air strikes on Baghdad were indeed dramatic and precise. The problem is that one's enemies don't necessarily respond to theories. Shock and awe, like blitzkrieg before it, would work superbly against Belgium. But its advocates failed to consider the nature of Saddam Hussein's regime.

No matter how shocked and awed the Iraqi leadership may be, surrender is not, never was, and never will be an option for Hussein and his inner circle. Because of the nature of their regime and its crimes, the contest is all or nothing for them.

Had the most senior officials surrounding Donald Rumsfeld paused to consider the enemy, instead of rushing to embrace a theory they found especially congenial for political reasons, they would have realized that you cannot convince Hussein, his sons, or his inner circle that they have been defeated. You must actually defeat them. And you must do it the old-fashioned way, albeit with improved weapons, by killing them and destroying their instruments of power.

Our attempt to baby-talk Iraq's elite military forces into surrender was humane in purpose and politically attractive, and it might have minimized Iraqi casualties. But it delayed essential attacks on Iraq's military capabilities. This encouraged at least some Iraqis in uniform to believe they had a chance to fight and win. Now our forces advancing on Baghdad face the possibility of more serious combat than would otherwise have been the case.

Some things do not change. The best way to shock and awe an enemy is still to kill him. Those who want to wage antiseptic wars for political purposes should not start wars in the first place.

A student of military history would recognize the ghost of Italian Gen. Giulio Douhet at work in the shock-and-awe theory. In 1921 Douhet published *The Command of the Air,* a book predicting that air power would prove so powerful in the next war that land forces would be of marginal relevance. In World War II, air forces did play a critical role—but the Army still had to fight its way across the Rhine to secure victory, just as our soldiers and Marines have had to fight their way across the Euphrates.

Without question, air power is performing magnificently in Iraq. Weapons technologies truly have improved by an order of magnitude over the past decade. The Air Force and the air arms of our other services are indispensable. But they remain most effective as part of an overall land, sea, and air military team. Once again, it has taken ground forces to provide the main thrust of military operations, to take and hold ground, to seize oil fields, airfields and bridges, and to force the war toward a battlefield decision.

Unfortunately, those ground forces are spread very thin. Military planners have argued for months that more and heavier ground forces were needed to ensure rapid and sustained success, as well as to minimize risk. Rumsfeld personally and repeatedly rejected calls for the deployment of additional Army divisions. Now, as our last major units move into the fight in Iraq, Gen. Tommy Franks does not have on hand a significant armored reserve he can commit to battle, should things go awry.

I do not doubt our ultimate success. But the impressive television images of tanks charging across the desert mask a numerical weakness for which technology may not fully compensate. One senior officer serving in the Persian Gulf complained to me that had we had sufficient forces on hand to deploy security elements along our routes of march—the usual practice—those American POWs who appeared on Iraqi television might not have been captured.

The troops at the front of our attack are performing superbly, but they are operating on adrenaline at this point. Four to five days into any conflict, another division should have conducted a "forward passage of lines" with the 3rd Infantry Division before the final push to Baghdad, giving the 3ID a chance to rest, rearm, and reequip before returning to battle. But no other heavy division is on hand in the theater of war to relieve or reinforce our tanks and infantry fighting vehicles. The closest unit is on ships in the Red Sea, at least ten days away from any ability to influence the battle.

Why did Rumsfeld and his most trusted subordinates overrule the advice of their military planners? For political, bureaucratic, and theoretical reasons. Rumsfeld, who is otherwise an inspiring wartime official, was out to prove a point. In his vision of the future—one shaped by technocrats and the defense industry—ground forces can be cut drastically in order to free funding for advanced technologies. To that end, Rumsfeld has moved to frustrate the Army's efforts to field medium-weight brigades that can be deployed swiftly to a crisis, which would have been invaluable in this conflict.

This war was supposed to prove the diminishing relevance of ground forces, while shock-and-awe attacks from the air secured a swift victory. Instead, the plan had to be rearranged so that ground forces could rush into Iraq to prevent economic and ecological catastrophes—you still cannot seize ground, prevent sabotage, halt genocide and ethnic cleansing, or liberate anybody from the sky.

We are headed for victory, but, as the Duke of Wellington observed of Waterloo, it may be a "near-run thing" on the ground.

Some lessons of this war are already clear: Ferocity, skill, and determination, not theories, win wars. And our nation will continue to require balanced, adequately funded forces—in all of our armed services—for a very long time to come.

# Knife Fight

## New York Post

*March 27, 2003*

No unit in the war thus far has fought longer and harder than the U. S. Army's 3rd Squadron of the 7th Cavalry. They have been in constant combat for three days, killing at least several hundred Iraqis without losing one American life and pushing almost to artillery range of Baghdad's suburbs.

When you read these lines, those troopers will have fought through their toughest night of the war.

The 3rd of the 7th's march northward through horrendous sandstorms and repeated enemy attacks at close range are being described in detail by a cherished friend of mine, Sean Naylor of *Army Times,* perhaps the bravest war correspondent I ever have known. As I write from the safety of America, he is sharing the dangers with the bravest of the brave.

The weary, dirty troopers of the Cav fought through one ambush after another, through blowing sand that rips the skin and clogs weapons, through heavy darkness and the bizarre twilight of noon in a sandstorm, with enemy rounds clanging off their armored vehicles. All the while, they have remained disciplined and determined, as fine as any soldiers who ever served our nation.

And they have been doing even more than they know in the heat of battle, where no man can stop to ponder greater questions. The hard-core fanatics they are killing on the move are not merely a menace to our Cav troopers, but to the peace that lies beyond Baghdad.

Were the savages loyal to Saddam to survive into the postwar months, they would be a menace to the reconstruction of the country. In a sense, Saddam is doing both us and his country a favor at last, sending his most vicious murderers to be slaughtered by the "Garryowen" troopers of the Cav.

Saddam believed he saw an opportunity. Although reports remain unclear in the "fog of war"—or the sandstorms of war—it looks as though he decided to roll the dice and send a large force of his Baghdad reserves into battle yesterday. He aimed them southward, to bolster the crumbling Republican Guard divisions—and on a collision course with the Cav.

Saddam and his last loyal generals calculated that their forces could move under the cover of the sandstorm, preventing the U.S. military from observing and attacking them from the air. They sent thousands of die-hard regime supporters, Iraq's Brownshirt and SS equivalents, to the front in as many as 1,000 vehicles of various descriptions. It's a desperate attempt to stave off disaster.

Certainly, the weather conditions make it tough for our aircraft and pilots. Some of our aviation gear does not work well under such circumstances. But we have other intelligence systems and weapons that can cut even through the haze of a sandstorm—as well as brave pilots who will take great risks to support our troops. Those Iraqi forces already have been surprised by attacks out of nowhere.

But these are irregular forces and fanatics who have no hope if Saddam's regime collapses. These men *will* fight to the death.

And the forces rushing south have at least one specific mission: Destroy 3/7 Cav. The Iraqis hope that the squadron has been weakened—although the best that Iraqi attacks along the route of march achieved was to disable—not destroy—three U.S. tanks.

Nonetheless, the Cav's toughest fight is on as I write. Because of the weather, some of those Iraqi fighters likely will get through, along with some Republican Guard armor. And the weather *does* hurt the ability of the Cav's tanks and infantry combat vehicles to detect and engage enemy targets at long range.

This battle is a knife fight.

Our gunners and dismounted troops are much more skilled than the Iraqis—and much better equipped in every respect, despite the degradation caused by the weather. And, in the confusion of a night battle under such conditions, I guarantee you that many Iraqis will wind up firing at each other, unable to maintain discipline and order in their attacks. Night combat quickly turns into nightmares for all but the best-prepared, most methodical troops. And the Iraqis are in a hurry.

Still, it will be a miracle if we do not end this days-long battle with painful friendly losses.

Other U.S. Army units have maneuvered to support the Cav. Iraqi attempts to cut off the 3rd of the 7th's troopers by retaking a bridge in their rear have been defeated. Still, the Cav faces extraordinarily intense combat. Those troopers are out there on the edge.

But when the sandstorms subside, ground and air forces working together will complete the destruction of Saddam's most-dedicated reserves, of any Iraqis in that column who have survived close-quarters combat with the Seventh Cavalry. Then our advance will continue northward, destroying the remaining threats from Iraqi units dispersed around the battlefield.

This battle—and it is and has been a true battle, not just an engagement—matters to me personally, because my friend is there, doing what he sees as his duty. Sean Naylor has always fought to cover the U.S. Army accurately and fairly, and he loves soldiers and their folkways. He has reported from Panama to Afghanistan. At the same time, hundreds of families are praying for their loved ones, and thousands of fellow soldiers are waiting for news of their comrades in the Cav.

Had Defense Secretary Donald Rumsfeld listened to his generals and given them more of the ground forces they requested for this war, the battle-weary soldiers of that Cavalry squadron would not only have plenty of reinforcements beside them, but would already have been replaced on the line by a fresh unit.

Make no mistake: The civilian planners, the shameless know-it-alls in expensive suits, who overruled the military's request for additional ground forces will bear a measure of responsibility for every American combat death caused because a soldier was simply too tired to react swiftly enough, because troopers were falling asleep over their guns, and because they were asked to achieve miracles—and have been doing so—on the cheap.

There are basic rules the military honors. One is that you always give the combat commander whatever he asks for. Secretary Rumsfeld did not do that. A dirty not-quite-secret in all this is that Rumsfeld wanted to send even *fewer* ground forces, because his civilian subordinates believed that airpower could do virtually everything by itself. The Rumsfeld Pentagon has been the defense industry's best friend, but not the soldier's.

The only reason we have even the current number of soldiers on the ground in Iraq and Kuwait is that General Franks fought for higher troop levels, month after month. Of course, he's a good soldier and can't speak of these matters while in uniform. But I hope the day will come when he writes his memoirs.

By the way—none of the self-important civilian experts has a son serving up there with the Cav or down-country with the Marines. Their children are too important to wear uniforms. But my friend is in the thick of it, writing the best combat dispatches of this war. Shoulder to shoulder with the soldiers who are going to give us victory.

This campaign has been magnificent, because our troops have made it so. Every day sees noteworthy progress. Saddam's latest moves are as desperate as many of them are criminal. I only hope the 3rd Squadron of the 7th Cavalry gets to lead the victory parade in Manhattan.

# Guts and Glory

New York Post

*March 28, 2003*

In southern Iraq, the last sandstorms faded away, allowing American bombs to drop from the skies with renewed intensity. In northern Iraq, 1,000 U.S. Army airborne soldiers also dropped from the skies—and paratroopers have an intensity all their own. South of Baghdad, Iraqi irregulars and war criminals were dropping dead in front of the U.S. Marines.

Not a good 24 hours for Brother Saddam.

Even the Iraqi defense minister admitted that allied forces would soon be encircling Baghdad. (Wonder if that bad boy's going to get a warning shot through the forehead from Uday or Qusay?)

Between Basra and Um Qasr, superb Brit troops simultaneously hammered the remnants of Saddam's supporters and delivered the first relief supplies to liberated Iraq. The Third U.S. Infantry Division, the "Rock of the Marne" blocked Iraqi attempts at piecemeal counterattacks.

Oh, and by the way: The 3ID got their nickname in the First World War, when they stood fast as the French were running away. The more things change . . .

The unsung heroes from our resupply and maintenance units performed more wonders in keeping huge volumes of fuel, ammo, and chow flowing to the advancing combat troops. Under fire from Iraqi terrorists, this war's "Red Ball Express" took enormous risks to deliver what the grunts and the gunners needed.

And anyone who doubts the dangers faced by our support troops in *any* war should recall that, in World War II, Army fuel-truck drivers took higher casualties, percentage-wise, than the Infantry.

We also suffered a painful incident. In a desperate night battle, two Marine units mistakenly fired on one another. While some Marines were wounded, none were killed—a blessing in the midst of tragedy.

Before anyone criticizes those Marines, let him imagine the confused conditions, the fanatic wave attacks those Marines had been fighting off in sandstorms and darkness, and the sheer weariness of fighting men on the front line without sleep for days on end. There is no blame. It's war.

And despite this sad incident, it's a war that is going astonishingly well.

We all need to pause after the war's first week to salute the remarkable progress our forces have made.

### The Troops

On the ground, the Army and Marines, supported by our Brit allies, carried out the swiftest, deepest attack in military history. And to put all of our supposed difficulties into perspective, the war to date has been fought with friendly casualties so low they are barely a fraction of the deaths and injuries that happened on America's highways in the same time-frame.

Certainly, we value every one of our soldiers, and mourn each loss. This is not a low-cost war to the families whose sons and daughters have been killed, wounded, or captured. But, by any standards, this campaign has been remarkable.

We even sought to spare our enemies. In the air, pilots from all of our services have done a marvelous job of striking Iraqi troops while limiting civilian casualties—despite Saddam's efforts, at every level, to use his own people as human shields.

The initial phase of our air campaign, although it did not succeed in its hope of toppling the regime, was a worthy effort. Because of political considerations, those air attacks were too cautious—frankly, too timid—but the principle of attempting to reach over the conscript army and past the innocent civilians to decapitate the regime itself, to eliminate the truly guilty, was morally sound and remains worth trying again in the future—but with more punch and less warning.

Now our air strikes are directed increasingly at killing our enemies, instead of just working on their nerves. As a result, airpower's value to the war will increase dramatically.

Attacks from the air still may not be able to win wars without boots on the ground, but I promise you that the troops locked in combat with the Iraqis love to hear those A-10 Thunderbolts come ripping in. Or to have the Air Force officer attached to their unit tell them, "On the way," followed by a pair of Navy F-18s streaking overhead to help Saddam's faithful achieve martyrdom.

From the ships at sea, to the youngest infantrymen on the land, this has been a proud week in American military history.

## The Press

I want to give credit everywhere it's due. In the first days of the war, I criticized the broadcast media for hysterical reporting, for declaring victory at night then declaring defeat in the morning. But the American media, too, has made rapid progress as it covered the dramatic advance of our troops.

The key to more reliable coverage has been the reporters "embedded" with the front-line units. Look, it takes guts to go out there—without even a sidearm to defend yourself. Several of those journalists—those who had covered military operations in the past—filed terrific stuff from the moment the troops crossed the line of departure. The novices, though, issued initial reports tinged with panic, as if each exchange of gunfire was the Battle of the Bulge.

It's said that everyone learns very quickly in combat. And I have been just plain impressed with the speed with which battlefield reporting has improved. Even the anchors back home are behaving a bit more soberly.

There's still a long way to go, and 24/7 news channels have a nasty appetite for sensationalism. But once journalists got out on the ground with our troops and saw just how superb those men and women in uniform really are—and how tough their line of work is—we began to hear a tone of respect that has not been accorded our soldiers in nearly half a century.

**The Enemy**

Now that I've praised the achievements of our troops and even of the journalists out there wearing flak jackets, let's take a look at where our enemies stand—to the extent that they're still standing.

Day by day, Saddam's attempts to lash out have grown more desperate. In the south, his regular army collapsed, surrendering or deserting, leaving his secret policemen, collaborators, and thugs sent down from Baghdad to terrorize the Iraqi population and try frantically to slow allied progress.

Let's be blunt. Those attacks on our rear area by war criminals dressed in civilian clothes (or even U.S. uniforms), using civilians as human shields, and employing other illegal techniques, such as false surrenders . . . well, the truth is those are mosquito bites on an elephant's rear end.

Those attacks may play well on television, and they certainly give some of our soldiers a few tense moments. But they accomplish nothing strategically.

Saddam's "elite" troops are fragmented—largely because of his own foolish strategy—and few of the Republican Guards appear willing to come out and fight unless the regime's enforcers literally put guns to their heads.

Saddam has squandered thousands of the die-hard regime loyalists he needs to control Baghdad in desperate wave attacks.

Saddam's air force has not gotten a single plane off the ground. Saddam's navy managed only to lay a few sea mines and delay humanitarian aid for the liberated Iraqis in the south before it ceased to exist.

**The War Ahead**

I see no reason why Week Two should not be as successful in its way as Week One.

- Our troops in the north will secure more of Iraq's oil fields, while speeding the dissolution of Saddam's forces.
- On the approaches to Baghdad, our air and ground team will complete the destruction of Saddam's Republican Guards and Special Republican Guards.
- Liberated Iraqis will be fed, and we shall see ever more enthusiastic and public expressions of support from these

long-suffering people—as they realize their torturers really are gone for good.

• And even if Saddam uses chemical weapons in a last-ditch attempt to stop our troops, we will overcome that, too.

My heartfelt advice to every reader is the same as it was on the eve of this war: Be patient with our troops. The collapse of Saddam's regime could be very sudden, or it could drag on for weeks. In either case, the outcome remains certain.

# How Long?

## New York Post

*March 29, 2003*

"As long as it takes": That's how long we'll stay in the fight in Iraq. President Bush put it as bluntly and clearly as possible. To the American people. To the world. And to Saddam Hussein.

No one can say exactly how long this war will take. But it is *not* going to be another Vietnam. No years of quagmire ahead. The attacks on our rear area by irregular forces are not signs of an endless struggle with guerrilla forces. That's utter nonsense.

Saddam's military shrinks by the day. Saddam's means of control are crumbling. His loyalists are dying in droves. And the atrocities the regime's terrorists are committing against their own people are not exactly winning domestic Iraqi support for Saddam and the kids.

While the regime in Baghdad may look surprisingly strong to some—especially to all you al Jazeera fans—it's important to remember that we only see the problems on our side. We have no clear sense of the internal pressures on Saddam's regime, of who's still alive, or of how desperate the survivors feel.

When a tyrannical regime finally starts to break, the collapse can go very fast—the Ceaucescu or Mussolini models. Or a fanatical ruling clique can sacrifice their people to the end while the rulers hold out in a bunker—the Hitler model.

So no one can fix a date for VI Day—Victory in Iraq Day (the acronym will be more interesting if we ever invade Denmark). But beware the pundits who, just last week, were predicting that shock-and-awe air strikes would end the war in days. Now the same voices are predicting a new Thirty Years War.

The likeliest scenario is that the major combat operations will be over in weeks—or perhaps a month, if Gen. Tommy Franks decides to wait for the arrival of the Fourth Infantry Division to deliver the *coup de grâce* to Saddam's military.

A siege of Baghdad and the reduction of Tikrit (Saddam's hometown) could take weeks, or a few months. And there will be plenty of small-scale mopping-up operations in the meantime.

But once the dictator is gone, the passion for the fight will go out of most of his surviving supporters. Some blood-drenched hardliners may attempt to go to ground in the cities or the mountains. But once they are certain Saddam is gone, the common people those regime loyalists have tormented will be our best sources of information as to their lairs.

What we have twitching before us is a reign of terror, not a government. The irregular attacks on our forces and the atrocities that regime die-hards are committing against their own people—including forcing children into battle—are the snarls and chokes of a dying regime, not a sign of a vast patriotic uprising against a hated invader.

I never become discouraged with our troops. But I'm dismayed, again and again, by those pundits who seem to be rooting for us to lose, who imply that the Iraqis are doing everything right and we're fumbling the ball. I'm growing weary of pointing out what a success this campaign has been to date. If you want perfection, join the Kirov Ballet.

Now the campaign is in a lull, what the military calls an "operational pause." Combat units that have advanced so far, so fast, need a break to rest and resupply, to perform maintenance on vehicles and weapons and to allow leaders to plan the next stage of operations, based on the developing situation.

Certainly, we would be better off had Gen. Franks been given all the troops he asked for to start with. Even the presence of one more heavy division would have allowed us to keep on punching without a break.

But in the deadly casino of battle, you play the hand you've got. And we've still got aces. While our forces are reorganizing for the next phase and cleaning up their lengthy supply lines, our aircraft are "tank plinking"—taking out the Iraqi armored vehicles concealed in towns and villages or dug into camouflaged positions. One by one.

Put yourself in the place of an Iraqi tanker who has just seen another tank go up in flames a quarter of a mile away—without even glimpsing the source of the attack. That psychological pressure is almost as important in triggering the final collapse of Iraq's military as is the physical destruction.

Meanwhile, more evidence emerges every day that this war is worth fighting. Cache after cache of Iraqi chemical warfare gear turns up. Our troops witness one atrocity after another. And there is ever greater proof that President Bush was right all along about Iraq's support of terrorism.

The recent report of an al Qa'eda cell in Basra, helping regime loyalists terrorize the population, is the smallest part of it. Our special operations forces in the north are going after thousands of terrorists who previously had crossed over from Iran to set up training camps.

Above all, it becomes clearer by the day that Saddam's Fidayeen thugs have been training for years on terrorist tactics—that's what they're using against our forces. In sheer numbers, Saddam's Fidayeen appear to be the largest terrorist organization in the world, an al Qa'eda on steroids, with a country to call their own.

Is this war worth fighting? Yes. For as long as it takes.

# Tragedy of the Arabs

## New York Post

*March 30, 2003*

TV networks in the Arab world gloat as they broadcast pictures of American prisoners. They report every Iraqi lie as if it contains unassailable truth, while mocking each report of allied success. They promise their viewers Iraq is winning the war.

They betray their own people by doing so, setting up Arabs for yet another psychological catastrophe.

Our natural response to the Arab world's phenomenal lies is anger: We resent their indecency in glorifying murder and war crimes. We cannot understand how anyone can believe these gruesome fairy tales for adults.

My advice is to ignore the Arabs. Hand-wringing about Arab TV disinformation or about the rage of the Arab street is a waste of our time. We cannot convince them and we cannot force them to change.

The best we can do—even for the Arabs—is to get on with America's agenda of liberation.

The most important thing for Americans to grasp about the impotent fury of the Arab world is that it isn't really about us. It's about their own internal demons.

The absurdities broadcast and printed throughout the Arab world are symptoms of a once-great culture's moral desolation, of the comprehensiveness of Arab failure. The Arabian Nights have long since turned into the Arabian nightmare.

The inability of the Arab world to compete with the West in any field of endeavor (even their efforts at terrorism ultimately fail) has been so devastating to the Arab psychology that they are desperate for someone to blame for what they and their grotesque leaders have done to their own culture.

Without the United States—and, of course, Israel—as excuses for Arab political squalor, Arabs might have to engage in self-examination, to ask themselves, "How have we failed so badly?"

They prefer to blame others, to sleepwalk through history, and to cheer when tyrants and terrorists "avenge" them.

On one level, Arabs know that Saddam Hussein is a monster. They know he has killed more Arabs than Israel ever could do. Saddam has been the worst thing to happen to Mesopotamia since the Mongols razed Baghdad. But Arabs are so jealous and discouraged that they need to inflate even Saddam into a hero. They have no one else.

Try to understand how broken the Arab world must be, how pitiful, if the celebrated Arab "triumph" of this war is the display of a few POWs on TV.

We would be foolish to descend to their level and gloat. The world would be better off were Arab civilization a success. We all should pray that the Arab world might, one day, be better governed and more equitable, that Arab peoples might join us in the march of human progress, instead of fleeing into reveries of bygone glories.

But the obstacles Arabs have erected for themselves are enormous. For all of the oil revenue that has flowed into the wealthier Arab countries, consider the overall state of the Arab world:

- It does not produce a single manufactured product of sufficient quality to sell on world markets.
- Arab productivity is the lowest in the world.
- It contains not a single world-class university.
- The once-great tradition of Arab science has degenerated into a few research programs in the fields of chemical and biological warfare.
- No Arab state is a true democracy.
- No Arab state genuinely respects human rights.
- No Arab state hosts a responsible media.
- No Arab society fully respects the rights of women or minorities.
- No Arab government has ever accepted public responsibility for its own shortcomings.

This is a self-help world. We can't force Arab states to better themselves. If Arabs prefer to dream of imaginary triumphs while engaging in fits of very real savagery, they're their own ultimate victims.

Is there any hope? Yes: Iraq.

While building the Iraq of tomorrow must be done by the Iraqis themselves, we would be foolish not to give them every reasonable assistance.

With their oil reserves, a comparatively educated population and their traditionally sophisticated (compared to other Arabs) outlook, the Iraqis are the best hope the region has of building a healthy modern state.

It isn't going to be easy, and it is going to take years, not months. But the Iraqis have the chance to begin the long-overdue transformation of Arab civilization.

For all the shouting and hand-waving in the Arab world, the truth is that Arabs have a deep inferiority complex. They're afraid they really might not be able to build a successful modern state—to say nothing of a postmodern, information-based society.

If Iraq could do even a fair job of developing a prosperous Arab democracy that respected human rights, it could be an inspiration to the rest of the states in the region—and beyond.

The Arab world desperately needs a success story. Let us hope, for the sake of hundreds of millions of our fellow human beings in the Middle East, that Iraq provides that example.

In the short term, though, the Arab world is in for a shock. By lying about Saddam's atrocities and promising an Arab victory, those Arab media outlets are doing all Arabs a cruel disservice.

Imagine the impact on the Arab world when Saddam lies dead and the oppression-stunned people of Iraq begin to tell their stories of suffering under his regime. What will Arabs do when their own fellow Arabs tell them Saddam's glory was all a big lie?

My prediction: They will turn on the Iraqis and accuse them of being tools of the United States.

But be patient. The cliché is absolutely true: Nothing succeeds like success.

Baghdad was once the center of Arab culture, of science and the arts, and a beacon of human progress. It should be our sincere hope that Baghdad one day might play that role again.

# U.N. Can't Take the Lead

## The Atlanta Journal-Constitution

*March 28, 2003*

Corruption will be the most important variable in the postwar reconstruction of Iraq. If not controlled, it will frustrate all of our hopes for Iraq's future, as it has ravaged the prospects of dozens of countries in the developing world. Yet, corruption is not even considered a strategic factor by planners and decision makers.

Corruption is the cancer that kills all else. It polarizes and balkanizes societies. It fosters mistrust and destroys incentive. The danger posed to Iraq's recovery by rampant corruption is the great reason our government must not hand over Iraq's future to the United Nations.

Contrary to a great deal of anxious speculation, the United Nations has not been destroyed or even much diminished by the dissension leading to the present war. We simply have been reminded, again, of the limits of the United Nations' abilities.

The organization can help feed and house refugees, it can support peacekeeping operations in relatively benign environments, it provides a global platform to the otherwise voiceless, and it serves as a tremendously effective employment agency for out-of-work bureaucrats from around the globe.

But what the United Nations cannot do is summon the will to depose dictators—too many dictatorships are represented in its body—and it lacks the integrity to reconstruct countries that tyrants have ruined. Do we wish to charge Libyan or Nigerian officials with rebuilding Iraq and setting the example for good governance? Nor can the United Nations ever bring a project to conclusion. Each new endeavor creates a self-perpetuating bureaucracy.

While it must be said, in fairness, that many honest and dedicated people do work for the United Nations, not one of my numerous friends working within or beside the United Nations in the field believes the organization is capable of honest management. The tales of corruption, from skimming relief funds to sexual exploitation of refugees, are so appalling that readers would be disinclined to believe them. The United Nations, at its best, does good work, despite its ethical laxity. At its worst, it contributes to the stagnation of troubled societies.

Current demurrals notwithstanding, the United Nations will maneuver to gain control of rebuilding Iraq—and not for humanitarian reasons. The ongoing oil-for-food program has been a huge source of income and employment for the United Nations. The United Nations takes a percentage off the top for administering the program. No bureaucracy, anywhere, wants to surrender tens of millions of dollars a year in income.

Oil-for-food also has fostered extensive corruption within and around the United Nations. While formal restrictions exist on how the revenue can be spent by the Baghdad regime, work-arounds tolerated by the United Nations enabled Saddam Hussein to buy French-built antitank missiles and Russian-made radars and jammers while continuing to purchase components for the missiles his forces have been firing toward Kuwait. In the tradition of U.N. aid programs around the world, the basic operating principle of oil-for-food has been "Don't ask, don't tell."

The income from future Iraqi oil sales must be used efficiently and honestly to benefit Iraq's people. Using the United Nations—an organization subject to far less scrutiny than Enron ever was—as a broker would mean the wrong people making the wrong spending decisions for the wrong reasons. Open books and transparent operations in Iraq's oil industry will be the single most important gauge of integrity in the redevelopment process, simply because that's where the money is.

When the United Nations, eager to retain its income stream and the bureaucracy it supports, comes to us to say, "Well, we've changed our minds now and we're ready to help out by taking over Iraq's reconstruction," we must say no—despite our national inclination to pass the buck once the bullets have stopped flying.

Some members of our own government who were impatient for this war to begin will be even more eager to evade our responsibilities after a military victory. But the future of Iraq is vitally important—to the Arab world and to us.

Behind their ornate rhetoric and bravado, Arabs suffer from an agonizing inferiority complex. They fear that they truly may not be capable of building modern, rule-of-law, market economies, to say nothing of postmodern information societies. And the challenges are daunting, given the low levels of education, the perversion of information, the oppression of women, the prevalence of kinship as the organizing principle of society and the economy—and, above all, the paralyzing levels of corruption endemic to Arab societies.

Iraq is the one major Arab country that has a fighting chance to break the pattern of failure. The odds are not as encouraging as we might like, but the effort is well worth the risk and expense that we will incur in helping the Iraqis build an even comparatively successful, reasonably liberal economy and state. They do have great advantages in their wealth of resources—oil—and in the education levels of an urbanized population. But the Iraqis will need the discipline of law and plenty of good examples during the initial phases of recovery from more than a generation of oppression.

The United States has accepted the responsibility for this war. Now it must accept a genuine responsibility for the peace.

U.N. participation must be limited to tasks that are subject to rigorous observation and that offer limited opportunities for graft. It is far too easy to say, "Tut-tut" about corruption, implying that things are just that way "over there." I always have found that attitude arrogant and racist, given the countries of which we usually speak in this regard. Corruption is as unacceptable in a country struggling to build a better future as it should be here in the United States. To suggest otherwise is to imply that we Americans not only enjoy superior privileges, but also are superior human beings.

As for U.N. corruption in the field, some of it is large-scale and daunting, while much appears minor, barely a nuisance, easy to dismiss. But it is often the small, personal instances of corruption that do the greatest damage over time. Even a tiny bribe extracted for a transient advantage destroys the trust of the local population. Other forms of U.N. corruption are institutional and focused on building power bases within the organization, or on protecting privileges and positions.

There is no effective mechanism for imposing discipline within the United Nations. Corrupt officials, even when caught red-handed, suffer at worst a transfer to another, similar post—and sometimes enjoy a promotion as a quid pro quo for going quietly.

Even at its best, the United Nations is an inefficient manager of resources. Nor can it make difficult decisions, always pursuing the course least likely to excite resistance. The goal of the United Nations—not unworthy—is to maximize cooperation between states. But the means used to achieve that goal generally lead to a minimum of effective leadership.

The oft-cited Marshall Plan worked well for many reasons, but one of the key factors was the "tough love" it imposed on the occupied states. The plan was not simply a matter of handouts. Especially early on, it was carefully regulated and demanding of results. And the earlier, pre-Marshall Plan phases of postwar reconstruction in Germany and Japan were even more stringent. We did not lower our standards—which academics consistently recommend—but forced the subject populations to raise their own.

If corruption is tolerated in Iraq's reconstruction, whether from U.N. agencies or our own contractors, it will send the message to the Iraqi population that nothing really has changed, that business as usual may continue. This is a mistake we have made elsewhere, and it is a painfully expensive one.

Our first error, consistently, is to fail to impose the rule of law. We hand over matters to the locals as quickly as possible because we want to do things on the cheap. In Bosnia, then Kosovo, our failures to impose the rule of law have left us with deeply troubled societies that will be on our hands for years to come. We look away as corruption flourishes, allowing aid to flow with few conditions—while our soldiers patrol the roads but do little more. To a disappointing extent, we simply have made the Balkans safe for black marketers.

Iraq is far too important strategically to receive the same treatment.

In a very real sense, President Jacques Chirac did us a favor by announcing, in advance, that France would veto any U.N.

proposal that would leave the United States and Britain in charge of Iraq's reconstruction. Good. The French would set a dreadful example, with their legendary affinity for nourishing corruption in developing countries. Chirac has given us the excuse we needed not to turn to the United Nations as the overall reconstruction authority.

Certainly, we cannot help the Iraqis rebuild without help from other states, but active participation on the ground should come primarily from the "coalition of the willing." Those countries that have supported the removal of Saddam Hussein should have exclusive call on submitting bids for reconstruction projects—at least until the Iraqis take over the management themselves. Then it will be Iraq's right to decide to whom contracts are allocated.

In the meantime, even companies and individuals from the friendliest states—as well as from our own country—must be subject to stern and constant scrutiny, as well as to meaningful penalties for engaging in corrupt practices. As a start, I recommend investing in a large number of polygraph machines.

The temptations to engage in corruption are going to be enormous, especially because that is how Iraq's economy has functioned in the past. The Iraqis are no innocents, and many of their businessmen and officials will take a quietly cynical view toward efforts to help the greater population. Human nature is a constant, not a variable. Those who are well aware of the money to be made through U.N. corruption will be the first and loudest voices within Iraq to call for a U.N. takeover of reconstruction efforts.

We must resist listening to those voices, too, although they will always find a hearing among those ill-disposed to any endeavor the United States undertakes. Long-term results are far more important than responding to transient complaints, and enduring success is of far greater value than brief popularity.

The battle against corruption is one we must fight with a perseverance equal to the military war. No matter what else we get right, if we get corruption wrong, Iraq will remain a danger to its people, its neighbors, and to us.

# Behind Enemy Lines

## New York Post

*March 31, 2003*

Have faith in the American soldier. Have particular faith in our special operations forces, the shadow warriors who are the most effective fighting men in history.

Over the weekend, special ops troops leading Kurdish freedom fighters overran a vast terrorist base near Iraq's border with Iran.

Perhaps a thousand members of Ansar al Islam, a group with direct ties to both al Qa'eda and Saddam's regime, had pledged to resist to the death. They ran like rabbits and died like sheep.

The surviving terrorists are now in detention in Iran. And their huge complex of caves and defensive positions is already yielding critical intelligence.

This victory in both the war against Saddam and the War on Terror was one of the rare times when our special operations forces stepped out into the light of day.

The Pentagon also showed a tape of Army Rangers raiding an Iraqi headquarters by night. Other reports tell of special operators tracking down a meeting place for over 200 leaders of Saddam's death squads in Basra. Allied aircraft wiped the building from the face of the earth.

Army Special Forces are active in An Najaf, rooting out the die-hards who have been tormenting the civilian population. Other special operators were in Iraq well before the start of the war, providing intelligence and locating Iraqi missile launchers.

We even have special operations forces operating in Baghdad, hunting for targets and killing Iraq's bloodstained leaders, one after another.

This is all mighty impressive. But it's only a fraction of what the Army's Special Forces, Rangers and Delta Force, the Navy's SEALs, and special operations elements from the Air Force and Marines are doing in this war—along with Brit, Aussie, and other allied comrades.

These men work best in the darkness, both figurative and literal. So they rarely get credit for their phenomenal skills and courageous accomplishments.

Far more is happening behind Iraqi lines than we ever will know. Our special operators have extraordinary capabilities that must be kept secret to remain effective. But I can assure you that some of the most effective actions taken against Saddam's regime are happening far from any TV cameras.

I was fortunate during my Army career and afterward to know many special operators, from brilliant generals down to sergeants so tough they make steel feel like a down comforter. I was never less than deeply impressed by their skills, professionalism—and intellect.

And that leads me to a general misunderstanding. Hollywood portrayals of special ops troops tend to portray them as wild men, hot dogs whose calling is to perform amazing stunts. Well, these guys are certainly amazing, but show-offs and braggarts don't make the cut.

Special ops troops are rigorously self-disciplined. Every man in a team must be able to depend completely on every other man. No drunks, no punks. These are men who must be ready to walk through fire, if the mission requires it.

Physically tough, you bet. But their *psychological* toughness is even more important, given the enormous stresses under which they operate. And many of them speak multiple languages, have advanced degrees, and possess such deep experience of the world that they are among the most intellectually sophisticated men I've ever known.

As for courage, well, it's required of many soldiers, often at unexpected times. But special operators know the risks they take going into a mission. And it's much easier to perform reliably when surrounded by hundreds of your buddies and backed up by armor and airpower, than when you are hundreds of miles from help, with the enemy all around you.

Our special operations troops aren't superhuman. But they're close.

Try to imagine the sort of courage it takes to serve in a hunter-killer team in downtown Baghdad. Or a Delta Force element on a direct-action mission deep in Iraq. Or an Air Force special ops pilot flying a helicopter in total darkness, skimming the sand, with only his skills and a pair of night-vision goggles to prevent a catastrophic crash that would kill the Special Forces A-team he's inserting.

These men are a breed apart. It is no slight to the magnificent performance of all our men and women in uniform to recognize the fearsome risks our special operations soldiers volunteer to undertake, or the extraordinary skills and dedication they bring to their missions.

Each one of these men is a national treasure, each one of them a strategic asset. As you read these lines, they are operating behind Saddam's lines, haunting him and hunting him. You may never see their faces. But you are going to see their results.

# Urban Warriors

## New York Post

*April 1, 2003*

Saddam had a plan. He intended to lure allied forces into the streets of his cities, where ambushes would turn the war into a bloodbath.

Unfortunately for Saddam, our troops failed to cooperate: The blood being shed is that of Iraqi terrorists.

Our troops didn't charge wildly into Basra or Nasiriyah as Saddam hoped. Instead, they methodically began to dismantle the resistance put up by the regime's die-hard thugs and party hacks—fighting on our terms, not theirs.

Saddam's response showed exactly how much regard he has for the Iraqi people: He began slaughtering them in an attempt to force us to come into the cities and save them.

Saddam, you see, has studied the lessons of history. He knows that urban warfare traditionally has been a blood-soaked affair, and he believes—wrongly—that the American people are cowards who can't bear casualties.

But he forgot that Americans aren't slaves to history. Americans *make* history.

And wherever the U.S. Marines, the U.S. Army, or the Brits have chosen to enter urban areas—often to protect innocent Iraqis from their own government—they have done it with great skill, patience, and determination. There will not be a street-by-street bloodbath in An Najaf or Basra, and certainly not in Baghdad.

Our forces are rewriting the book on how to conduct the toughest sort of military operations efficiently, effectively, and with an unprecedented degree of humanity.

To put it even more accurately, our military already *had* rewritten the book—literally—before this war began. While cliques of self-appointed experts in Washington did their best to divert funds away from our ground forces (to lavish the money on defense contractors, instead) the Marine Corps marched ahead with its decade-long project to create new doctrine for urban warfare and to train Marines for a type of fight their leaders knew was coming.

Under a series of visionary commandants, the Corps ignored the flashy theories of sterile high-tech war and prepared for what they believed the country would need them to do. And the Marines, not the technocrats, were right.

The U.S. Army, too, began to follow the USMC's lead back in the 1990s, constructing new urban-warfare training sites at various military bases and revamping combined-arms doctrine for the urban fight. As a result, our troops today—along with the Brits, thanks to their long experience in Northern Ireland—are the best-prepared in the world for combat in cities.

As you read, our Marines continue their steady, successful operations to secure Nasiriyah. Any couch commandos out there who think the effort should have gone faster should consider how much the Marines have done with remarkably low casualties by historical standards. "You want it bad, you get it bad," is the No. 1 maxim of warfare in built-up areas. The Marines are doing it right.

On Monday, two brigades of the Army's 101st Airborne Division—a unit that has trained hard for this type of combat—launched a squeeze play on the terror detachments in the city of An Najaf. Thus far, two American lives have been lost—each soldier mourned and honored—but the Iraqi death machine has lost several hundred killed, still more wounded, and a large number of thugs and hit men captured.

Every hour, more of An Najaf's citizens are safe and free.

How have the Marines and the air assault troops from the "Screaming Eagles" upset the traditional wisdom on urban combat, winning big with low casualties?

Training. Leadership. Doctrine. Courage. And innovative techniques of coordination and cooperation literally incomprehensible to Iraqi bully-boys and butchers.

Instead of sending the infantry headlong into ambushes, our officers and NCOs employ precision air strikes, direct fire from tanks, skilled infantry, special operations forces, and pinpoint artillery fire in varying combinations to get the job done. Teamwork, American style.

Urban combat remains fierce, deadly, and indescribably stressful. But our troops are so disciplined that the Iraqis have not been able to excite them into firing on innocent civilians, no matter the treachery or provocation.

And what about those civilians? We've all heard the studio-strategists in the media jeering that the Iraqis didn't welcome us with open arms, after all (how about all those cheering Kurds, folks?). Well, it happens that our best sources of intelligence in these urban operations are, in fact, Iraqi civilians who can't wait to see the back end of Saddam's regime.

The Shiites in the south of Iraq have been living in a trance, in a daze of oppression. Now they realize that Uncle Sam's serious, that Saddam is really going to fall. And they are flocking to provide us with intelligence.

Iraqi civilians and deserters are telling us where the safe houses are, where the ammo is stored, where the death squads have prepared strongpoints or bunkers—and even the best routes to get at them. Instant judgments to the effect that the Iraqis were not welcoming us were just plain wrong.

Tragically, we are going to see continued atrocities as murderers and torturers with no way out find themselves pressed ever more tightly against the wall. When they cannot beat our troops, they take it out on the people of Iraq.

But now the people of Iraq are beginning to take their revenge.

# On to Baghdad!

## New York Post

*April 3, 2003*

As the U.S. Army and Marines race each other to Baghdad—traditional service rivalry at its best—American battlefield innovations have come so fast it's hard to keep up with them. Theory failed, but ferocity saved the day.

The ultimate technology in this war hasn't been a smart bomb, but the American soldier. Again.

Critics at home and abroad have complained that it's taking us *weeks* to conquer Iraq. Wait until the truth sinks in that we conquered Iraq in just weeks.

In the heat of the moment, few kept their perspective, and enemies elsewhere indulged in some preposterous wishful thinking, predicting another Vietnam or even worse. Now the terrorists and despots are learning, yet again, that America's power is irresistible when aroused.

This truly has been a revolutionary war, though not the way the think-tank crowd expected. The apostles of victory-through-technology-alone have been disappointed to find that GI Joe still leads the way. And the past several days of hyper-velocity combat south of Baghdad have repackaged a very old form of warfare for the twenty-first century.

The fighting as our forces close on Saddam's citadel has become a battle of attrition—but not in the manner our enemies expected. Wars of attrition have a bad name, but there's nothing wrong with them as long as the attrition is all on the enemy side.

And it is.

This isn't the attrition of the Great War's Western Front, with its trenchlines and stalemate. This is *dynamic attrition,* inflicted by air and ground forces moving so swiftly that the enemy is kept hopelessly off-balance and bewildered. It's shoot-on-the-move warfare in fast-forward against a paralyzed opponent.

There are no instances in modern warfare, and few examples from antiquity, of such one-sided battlefield success.

We have attempted to wage this war as humanely as possible, giving the Iraqi military the opportunity to lay down its arms. The secret police commissars of the Baghdad regime prevented extensive surrenders among the Republican Guards. So the time came to take aim and kill them.

And we did. As with our innovations in urban warfare, this supercharged combination of mobile firepower moving through the dirt with see-it-kill-it aircraft ruling the sky has deep roots. For decades, our military thinkers have struggled to peer into a dangerous future, to imagine the threats we would face and the combat techniques necessary to defeat them. Debates raged over desks before the bullets flew. And the inquiring, forward-thinking nature of *all* the military services has served us very well in this essential war.

We saw the first, rough-hewn versions of the new American way of war in Desert Storm. But the progress made since then in our ability to understand the battlefield in "real time" and to coordinate the effective application of all our tactical and even strategic systems has given us both a lethality and level of friendly security that has exceeded the expectations even of those pioneer thinkers in uniform.

Of course, the armchair generals who compose Defense Secretary Rumsfeld's braintrust believed that the decisive role would be played by the strategic application of air power. Wrong, as usual. But the increase in airpower's ability to advance a ground campaign from the sky, to work with the troops down in the sand and dust, has been stunning.

Right now, our forces are punching through great holes torn in the Iraqi defenses and closing on Baghdad. Those gaps were created by the entire military team, all working together. Heroism comes in every service uniform. It is the combination, the teamwork, that is delivering such a striking victory—despite real flaws in a generally good war plan.

If we stand back a bit from the torrent of American steel flooding past Al Kut and Karbala, backing up a step from the tanker's swift engagement of enemy targets too confused to escape and the adrenaline rush of mounted infantry rolling forward in their war machines, we can learn even more about the varieties of warfare in the twenty-first century.

The war in Iraq to date has included multiple sub-campaigns:

- We've seen the full range of special operations activities throughout the area of operations.
- In the north, another variant of the Afghan model developed in which Special Forces, light infantry, and local militias teamed up with allied airpower.
- In the swift march to Baghdad, we've seen the enduring importance of armored ground forces in this new century, the

decisive effect of the heavy-metal fist (further empowered by information technologies—a fusion of tradition and innovation).

• Along the supply lines, our forces have had to contend with terror attacks, enemy irregulars, and regime gangsters, none of whom observe the laws of war or any international convention.

• And yes, in the skies over Baghdad we've seen how far airpower has advanced in precision targeting and the ability to spare civilian lives and infrastructure, even if it can't win a war by itself.

We've come a long way since the carpet bombings of World War II. Because civilians in the Pentagon over-promised as to what airpower could do, it's all too easy to overlook the remarkable operational successes our Air Force has achieved in this war.

Even if airpower failed to win a strategic decision by itself, the velocity of this victory would have been impossible to achieve without the pilots and aircraft from all of our services. The easiest way to rule the ground is to begin by ruling the skies.

It cannot be said often enough: The unprecedented results our forces have achieved came because of teamwork, because every service made its contribution.

At present, our troops are *winning big*. Risks remain. Saddam still could attempt to employ his chemical weapons. There is even a slight possibility that his dead-enders will try to unleash biological weapons.

The end game in Baghdad could proceed with dazzling speed—or our military commanders could decide, for pragmatic and humanitarian reasons, to slow down and finish the job methodically. No one can predict the final moment of hostilities. Even after the regime's collapse, there will be plenty of Ba'ath Party criminals and terrorists to round up (a task with which we will have plenty of local help, as people throughout Iraq realize they need not fear Saddam any longer).

But one thing is already certain. Beyond the practical lessons we have learned on the battlefield, the world has been learning a lesson of which it must periodically be reminded: When America takes on a mission the American people support, nothing can stop us.

# The Rashomon War

## New York Post

*April 5, 2003*

The classic Japanese film *Rashomon* relates the same incident from several points of view. Each successive narrator's perspective on events is jarringly different—yet each version of the tale might be equally true. The film is a brilliant early example of "spin" and an uncanny metaphor for our present war.

Ground commanders complain that they were not given the resources they required, while Defense Secretary Donald Rumsfeld counters that the war is going remarkably well. Troops in combat insist that the kinds of Iraqi resistance encountered were unexpected, but Gen. Tommy Franks states firmly that the war is going according to plan.

Retired generals accuse the Office of the Secretary of Defense (OSD) of interfering amateurishly in war planning and refusing to send enough ground troops to win quickly, while minimizing risk. OSD responds that more troop deployments were planned all along. President Bush announces that this war is one of liberation for the Iraqi people. The Arab media declare it an unwelcome invasion.

Each of these statements is true from the standpoint of the advocate. But several of the truths mask lies.

The least credible version of the war—at least outside of the Arab media—is that repeated daily in the Pentagon. While there should be no doubt that American and allied armed forces are winning impressively, OSD's adherence to a party line of almost Stalinesque rigidity becomes more untenable with each press briefing.

Unable to admit that errors of any kind might have been made in planning the war, OSD spokespersons engage in a combination of outright lies, attacks on critics, and highly selective memories.

As far as events proceeding according to plan, well, if your plan is vague enough, with a sufficient number of "branches and sequels," as the military puts it, even defeat might be presented as having been anticipated.

Fortunately, we are not faced with failure. The outcome of this war, if not the timing of that outcome, truly is not in doubt. But events did *not* proceed according to plan.

The much-heralded initial air strikes failed and are now conveniently forgotten. The ground campaign assumed the lead from the first days of the war—which definitely was not according to the plan. And the number of ground forces permitted to the theater commander was inadequate by any honest measure.

Yet, the bare-bones forces we have in Iraq are far more in number than OSD wanted to send. At one point in the long planning process, Secretary Rumsfeld's civilian advisers—not one of whom had served in the military—insisted the ground campaign would require less than 10,000 combat troops, who would take a Sunday drive to Baghdad after the regime had been toppled by technology. The generals had to fight bitterly to overcome such madcap notions.

The resulting war plan was one for which the military was forced to settle. It was an ill-tempered compromise. And even after the plan had been agreed upon, OSD continued to interfere with the process of troop deployments, convinced to the end that airpower alone would determine the war's outcome.

Embarrassed by its miscalculations, OSD now insists that the deployment of additional heavy divisions from the United States had always been part of the plan. This is technically correct, but only because of the way formal military planning proceeds during any build-up to a crisis. If those troops actually had been intended for this campaign, they would have been sent to the Gulf months ago. Fortunately, the 4th Infantry Division, denied access through Turkey, unexpectedly became available to rush to southern Iraq, where it has been much-needed. Secretary Rumsfeld may lack humility, but he does have good luck.

Still, Secretary Rumsfeld cannot have it both ways. Either he expected a short war, in which case he did not intend to deploy those heavy divisions from the States, or he expected a long war all along.

The truth is that OSD expected a brief, nearly painless conflict, despite months of warnings from those in uniform. The deployment of units Pentagon spokespersons now insist were "always in the pipeline" was simply a matter of pro forma military planning. The military bureaucracy so despised by the secretary of defense has provided him a fig leaf. But it does not help the troops in the field, who have been deprived of the back-up forces essential for security and a margin of safety. The troops are winning impressively—*despite* Secretary Rumsfeld's micromanagement.

In addressing his critics last week, Secretary Rumsfeld demonstrated the low regard in which he holds military personnel, active duty or retired. He mocked his critics as "military retirees" and "armchair generals." In fact, the secretary's leading critic has been retired U.S. Army Gen. Barry McCaffrey, the nation's most decorated senior officer and a hero of both Desert Storm and Vietnam—where he was painfully and graphically wounded.

Gen. McCaffrey, who has nothing to gain and much to lose by speaking out, undertook to express the anger felt by serving officers toward Secretary Rumsfeld for his refusal to honor repeated requests for more ground troops.

As for the existence of a plague of "armchair generals," the secretary is correct. They occupy the highest-level civilian positions in the Pentagon, where these amateur theorists of warfare have treated career officers as if they were servants—or worse than anyone should treat a servant. Dismissed as unimaginative and insulted in front of their subordinates, the generals and colonels could not respond in kind. They could only stand there and take the abuse—or face a court-martial by replying.

As it became evident that more ground troops would have been a great help to the campaign, the secretary of defense denied any responsibility for capping troop levels. This is breathtaking: the first-ever doctrine of secretarial infallibility. It is a display of moral cowardice by an arrogant man who was dangerously wrong.

Our troops will continue to save the secretary's strategic bacon. Secretary Rumsfeld will be heaped with laurels earned by our combat soldiers. But, even now, those troops continue to face higher than necessary risks because they were deprived of the additional ground forces for which commanders and planners asked.

We shall, of course, hear continued denials that anything ever was amiss from Gen. Richard Myers, the chairman of the Joint Chiefs of Staff, and from Gen. Franks, the theater commander. They are loyal subordinates and, at least for the duration of the war, cannot and should not break ranks with the Secretary of Defense. They must present a unified front to our enemies.

But honest criticism from those outside the chain of command is another form of loyalty. It is the role of the retired officers whom Secretary Rumsfeld publicly despises to speak for those in uniform when they cannot speak for themselves. And to insist that our troops be given all the support they need.

# Beyond Baghdad

New York Post

*April 6, 2003*

Two task forces from the U.S. Army's Third Infantry Division just took their first tour of downtown Baghdad. The 3ID controls the city's international airport, while our air power dominates the capital's skies. And the Marines are sweeping in from the Southeastern flank.

Iraq's surviving "elite" soldiers are fleeing, leaving the fight to the thugs and fanatics. Iraq's civilian leaders are bailing out of Baghdad with suitcases full of cash. The defensive positions of the Republican Guards look like the world's biggest gunnery range, hundreds of square miles of burned-out wrecks.

And the Iraqi regime predicts victory. Warfare, which we are taught is a relentlessly grim affair, is not without moments of humor.

And the silliness has not been all on the Iraqi side. Surely, readers will remember the recent predictions from countless pundits that the Republican Guards would put up a ferocious fight and that Baghdad would prove a bloodbath for American troops. The Midtown edition of the *Village Voice*—also known as *The New York Times*—salivated at the prospect of an American defeat.

Eat a big hunk of dead Iraqi crow. And the next time GI Joe goes out to thrash one of your pet dictators, ask a military man what's going down, instead of trusting the croissant commandos on your staff.

As predicted by the *Post*, our field commanders fought smart all the way. Arriving at Baghdad *ahead* of their own expectations and with a limited number of combat troops for a huge mission, our generals and planners had to improvise. But improvisation, recognizing battlefield opportunities, and acting upon them before the enemy has a clue, has long been an American specialty.

Lacking the ground strength to encircle Baghdad, our forces made a virtue of necessity. They employed a technique perfected by Prince Eugene of Savoy in his wars against eastern Europe's Turkish occupiers three centuries ago. It's call a "golden bridge."

This strategy leaves the enemy an escape route so he won't feel obliged to fight to the death. That's why we haven't bombed that stream of Iraqi forces running for their lives. No "highway of death" this time. Just a highway of cowards. We *want* the remnants of Iraq's military to leave Baghdad.

Even if significant forces escape the immediate battle, they'll be in disarray and psychologically beaten. They can be cleaned up later. With far fewer friendly and civilian casualties.

The Iraqi forces fleeing Baghdad, intermixed with civilians and the dying regime's bureaucrats, will never again be a coherent fighting force. They're dissolving as they distance themselves from Saddam's fabled fortress.

The violent actors who remain in Baghdad will be the diehards. And our forces will see to it that they die very hard, indeed.

This is not meant to suggest that the struggle for Baghdad is over. There still could be plenty of nasty tactical encounters. Shrinking bands of thugs might trouble the city for weeks. The prospect of painful—though not extreme—friendly losses remains. But, at the operational and strategic levels, the campaign for Baghdad already has been won.

What remains are questions of time and ultimate cost, not of the final result.

The final fall of Baghdad will be the decisive event of the war. But it will not bring an automatic end to the fighting. Certainly, increasing allied control over more and more of the city in the days ahead will take the wind out of most Iraqi resistance. But a variety of remaining threats will keep our forces busy for weeks after the capital's fall.

Some regime elements, with nowhere to turn and a fanatical commitment to the privileges of tyranny, will resist in pockets scattered throughout the country. Ba'ath Party torturers and bully-boy thugs, especially, will fight on because they fear justice.

Some of those hardcore murderers may try to cut deals. We should not accept anything short of "unconditional surrender" from these criminals of war and peace. That's one thing about which our defense secretary is correct, and we must hope he lives up to his own rhetoric.

The last semi-coherent shreds of the regime may attempt a stand around and in the city of Tikrit, Saddam's hometown. If they do, that is the one locale where we should take off the gloves.

Our forces have waged a remarkably humane war thus far. But Tikrit is a cancer on Iraq, a privileged city under Saddam's rule and a source of strength for his savage clan. If necessary, we should make an example of it.

Some diehards may take to the hills. We will root them out. With Iraqi help.

The greatest long-term threat would come from regime elements that managed to flee to Syria or, perhaps, Iran, hoping to foment instability from across the border. Our approach to any government harboring Iraqi war criminals—especially the Ba'athist sister regime in Damascus—must be uncompromising.

A terrorist regime only slightly less sinister than Saddam's, Syria cannot be allowed to shelter either high Iraqi officials or low-level terrorists. Bashar Assad must be reminded that Damascus would be even easier to take than Baghdad, while the benefits to the entire Middle East might be even greater.

As for Saddam himself, he may be dead—despite the stream of artless videos broadcast on Iraqi TV. He may have fled Baghdad weeks ago, preferring to hunker down in a bunker in or near Tikrit. Or he may be in Syria.

Wherever he is, he must be brought to justice, along with his sons and his government ministers, no matter the cost.

Then the great strategic challenges will begin: Helping the Iraqis reconstruct not only their government but a battered society. Dealing with the regional challenges and opportunities this war will create in neighboring states. Re-evaluating our strategic partnerships, from Turkey to Saudi Arabia. And staying the course to win the peace.


The United States will be accused of arrogance and violations of international law by the jealous, the jilted, and the jittery, from Paris to Pyonyang. We will be warned, even threatened.

We must ignore such voices and show the firmness to move forward as obsolete powers struggle to tug us backward to their old, decayed, dysfunctional, cherished order.

If doing that which is right is arrogant, then arrogance is preferable to the alternatives. America is, indeed, the modern Rome. And Rome does not ask permission of Thebes or obey the orders of Gaul. The more bitterly we are criticized by yesterday's powers, the more certain we may be of the rightness of our course beyond Baghdad.

# Laboratory of War

## New York Post

*April 9, 2003*

America's armed forces entered the war in Iraq with the finest equipment, the best training, and the most advanced doctrine in the world. Our military will end the war with priceless practical experience of what works on the twenty-first century battlefield and what doesn't.

No matter how much thought is applied to war, theory is never a substitute for experience. Even the most insightful military thinkers will not get everything right. We know that.

That's why we stress flexibility at all levels of training and planning. Our military is better than any other at adjusting to new realities while the bullets are still flying.

Many of the nitty-gritty lessons learned will only emerge after the dust settles and the services can audit everything from specific weapons effects to the most appropriate basic load of ammunition for tanks in urban combat. But, at a broader level, critical lessons are already evident.

Perhaps the greatest revelation has to do with the continuing value of ground forces. Every few years, critics who insist that, *this* time, technology will win the war with little or no help, must be proven wrong. And while the remarkable advances in precision weapons delivered from the air have enhanced our ability to make war more efficiently while reducing the price civilians pay, what has gone largely unnoticed is the emergence of another form of precision weapon: ground troops.

Traditionally, ground forces have been war's blunt instrument. But, in this campaign, our Army and Marine units have been applied throughout the depths of the battle-space with unprecedented efficiency. Our troops have done more with less than any army previously has done.

Dramatic improvements in intelligence and communications allowed our forces to focus combat power at the right place and time—before the enemy could begin to react—in a manner that gives one Army division the battlefield effect of multiple divisions in past wars.

This does not reduce the need for any of the divisions currently in our inventory—a meager ten in an Army with global commitments. On the contrary, our Army and Marine Corps are sized austerely for our country's responsibilities. But it does revolutionize the impact of ground forces.

More and more, our forces resemble the Roman legions of the empire's golden age, invincible against all threats posed by barbarians.

This isn't a revelation to military professionals. Planners and force designers have been working toward this goal of intensifying combat effectiveness for more than a decade. But the doctrine and technologies had to be proven on the battlefield. Now the military's forward-thinkers have been vindicated.

That said, numbers still matter. While our forces have conducted the most impressive military campaign in history, another heavy division on the ground would have allowed them to press on *immediately* to Tikrit, the regime's last citadel, and to open the back door to Mosul and Kirkuk in the north. This role will fall to the hi-tech 4th ID as it enters the war zone, but there has been a time lapse between opportunity and our capability to exploit it.

Our troops fighting in Baghdad would also welcome additional comrades beside them. They're doing a spectacular job under tough conditions. But more troops on the ground would enable us to finish the Iraqi resistance even more swiftly and safely. In urban operations, sheer presence can be decisive.

Other advances that have proven their worth include twenty-first-century joint operations—all the services working in much-improved cooperation with one another—and the increasing integration of special operations forces into conventional operations and even tactical encounters.

While the strategic air campaign did not meet initial expectations, it remains a worthy effort to attempt to reach beyond intervening armies and innocent civilians to destroy an oppressive regime's leadership. Attacks against leadership targets, even when the immediate results are disappointing, send a valuable warning to other dictators that they will not be able to hide behind civilians forever.

Practical lessons include the need for the Marine Corps to receive more funding to beef up and refresh its inventory of combat vehicles. Performing valiantly, the Marines have disproved the old adage that the Corps cannot sustain a fight deep inland. But the likely contours of future wars mean our Marines need to be supplied with upgraded equipment for future campaigns. The Marines are particularly good stewards of tax dollars. We are foolish not to treat them more generously.

Our attack helicopter fleet faced unexpected levels of risk on the battlefield, with Apache tactics leaving aircraft more vulnerable to ground fire than anticipated. Yet, the Apache pilots—and those flying all other types of helicopters—swiftly adjusted their techniques, determined to get right back into the fight. No one has been more courageous in this war than our tactical aviators.

Our attack helicopter doctrine will be heavily rewritten after this war, based on lessons learned. That's in the normal order of things. Friendly fire incidents also continue to bedevil us—a problem that may never be solved entirely on the hyper-velocity, fluid battlefields of this century.

No military gets everything right, no matter the intensity of its efforts to forecast the future. The goal is to get it right to a decisively greater degree than your enemies have done. We have passed that test with the highest marks in history.

# A New Age of Warfare

## New York Post

*April 10, 2003*

With the Iraqi people dancing atop a dictator's fallen statue, the pundits who forecast an American bloodbath have begun to change their story. Implying that our military achievement wasn't all *that* grand, they tell us Saddam didn't even have much of a plan to defend his country.

Absolute bull.

Saddam had a classic twentieth-century, industrial-age war plan. But our forces fought a twenty-first-century, postindustrial war.

We have witnessed the end of an era along the road to Baghdad. Every other military establishment and government in the world witnessed it, too.

We shall hear a great deal from think-tanks in the coming months, warning that other armies have learned their lesson and will devise clever, asymmetrical strategies to defeat the United States armed forces.

To an extent, that's a valid concern. But it's also secondary. The basic lesson that governments and militaries around the world just learned was this: Don't fight the United States.

Period. This stunning war did more to foster peace than a hundred treaties could begin to do.

Our officials are right to warn that there's a great deal of work still ahead to complete this victory. But the world knows that Saddam lost, the allies won—and there ain't going to be no rematch.

So which military lessons will potential enemies and even our allies draw from this grand American triumph?

Yes, Saddam's forces may have failed to fight for him as stalwartly as he hoped. And no one can deny the technological overmatch between the rival armies. But generals from Moscow to Damascus to Pyongyang will look at how Saddam *planned* to fight and recognize their own weakness.

Far from technically incompetent, Saddam's plan was right out of Clausewitz. Its models were the lessons of the Russian defeat of Napoleon in 1812 and the Soviet victory over the Germans in the Second World War.

The principles were: Delay your enemy, attrite his forces, trade space for time, harass his supply lines, and husband your best forces for a mighty counterattack. Wait until the attacker has advanced so far into your country that he reaches a "culminating point" at which he has lost his momentum and his supply lines are overextended. Then strike.

Saddam didn't so much plan the defense of Baghdad as he tried to refight the defense of Moscow.

His plan was a textbook model for a modern war to be fought by a nation in arms, containing the wisdom of historical experience. Had Saddam faced any other military in the world, he would have extracted a far higher price—and might even have won in a war of attrition.

But the campaign the U.S. military fought cast off the rules of the modern era. We fought the first postmodern war.

In the final grudge match between Clausewitz and GI Joe, it was a shutout. And no other military on earth could have done it.

What remains remarkable is how little the Iraqis—and the Russian advisers who helped plan their defense—grasped the profound changes in our military and the American way of war. They clearly had no sense of the battlefield awareness, speed, precision, and tactical ferocity of America's twenty-first-century forces.

The Iraqis had not advanced beyond Desert Storm in their understanding of our military. The Russian generals—one a former paratrooper chief, the other an air defense expert—who advised them don't seem to have advanced beyond mid–Cold War thinking.

There was no appreciation of the effect of combined arms and joint synergy supercharged by information systems, of American flexibility and agility, of our intelligence capabilities—or even of American grit and determination.

But the worst sin in which the planners indulged (and it's one to which Russians and those they've trained are particularly susceptible) was to rely too much on the book. They fought a printing-press war. We fought a digital one.

Consider the fear and impotent anger would-be opponents of the United States must feel today. Begin with the Russian military, in which a generation of mentally poisoned generals must die off before we can begin to build a healthy, cooperative relationship.

First, the Russian heirs of the once-dreaded Soviet military had to watch in humiliation as a handful of U.S. forces in Afghanistan did in a few months what they could not do in a decade. Now they have witnessed the swift collapse of a conventional military that Moscow had equipped, trained, and advised.

Iraq embraced the Russian general staff academy's "school solution" for this war. The potbellied generals in Moscow must be squirming in their vodka-addled shame. Meanwhile, the Russians can't even defeat a provincial rebellion in Chechnya.

After its inept attempt at strategic blackmail, North Korea has grown very quiet. Doubtless, we shall hear a great deal more rhetoric as the shock of our victory begins to wear off. But North Korean tanks are not going to head south anytime soon.

Syria is getting a well-deserved helping of fear served up on its bloodstained plate. Bully-boy Bashar Assad may hate us, but he is unlikely to make a further move to harm us. And if he does, it will be an act of folly tantamount to Saddam's defiance.

One does not imagine that the Syrian military is anxious to face the armed forces of the United States.

The Chinese long have studied our superiority—yet nothing could have prepared them for the effectiveness and efficiency of this campaign. When even our own military is surprised at how well things went, you may be certain that the boys in Beijing are following events avidly.

The Iraqi defeat was a defeat for every other military in the world—in a sense, even for our allies, whose forces cannot begin to keep pace with our own. Faced with America's military might and prowess, no other power could have devised a better general war plan than the one Saddam tried to execute.

The Marine Corps Hymn might serve uncannily well as this campaign's anthem, with its opening line, "From the Halls of Montezuma . . ." Although the lyrics refer to America's Mexican War, we have just witnessed the destruction of one military civilization by another immeasurably more advanced. The impact is as shattering and epochal as the triumph of Cortez over Montezuma's Aztecs—a regime with marked similarities to Saddam's.

# What Do We Do Now?

## New York Post

*April 12, 2003*

Our military success has been spectacular. Key phases of the campaign, such as the fall of Baghdad, came even more swiftly than the most optimistic observers believed possible. But sudden victories bring sudden dilemmas.

After several days of liberating additional cities with hardly a shot fired and taking the surrender of an entire Iraqi army corps, our forces are in the position of the dog that caught the fire truck.

What do we do now?

The good news is that Americans are the world's best problem-solvers. We don't sit around drinking tea and blaming history when the plumbing doesn't work. We like a good challenge. And challenges will not be in short supply in the coming months.

But the incidents of which the media makes so much today, from looting to local resistance, are vastly preferable to the problems so many pundits predicted just one week ago, before our troops entered Baghdad.

We were warned of a slaughter of our soldiers in the streets, but the most common challenge in the Iraqi capital turned out to be how to keep people from stealing office furniture. Far from a bloodbath, we just need to get the water turned back on so folks can take regular baths.

As problems go, things could be a great deal worse.

Certainly, the breakdown of law and order is a serious matter—establishing the rule of law is essential to all other forms of progress. And we still have a war to finish, with the possibility of nasty fighting around Tikrit. But the exuberant thievery we've seen in Iraqi cities came in two forms.

Some of it has been common criminality, worsened by the regime's spiteful release of criminals from Iraq's prisons to destabilize the cities officials deserted. But there is undeniably an element of catharsis, a great blowing off of steam, in most of the looting.

People held in bondage for more than a generation are getting a bit of their own back. The regime stole from them, now they're stealing from the regime. It's their slight, pathetic revenge.


This petty rampaging cannot be allowed to continue indefinitely. But, to be clear-eyed and cold-blooded, the current spate of revenge killings against Ba'ath Party officials is not a bad thing. *We* cannot yet identify, let alone punish, the men who have tormented the inhabitants of countless city neighborhoods and villages. The locals are meting out justice with ropes and clubs. Ugly, yes. But it is, undeniably, justice.

And the fear these acts of retribution put into surviving party officials will keep them subdued as we begin the long and difficult task of helping the Iraqis rebuild their society, economy, and state.

The aftermath of this war will be indescribably complex. Danger will haunt our soldiers. In coming months, we'll see additional terrorist attacks, as well as eruptions of discontent and discord. Evil does not die a clean death.

Iraqi society is a pressure cooker of grudges and resentments long suppressed. Not all will be contained. After the outbreak of peace, expect the outbursts of demagogues. Before long, cynical Iraqi politicos will accuse us of favoring one faction over another, no matter how equitably we behave. Others will trumpet demagogic messages that divide Iraq's people, rather than uniting them.

We will make mistakes. Goes with the territory. Elements within the administration already made an embarrassing error by backing the exile leader Ahmed Chalabi and shipping him back into southern Iraq with a motley battalion of his supporters. No sooner did Chalabi hit the ground than he began, disingenuously, to accuse the United States of not doing enough for the people of Iraq in their hour of need.

Spectacularly ungrateful, Chalabi also attacked Gen. Jay Garner, the retired U.S. officer charged with getting the interim administration of Iraq up and running. Chalabi's self-promoting message was: *I should be put in charge of this country. I'm the indispensable leader for Iraq . . .*

Plenty of such hustlers will pop up in the days to come. But whenever things seem to be going awry—which the media will report with urgent glee—be patient. Step back and look at the big picture. No matter the disappointments we may encounter, ask yourself the same question: Are we all better off now than when Saddam Hussein was in power? No matter how nasty things get on the ground, the answer will always be yes.

For now, Iraq is in a difficult, confused stage between war and peace. Some of our troops face more combat. Others will have to assume policing functions, which are never popular with the military—although we fielded effective constabulary forces time and again, from the Philippines to postwar Germany and Japan. It's frustrating work for soldiers, but GI Joe and GI Jane can do that mission, too.

Eventually, Iraqi police forces will be reborn. Other nations will begin to contribute to interim policing capabilities. But, for now, the burden of a peace still in its birth hours falls as squarely on the shoulders of our troops as did the burden of this war. And we must beware foolish shortcuts, such as re-empowering police elements from the old regime. We cannot be seen as reviving any aspect of the old regime's security apparatus. In a broken country, the easy solution is often the very worst solution.

The most important thing is to remain calm and stay on course when faced with disappointments and complaining headlines. We've caught the fire truck. The men and women in uniform will figure out how to drive it soon enough. Trust them.

# The Key Decisions

New York Post

*April 15, 2003*

Plans don't win wars. Soldiers do. But good plans and sound decisions aid the fighters in the field enormously, easing success and saving lives. In the course of this war, four key decisions helped insure our swift, decisive victory. Two other decisions—poor ones—were redeemed by the valor and skill of the men and women in uniform.

The first powerful decision of the campaign was to launch the ground attack ahead of schedule.

The immediate goal was to prevent the destruction of Iraq's southern oil fields. But the practical effect was much greater. Although the Iraqis had been warned that there would be no lengthy air campaign before the armored vehicles started their engines, they did not expect the allies to *lead* with ground troops.

The decision to throw the first big punch on the ground required great confidence on the part of the coalition leadership, since it defied the conventional wisdom that air power must "shape the battlefield" before land forces are committed.

Taken by surprise, the Iraqis never recovered. Despite the lack of extensive air strikes to soften up the enemy, our forces consistently moved ahead at a speed so great the Iraqis never managed to react in an effective, coordinated manner. In military parlance, we operated ever deeper within their decision cycle.

The second crucial decision came early on, when an unanticipated degree of resistance from irregular forces threatened to bog down the campaign in Nasiriyah and other urban areas. Some tactical commanders wanted to secure their lines of communication before pressing on.

The call to push on toward Baghdad, despite the risk to an austere ground force, had to be made on high, where decision-makers could look beyond immediate tactical concerns. The decision to strike deep and "damn the torpedoes" was critical and correct.

The lesson is not that higher-level decision-makers always know best. War is more complicated than that. Sometimes the guy on the ground knows what presidents and their advisers cannot know. But there are also times when a president can see what Captain Jinks can't. The rule is that there is no iron-clad rule in wartime decision-making.

The third critical decision was to reinvent the air campaign. As results of the strategic bombing offensive proved disappointing, the proportion of air power dedicated to supporting the advance of the Army and Marines was increased dramatically.

This turbocharged an already rapid advance. With joint operations of unprecedented intensity directed against Iraq's remaining defenders, both their will and practical ability to resist our forces collapsed.

The fourth key decision involved an abrupt change of plans. The allies expected to besiege Baghdad. But when our military leaders spotted a chance to leap ahead and grasp the prize, they didn't hesitate.

First, they "developed the situation" with a large-scale reconnaissance-by-fire, an armored thrust toward the city's heart. The raid drew a furious response, but the generals read it correctly: The desperate attacks on the task force came from irregulars, ragtag military remnants and foreign fighters, not from disciplined troops.

The Iraqis were slaughtered in the streets. The chain of command realized that Baghdad no longer had a coherent defense. The next morning, the 3rd ID rolled downtown.

Daring, fortitude, and flexibility throughout the campaign paid off hugely. But errors were made, as well. And the two most serious mistakes were made at the highest levels.

First, the shock-and-awe air campaign was such a disappointment that Pentagon briefers immediately wrote it out of the war's history, much the way Stalin's Politburo used to erase purged figures from official photographs.

The truth is that the strategic air campaign was worth trying. And we may yet learn of unexpected results from the attempted decapitation strikes. But no air effort could have lived up to the hype civilian "experts" imposed on it.

For shock-and-awe type air campaigns to work, there are three requirements: Surprise, truly overwhelming blows, and an enemy leadership that regards surrender as an option. But months of schoolyard threats from Pentagon staffers as to what the air campaign would do to Saddam's regime both ruled out surprise and prepared our enemy psychologically. When they finally came, our air strikes on Baghdad were colorful, but cautious and slight in effect. And Saddam and his cronies never viewed surrender as an option.

The second, graver error was the ideologically motivated refusal to send more troops to the theater of war prior to hostilities. When commanders in combat complained that they needed more troops, senior leaders silenced them. When retired generals insisted that more troops should have been sent, the Office of the Secretary of Defense (OSD) shamelessly branded them as disloyal, portraying war heroes as defeatists and distorting their comments to a degree worthy of the Iraqi information minister.

Wait until the soldiers who fought this war write their memoirs. Then judge.

Certainly, we won a magnificent victory. But our military won it *despite* OSD's micro-management.

Size matters. More troops would have allowed us to seize Tikrit and close the roads to Syria a week earlier, preventing the flight of key Iraqi officials. We lacked the forces to seize Baghdad and continue the attack simultaneously.

Our inability to guard hospitals and the failure to protect Baghdad's National Museum of Antiquities from looters are undeniable stains on an otherwise unblemished record. We needed more troops on the ground to establish a presence throughout Baghdad and elsewhere. Out of sight, our troops were out of mind.

Despite denials from the secretary of defense that more troops were needed, the 4th Infantry Division had to be rushed to Iraq. Other reinforcements—hastily flown in— included an airborne brigade, an armored cavalry regiment, an additional heavy brigade and another light brigade, with more units slated to follow. Have they been hurried to Iraq because they were unnecessary?

This has been a brilliant campaign. But it was won by soldiers, not by civilian "experts" who regard our troops as nothing more than strategic janitors. The recent suggestions by party hacks who disdained military service to the effect that they and their ideas won the war is conduct unbecoming. Even by Washington's standards.

# Heroes In Iraq

## New York Post

### *April 16, 2003*

Now that our troops have given us victory in war, the battles of
peace have resumed. As our soldiers and Marines continue to
risk their lives clearing out pockets of fanatics, Washington's
masters of spin have begun to twist the facts, lying about this
war for advantage and profit.

Business as usual. Except that the Beltway parasites are
spitting in the blood of heroes this time.

Doesn't bother 'em, though. There are ideological points
to be driven home and—more importantly—there's a great
deal of money to be redistributed from the forces that won the
war to the defense contractors who always win the peace. Bob
Dylan's old line, "Money doesn't talk, it swears," should be
engraved above every entrance to the Pentagon.

This war was not supposed to unfold as it did. Civilian theorists, technocrats, and defense industry lobbyists yearned for
it to prove that air power and technology can now win wars
without much help from ground troops. The Office of the Secretary of Defense hoped to cut three Army divisions, out of
ten, and to divert the savings from the personnel account to

defense contractors. Such deep cuts have been a core goal of Defense Secretary Donald Rumsfeld's since he took office.

The war in Iraq was supposed to provide an irrefutable justification for slashing ground forces. As America witnessed, the campaign turned out differently. Our soldiers and Marines fought their way to Baghdad in a running gunfight. They did not even stop marching when sandstorms grounded most of our aircraft.

It wasn't that our Air Force performed badly. On the contrary, it was brilliantly effective, especially after aircraft were diverted to support joint operations with our ground forces. As this column has insisted throughout the war, no single service won the victory. All of our services, working together, delivered such a stunning combination of effects that the Iraqis literally never had a chance. Our military works best as a team, not as solo-service prima donnas competing for the battlefield spotlight.

Yet now we have begun to hear that the ground troops we saw fighting their way to Baghdad really didn't do that much, that they only served to herd Iraqi forces into kill zones where air power destroyed them.

Tell that to the Marines who fought from building to building in Nasiriyah. Tell it to the troopers of the 3rd of the 7th Cavalry who fought the longest uninterrupted series of engagements, in time and distance, in U.S. military history—while blowing sands reduced visibility to handgun range. Tell it to the soldiers and Marines who had to fight their way into, then pacify Baghdad, An Najaf, and Karbala.

You can't even take a surrender from 25,000 feet.

Yet no soldier or Marine would be foolish—or cynical—enough to insist that their service had won the war by itself. The Air Force, though, delivers such tremendous profits to the defense industry that its partisans will insist, despite all evidence to the contrary, that this war really did prove that ground forces are outdated and that air power trumps all.

The defense industry wants to sell 200-million-dollar aircraft, not inexpensive rifles, canteens, and boots. The amounts of money at stake run from hundreds of billions of dollars in the near term to trillions in the out-years. GI Joe can defeat our nation's enemies, but he can't beat the forces of greed inside the Beltway.

Yes, military technology is a wonderful enabler. Give us more. But make it appropriate technology, not just what corporations want to sell. Demand a strict accounting and rigorous oversight. And don't succumb to the accountant's desire to free up funds by cutting the people our military sorely needs.

Nor is this an argument against adequate funding for our Air Force. The service badly needs more transport aircraft, a follow-on system for the superb, but aging, A-10 Thunderbolt ground-attack aircraft and a new bomber program to design a cost-effective replacement for the B-52. But it does *not* need platinum-plated, Rube Goldberg systems such as the F-22, an aircraft loved by lobbyists alone.

As carrier battle groups sail homeward for a well-earned rest and aircraft lift off from the Gulf to return to their peace-time bases, more than 100,000 soldiers and Marines will remain behind to do the unglamorous work of winning the peace. As they remain in Afghanistan, in Kosovo, Bosnia, and the Sinai. We must not forget them when the parasites and ideologues attempt to falsify the history of this war.

America's balanced armed forces won this war. We would be very foolish to let anyone upset that balance to advance a theory or line a contractor's pockets.

# The Enemy's Smile

## New York Post

*April 18, 2003*

The instant cliché of the moment is that, with the war essentially over, the hard part's about to begin. Nope. War's always the hardest part. But the aftermath of combat operations *is* likely to be the most *exasperating* phase of our involvement in Iraq.

War is drama. Reconstruction is drudgery, with occasional spikes of danger.

We have the skills and resources to get our part right in postwar Iraq. But that doesn't guarantee the Iraqis will get their part right.

We shall experience no end of minor—and some major—frustrations. But quitting without a serious effort to help Iraq redesign itself would be the fool's option.

Even the Iraqi interpretation of freedom may leave us scratching our heads. Most Iraqis welcome the departure of Saddam's regime. But they will not necessarily define freedom in terms that appeal to the average American.

For some, it will be the freedom to settle old scores or to advance programs of religious repression. Iraq's borders contain more competing agendas than Manhattan has would-be actors waiting tables.

Identifying those agendas and sorting implacable foes from potential allies is a pressing task. And, in the Middle East, today's ally may become tomorrow's enemy. The sands are always shifting.

While our intelligence capabilities continue to improve, we remain superb at collecting technical data, but poor at assessing the human factor.

There are times in the intel game when the ability to speak a local dialect is more important than all the satellites in the sky, and a feel for the hidden allegiances within a population can save more lives than all the technical data in the National Security Agency's computers. We're still a bit amateurish at peeling the human onion.

Consider the challenges a military intelligence officer—probably a captain or major—faces on the ground in the ethnically mixed city of Mosul, where days of provocative demonstrations forced our Marines to fire on "civilians" who were doing their best to kill them—while robbing a bank on the side.

At least ten of the "civilians" died, a matter of which the media, newly starved for headlines, made much. Yet, as a former intel hand, I suspect the problem may be that we did not kill enough of the attackers to demonstrate our resolve. When you come up against the hard boys, you must shock them with your strength and resolution.

Various Iraqi factions are going to test us in the coming months to see if we're up to the job of pacification. If they sense weakness, our problems will expand geometrically.

Developing peace in a broken country demands a two-handed approach—an iron fist to crush the incorrigible, and a hand gloved in velvet to stroke those who behave. An excess of politically correct restraint in the early days of peacemaking may save us a few annoying media headlines, but damn us to ultimate failure.

If we do not punish murderers and thugs, ever more Iraqis will see an advantage in becoming thugs and murderers. The Middle East is not a region where restraint in the face of criminal violence wins respect.

We must not confuse justice with weakness, or we shall be perceived as both weak and unjust. This does not mean that we should be wantonly violent, but that we must be intelligently fierce.

Back in Mosul, that Marine intel officer has to attempt to sort out a very complex series of issues—and he probably isn't a regional specialist or an Arabic speaker.

First, he must determine the ethnicity of the demonstrators: Ethnic Arabs? Turkomen?

Second, and much tougher to answer, who was *behind* the demonstrations? What was the motive beneath the surface explanations—which are rarely sufficient in the Middle East?

Here are just a few of the possibilities through which that intel officer and his tiny staff must work:

• Was the violence spurred by unrepentant regime supporters determined to undermine local stability? Or were these just Arabs or Turkomen who fear Kurdish retribution for past wrongs?

• If Turkomen were involved, was our "ally" Turkey fomenting unrest to insure that we would not be able to hand over Mosul to the Kurds, a Turkish nightmare?

Are the Turks working to set the stage for an eventual intervention in the north? Perhaps after driving U.S. forces out through a terrorist war of attrition, of which Ankara would disclaim any knowledge?

• If Arabs staged the provocations, which faction did they belong to? A local political group, or a clan gang? The vanquished regime? How much support could they arouse among the greater population? How fast could they do it? What would be the triggers?

• Might a Kurdish faction be stirring up Arab unrest to push America into a greater reliance on Kurdish warriors to enforce the peace, thus speeding the return of Mosul to Kurdish suzerainty? Or to steal an advantage from another Kurdish party?

• Was this really a protest against the appointment of a U.S.-backed official to the local administration, or just a cover for a bank robbery? Or was it a display of heartfelt nationalism?

In a society such as Iraq's, these are only the initial questions. As the weeks turn into months, we are going to see devious and deadly efforts by Iranians, Syrians, our Turkish "allies," Saudis, assorted Islamic terrorists, and our dear European friends to make life as difficult as possible for our troops.

Our open opponents and false friends understand all too well that we won the war with American military prowess. But many are convinced that they can make us lose the peace through America's political impatience. Precious few parties wish us success.

We planned well for this war, but less well for the peace. We need to work hard to catch up with the pace of events. We must be patient, determined, alert to the unexpected, endlessly skeptical, and when necessary, fierce.

# Must Iraq Stay Whole?

## The Washington Post

*April 20, 2003*

Traditional wisdom insists that Iraq must remain in one piece. Washington subscribes to that belief. The Bush administration insists it will not permit the breakup of Iraq.

But what if some Iraqis prefer to live apart from others who slaughtered their families?

Certainly, our efforts to rehabilitate the region would go more smoothly were Iraq to remain happily whole within its present borders. Our initial efforts should aim at facilitating cooperation between and the protection of Iraq's ethnic and religious groups. But we also need to think ahead and to think creatively if we are to avoid being blindsided by forces we cannot control.

What if, despite our earnest advice, the people of Iraq resist the argument that they would be better off economically and more secure were they to remain in a single unified state? What if the model for Iraq's future were Yugoslavia after the Cold War, not Japan or Germany after World War II?

The key lesson of Yugoslavia was that no amount of diplomatic pressure, bribes in aid, or peacekeeping forces can vanquish the desire of the oppressed to reclaim their independence and identity. Attempts to force such groups to continue to play together like nice children simply prolong the conflict and intensify the bloodshed.

We are far too quick to follow Europe's example and resist the popular will we should be supporting. If the United States does not stand for self-determination, who shall?

This is not an argument for provoking secession by Iraq's Kurds or Shiites. Objectively viewed, Iraq's advantages as an integral state are indeed enormous, while the practical obstacles faced by any emerging mini-states would range from the problems of a landlocked Kurdistan in the north to the threat of religious tyranny in the Shiite south.

But reason does not often prevail in the affairs of states and nations. Passion rules. Kosovo, Macedonia, and Bosnia remain dependent on foreign donations, black-marketeering, and debt for their survival. Two of the three were born anew in blood, and all are troubled. But none of this matters to those who could not bear the arbitrary borders imposed on them by diplomats whose concerns did not include the popular will.

We live in an age of breakdown, of the dissolution of artificial states whose borders were imposed arbitrarily in the wake of the Versailles conference that concluded the Great War with peerless ineptitude. The world has suffered for nearly a century for the follies and greed of the European diplomats who redrew the world to suit their foreign ministries.

Unthinkingly accepting this legacy, we Americans assume we might convince one people after another that they cannot constitute a viable state on their own, that they must see reason. We might as well try to talk a friend out of a foolish love affair. Entire peoples, like individuals, must learn the hard way.

After the collapse of these rotting states, many a newly liberated population will indeed find that it cannot thrive on its own. Then these populations will begin building new, larger entities. But we cannot short-circuit the system of change and force them to see reason before they have tried the course of passion. Human beings are not made that way.

As we try to help the Iraqis rebuild their state, we should spare no reasonable effort to demonstrate to all parties concerned the advantages of remaining together. But we must stop short of bullying them—and well short of folly.

Even as we aim for a democratic, rule-of-law Iraq, we must consider alternatives if we are to avoid being bushwhacked by the guerrilla forces of history.

Iraq's Kurds, Shiites, and numerous minorities long have suffered under the rule of Sunni Arabs from the country's middle. We have witnessed widely varied reactions to the arrival of U.S. troops in Iraq. Kurds welcomed us with flowers. Some Shiites cheered and applauded, but others—influenced by Iran—have been far more reticent, even hostile. The Sunni Arabs in the nation's heartland were Saddam Hussein's most enthusiastic supporters, although many also suffered under the old regime.

All the peoples of Iraq need to adjust to a new reality. But Washington may need to adjust to new realities of its own. Having caused so much change, we dare not insist categorically that nothing else may change.

Above all, we should champion the Kurds, who have earned the world's respect. A long-suffering people divided by cruel borders, they seemed to pose an insoluble dilemma, given the strategic dictates of realpolitik. The United States needed bases in Turkey, and Ankara would not countenance a

Kurdish state. Turks, Arabs, and Iranians all insisted the Kurds must remain divided, poor, and powerless.

Now Turkey has betrayed us, while the Kurds fought beside us. In a decade of de facto autonomy in Iraq's north, the Kurds proved they can run a civil, rule-of-law state. Cynics point out that a "free Kurdistan," surrounded by enemies, would lack access to the sea. But the Kurds would have oil, and oil can buy access. Furthermore, regime change in Iran is only a matter of time.

The situation in Iraq is far more complex than any commentary can describe. But a few things are clear. The United States throughout its history has been the world's most positive force for change. Now we must prepare ourselves to help shape further changes we cannot prevent. We must concentrate on building a better future, not on defending Europe's indecent legacies.

At the end of the Iraqi experiment, our most important goal should not be preserving the relics of Versailles but promoting human freedom and security—whether that means one Iraq, or several.

# Palestinian Reality

New York Post

*April 21, 2003*

In the aftermath of the allied victory in Iraq, the international pressure to create an independent Palestinian state will be irresistible. And the Palestinian people unquestionably deserve a government and homeland of their own.

Israel's vital interests must be protected, but even Prime Minister Ariel Sharon recognizes that some West Bank settlements must be vacated. Despite legitimate misgivings in Jerusalem, Palestinian statehood is on the way.

We may hope that this new state will honor the dignity of its own people and the security needs of its neighbors, that democracy—and peace—will be given a chance.

But extravagant optimism guarantees disappointment. This politically independent, but financially dependent Palestinian state is likely to disappoint everyone except the most corrupt Arabs and the most cynical Europeans.

For the United States and Israel, the greatest disappointment will be that Palestinian statehood will *not* put an end to anti-Israeli terrorism. There may be an initial drop in suicide bombings, but terrorism will remain a fact of life. Palestinian authorities will sign the treaties and make the right noises but will take only limited action—under duress—to suppress violent extremists.

Even were a Palestinian government to behave with flawless integrity, terrorists would simply stage their operations from Lebanon or elsewhere. The key fact that Western advocates for the Palestinian cause refuse to recognize is that the terrorism directed toward Israel is only superficially about Palestinian independence. At its core, it is about the old passion for killing Jews.

Once there is an independent Palestinian state, Israel will be accused of countless other sins—among them hindering the economic and political development of the new entity. While many Palestinians do, indeed, yearn for freedom and a just society, the hardline killers desire the complete destruction of Israel. Nothing less will do.

For the profoundly unscrupulous Arab governments of the region, the Palestinian cause has been a cherished convenience. All home-grown ills could be blamed on the need to sacrifice for the Palestinians—although the Palestinians never received sufficient aid from other Arabs to build decent lives. The image of Palestinian poverty and deprivation has been essential to the Arab world's myth-making.

Now Arab insistence and rhetoric have backed the myth-makers into a corner: For the region's decayed regimes, continuing Palestinian misery and powerlessness remain preferable to a Palestinian state. But the United States and even Israel now seem to accept the inevitability of free Palestine.

The Arabs have gotten their public wish, but will regret it in private.

The Arabs still need someone to blame for their failures. And they will continue to blame Israel and the United States.

The Arabs will find countless faults with Israel's implementation of any accords. Then they will attack the accords themselves as unjust.

The Arab world is as addicted to blame as any junkie was ever addicted to heroin.

There may be some meaningful efforts to place new limits on terrorist operations from the soil of states such as Jordan and Egypt. But the terrorists will find ways around any restrictions. They are so consumed with the vision of Israel annihilated that many will never be able to tear themselves away from the delicious comforts of hatred, blame, and slaughter.

The best hope for peace would be a regime change in Syria and the expulsion of all terrorist organizations from Lebanon. That may happen. Operation Iraqi Freedom provided the spark that could ignite the entire region, leading to the eventual collapse of one illegitimate government after another.

Anti-Israeli terrorism will never cease entirely—it's simply too alluring to the spiritually dispossessed of the Arab world—but the transformation of surrounding governments into states even moderately observant of human rights, the rule of law, and the popular will would seriously hamper terrorist operations.

The other great disappointment will be visited upon the Palestinian people themselves. Most Palestinians would welcome a chance to better their lives—or at least the lives of their children—and to determine who will lead them through free and fair elections.

But the other Arab states will never permit it—at least not until they change themselves. The last thing any of the surrounding regimes wants is a successful, economically thriving, rule-of-law, freely elected Arab government in their midst. The example to their own people would be unbearable.

It's critical to Arab leaders that a Palestinian state remain corrupt, malleable, and governed by gunmen—even if the gunmen wear tailored suits to the conference table.

Arab states want the Palestinians to remain needy clients, not to become apostles of change. The situation in Iraq is worrisome enough to Damascus, Cairo, and Riyadh.

Elections will be the first real test. Other Arab states will do all in their power to insure they don't happen freely and fairly. A leader like Yasser Arafat is ideal from the perspective of other Arab governments: He's impeccably dishonest, careless of the welfare of his people, and contemptuous of individual rights. He's not only willing to be bought, he's willing to be bought cheap.

Any brave Palestinian who attempts to stand for election on a platform of genuine reform had better have the world's best bodyguards.

Israel will get through all this. Israelis know what is at stake, and they will adjust to new realities as necessary. Israel even may be a bit less embattled as long as the celebrations continue in the West Bank, Gaza, Paris, Berlin, and other anti-Semitic hotbeds.

The real losers in the new state will be, as always, the Palestinians. They deserve freedom and a real chance to build a decent civil society. But the Europeans don't really care, the Arabs care about all the wrong things, and the current Palestinian leadership cares only about its own continued tenure in power.

A Palestinian state is on the way. Palestinian freedom will remain a dream.

# Test-Driving Freedom

## New York Post

*April 23, 2003*

Demonstrators in the streets of Baghdad, shouting that American troops must leave Iraq. Shiite pilgrims chanting, "Death to America!" Interviews with angry Iraqis who insist the Americans only want their oil.

Judging by the cable-news offerings, we seem to have lost the peace before the official end of the war.

Or maybe not.

As my favorite philosophers, the Bowery Boys, used to say, "Don't jump to contusions."

We will not know for a decade or more, after a good deal of tumult and noisy elections, whether we have "won" or "lost" the peace. For now, President Bush is correct to dismiss alarmist reporting about demonstrations in Iraq as simply people trying out new freedoms—the first, crude, rambunctious stirrings of democracy.

Doubtless, there will be days ahead when we all get the Baghdad blues, discouraged by the furor of a mob or the folly of Iraqi political factions. But anyone who imagines that democracy can roll right out of the showroom and cruise down the highway should review the first decades of our own nation's freedom, when the accusations the Founding Fathers hurled at one another make Michael Moore's tantrums seem downright mannerly.

Then there was that little civil war of ours 80 years after we gave the Brits the boot.

Is it sensible to believe that the Iraqis will get everything right on the first ballot?

Our intervention in the Middle East is—and will remain—necessary, thanks to the region's unique blend of viciousness and torpor. Our troops may come and go, but we're in for the long haul. Uncle Sam's going to have sand between his toes for decades.

Whatever the intellectual or ideological arguments against this involvement, it is indisputably better to take the fight to our enemies than to let them bring the fight to us, as they did on 9/11.

This does not mean we must occupy Iraq indefinitely, but it definitely means we will remain occupied by the Middle East's genius for failure.


Meanwhile, what about those demonstrations? What do they really mean?

Not much. At least for now.

It's far too early for pundits to analyze what the Iraqi population thinks. The Iraqis don't know themselves. Some are test-driving freedom of speech for the first time. Others, savvy and devious, are exploiting the "CNN effect" to advance political agendas. But the silent majority is still silent.

Right now, the average Iraqi is bewildered, frightened, and worried about his future and that of his family. If he lives in

Baghdad, he's downright angry about the lack of basic utilities. (How cheerful would New Yorkers be after a few weeks without water and electricity?)

And he's lived his life in an information vacuum. He truly doesn't know what the Americans are up to—but his own experience has made him suspicious of the promises of the powerful.

While the protests may evolve into serious threats, our restrained approach to the situation—let the kids make a mess, as long as they stay in the sandbox—is the wisest course of action for the present.

The massive demonstrations accompanying the revival of long-forbidden Shiite pilgrimages reflect decades of pent-up emotions. The haters make the best headlines, but the bulk of Iraq's Shiites are politically undecided—they're still in a trance of conflicting feelings and haven't yet settled down to the business of thinking.

Hardline clerics appear to have gotten some initial traction, but may overreach and alienate their co-religionists. Reason may prevail, as voters in a future election realize that a victory for religious extremists would mean the breakup of Iraq. Or emotions may run so high that reason is cast aside. That, too, is democracy.


Perhaps the most dangerous factor at work in southern Iraq is the infiltration of provocateurs from Iran. They're being sent in to radicalize Iraq's Shiites—not because Iran is strong, but because its aging, rotting leadership is fearful.

The bitter mullahs in Tehran hope that, by extending religious rule into southern Iraq, their own regime might gain a new lease on life.

Tracking down and neutralizing Iranian agents is a job as essential as it will be sensitive. The Iraqi people have a right to make their own decisions. They don't need Iranian help. We may have to take a very hard line with the old men in Tehran.

As for the demonstrations in Baghdad, never assume that what you see is what you get. None of those photogenic mobs bawling for the Yankees to go home approached the numbers of demonstrators we saw marching in support of Saddam in Manhattan and Washington.

The antiwar demos in our own country did not tell us much about America's future. And the current barking in Baghdad will not determine the future of Iraq.

Far from being spontaneous outbursts of discontent, those demonstrations could have been provoked by supporters of the old regime, by clerics with political agendas—or by elements within the broad and quarrelsome exile community determined to rule Iraq, one way or the other. Some among the Iraqi exiles will do everything they can to force us to turn to them for help, including provoking attacks upon our forces.

Corrupt exile groups threaten the future of freedom in Iraq—and the image of the United States throughout the Middle East. Our claims not to favor any faction ring hollow when we fly in exiled leaders and uniformed personnel on our military transports.

Backing unscrupulous Iraqi exiles may be the factor that causes us to "lose" Iraq in the end, a moral Bay of Pigs. The most foolish act we could commit would be to betray our promise to let the Iraqi people decide for themselves who will lead them. We don't have to like their choices. But we do have to respect them.

Iraq doesn't need another strongman. But it could use a few honest ones.

# Wishful Thinking

New York Post

*July 7, 2003*

President Bush is accused of unfairly falsifying intelligence. He didn't do it. That's not the way the system works.

On the other hand, I have no doubt that the president and his deputies read intelligence reports selectively and talked themselves into believing what they wanted to believe.

That *is* the way the system works. For *all* presidents.

In fact, President Bush is far from the worst, as I can attest from personal experience. I spent most of my military career in intelligence work. During the Clinton years, I served in the Pentagon and on detail to the Executive Office of the President. The experience was discouraging, to say the least.

Since the early nineties, a number of us had been warning, both in classified forums and in the open press, about the threat from asymmetrical warfare, from terrorists, from warriors unconstrained by any laws, and from religion-obsessed madmen.

The evidence mounted. Terrorists attacked us in New York—the first attack on the World Trade Towers—and around the world. But contrary to the revisionist history churned out by loyalists, the Clinton administration just wanted the problem to go away, to pretend as long as possible that terrorism by Islamic zealots was a passing issue, and to avoid the politically painful costs of mounting a serious effort to counter such threats.

The fundamental difference between the Clinton and Bush administrations' use of intelligence is that Clinton consistently refused to acknowledge the threats we faced, while Bush sometimes sees threats as more immediate than they may be.

The Clinton approach led directly to 9/11. The Bush approach led to Baghdad. Guess which one makes more sense for a nation under threat of deadly attack?

Governments are made up of human beings, and human beings are imperfect. While many of President Bush's policies may merit closer scrutiny, the claim that he and his deputies lied about intelligence is politicized nonsense.

First, they couldn't get away with an outright lie. Our system just can't keep a secret. As it is, we hear complaints from analysts who don't believe proper attention was paid to their dissenting views.

Unfortunately, no administration pays adequate attention to dissenting views.

Governments graze in the classified pastures until they find a patch of "facts" to their taste, I know. I was one of the dissenters in the Clinton years. And Clinton came closer to outright lying about intelligence than any president since the Spanish-American War. Bill Clinton made LBJ and Nixon look like models of integrity.

Yet even Clinton didn't quite lie (not about intelligence, anyway). He just ignored uncomfortable facts, clinging to those reports and analyses that buttressed his huckster's, they-gotta-love-me view of the world. But even the charm that worked with interns fell short with Osama bin Laden.

The intelligence community can't win. Neither Republicans nor Democrats are interested in objective analysis. It's always about supporting an administration's goals. Republicans do, however, make somewhat better use of intelligence in the foreign policy arena simply because they tend to have a more mature sense of global realities.

Republicans stretch the facts, while Democrats ignore the facts. And GI Joe cleans up the mess.

Were there serious indicators of the presence of weapons of mass destruction in Iraq? No question about it. Even Rolf Ekeus, the U.N.'s Mr. Find-the-Nukes, stresses that the evidence was there.

Was there reason to believe that Saddam had bugs and gas, and that he intended to use them? You bet. He already *had* used them.

Was the intelligence community able to pinpoint WMD stockpiles with absolute certainty? Nope. But if you believed—rightly—that Saddam was evil and needed to go, and if you weighed the available evidence, in bits and pieces, among like-minded advisers, it's easy enough to see how the strong possibility that Saddam had active WMD programs became first a probability, then a certainty.

Evidence to the contrary? All too easy to ignore. And the truth is that there wasn't much of it. We're *still* likely to find some of the stuff hidden away.

Another problem, of course, is that intelligence remains more of an art than a science—it's never perfect. I've seen, many times, how different decision-makers, presented with the same set of facts, come to different conclusions.

But none of this really matters. Because President Bush's accusers know all this as well as I do. They're far less interested in the facts than Bush and his advisers were. There's a presidential election coming, and the Democrats are desperate to score any points they can.

Of course, the issue hasn't caught fire with the American people—and it never will. Except for a few Columbia professors, we all know that Saddam truly was evil and that getting rid of his regime was a virtuous act, whether or not he had WMD downstairs in his home workshop. Splitting hairs about who knew what when just doesn't resonate.

Nor should it. In their pathetic disarray, the Democrats are betraying a greater trust. Making the political reconstruction of Iraq a success—to the extent possible—is in America's interest, in the interest of the Middle East, and in the world's interest. This petty sniping and the insistence, day after day, that the sky is falling is conduct unbecoming. It truly does provide aid and comfort to our enemies.

Democrats would better serve themselves and our country if they would challenge the president with a *positive* vision of the future, with better ways to do what must be done, rather than siding with those Europeans who want American foreign policy to fail.

The truth is that President Bush *is* vulnerable domestically. But his foreign policy is unassailable.

I hope that one day we will see the strictly ethical, objective use of intelligence by all presidential administrations, Republican or Democrat. But I don't expect to see it in my lifetime.

# We're Doing Fine

## The Washington Post

*July 20, 2003*

In the summer of 1945, occupied Germany's cities lay in rubble, hunger and disease prevailed, and tens of millions of displaced persons foraged to survive or lived behind barbed wire. Criminals thrived on the black market. De-Nazification had barely begun. That July, three months after the war's end, no one could have foreseen Germany's political future, its economic miracle, and astonishing reconstruction.

During the federal occupation of the South after the Civil War, a hostile, impoverished population lived amid ruins and cholera. Deadly riots and murders were common. The terrorists of the Ku Klux Klan enjoyed far greater support among the population than do today's Ba'ath Party dead-enders in Iraq. Attempts to achieve inclusive democracy were frustrated for a century.

By historical standards, our progress in Iraq is extraordinary. While we cannot predict the character of the future Iraq with precision—and we must have realistic expectations— we already may claim with confidence that we will leave the various peoples of Iraq a more humane, equitable political environment than they ever have experienced. It will then be their own to improve upon or ruin.

With unprecedented speed, we overthrew a tyrannical regime that ruled twenty-five million people. A few million of Iraq's citizens had personal stakes in that regime as the source of their livelihoods and privileges. Should anyone be surprised if hundreds of thousands passively resist the occupation forces and some tens of thousands are willing to engage in or support violence against the force that robbed them of their power? Theirs is the violence of desperation, not of confidence. We face criminals, not a quagmire.

Yet the breathless media reporting of each American casualty in Iraq implies that the occupation has failed. Yes, every soldier's life matters. But we also need to keep the numbers in perspective. In one recent week, as many Americans died in a workplace shooting in Mississippi as were killed by hostile action in Iraq. The total casualties for the war and its aftermath hardly rise to the number of deaths on our highways over a long holiday weekend. Considering the dimensions of our victory, the low level of our losses is something entirely new in the history of warfare. But the quest for daily headlines is not synonymous with a search for deeper truths.

Most of Iraq is recovering—not only from the recent war, but from a generation of oppression. The Kurdish region is prospering, a model of cooperation, and the Shiites have behaved far better than initial worries suggested. The violence is isolated in the Sunni-Arab-minority region, a sliver of the country just west and north of Baghdad, which benefited most from Saddam's rule and has the most to lose under a democratic government. The absence of broad support for anti-coalition attacks is heartening. There is no general insurrection, and there are no violent, massive demonstrations. Individual soldiers are assassinated, but our overall presence is not endangered. The resistance of die-hard elements should surprise no one but the most naive neoconservatives in the Office of the Secretary of Defense.

Meanwhile, our focus on micro issues such as individual casualties or a disgruntled shopkeeper's complaints obscures our macro success, both within Iraq and beyond its borders. Change has come to the Middle East with remarkable force and velocity. The notorious "Arab street," far from exploding, is the quietest it has been in decades. Syria has sharply reduced its support for terrorism as it weighs its future. In Iran, the young are encouraged by the atmosphere of change, while the bitter old men in power glance nervously at the U.S. military forces positioned to their east and west.

There is genuine if imperfect progress on the Palestinian dilemma. The necessity for American bases in benighted Saudi Arabia has faded. Arab intellectuals and journalists speak more frankly of the need for change than they have in four decades. And, depending on how the situation in Iraq develops, the United States may have the opportunity to right one of history's most enduring wrongs by fostering the establishment of an independent Kurdistan.

Instant judgments that our occupation is somehow failing, though politically gratifying to a few, are inaccurate, destructive, and ill-judged. It will be at least a decade before we can read the deep results of our actions in Iraq, but the initial indications are that they will be overwhelmingly positive. By choice, we may retain a military presence there ten years hence—or we may be long gone. It is simply too early to say.

# Au Revoir, Marianne . . .
# Auf Wiedersehen,
# Lili Marleen

# The End of America's European Romance

## Frankfurter Allgemeine Zeitung

*May 15, 2003*

The societies of "Old Europe" remind Americans of the Arab Street. Preferring comforting delusions to challenging realities, Europeans talk a great deal, do very little, and blame the United States for homegrown ills.

The recent chants in the boulevards of Berlin were almost indistinguishable from those heard—until recently—in downtown Baghdad. Europe's culture of complaint, its enthusiasm for accusing America of every wickedness while assigning every virtue to itself, and its stunning lack of self-examination leave Americans bewildered.

We thought you were adults, but, from across the Atlantic, you look like spoiled children. And your recent tantrums have convinced Big Daddy America to deposit you on the steps of the strategic orphanage.

The damage done by the recent confrontation between the United States and those nations whose vocabularies collapsed to the single words "Nein!" or "Non!" will be repaired—on the surface. We shall continue to cooperate on matters of mutual interest. But, on a deeper level, the exuberantly dishonest attacks on America heard from France and Germany (Belgium simply doesn't count), along with the shameless grandstanding of Mr. Schroeder and Mr. Chirac, appear to even the most pragmatic Americans as grounds for divorce from our long marriage of convenience.

The divorce is long overdue. Ignoring "Old Europe" on questions of grand strategy will liberate the United States, freeing us at last from the failed European model of diplomacy that has given the world so many hideous wars, dysfunctional borders, and undisturbed dictators. The recent mischief wrought in Paris and Berlin has enabled Washington to escape a long thrall of enchantment, a slumber of sorts during which America allowed Europe's ghost to haunt its decisions.

Now you have awakened us, and we see that Europe's influence was nothing but a legacy of nightmares. We shall no longer subscribe to your bloodsoaked, corrupt rules for the international system but will forge our own.

You will not like many of our new rules. But to paraphrase Frederick the Great's remark about Maria Theresia, you will cry, but take your share of any available spoils.

As a result of a series of remarkable strategic miscalculations, France and Germany have lost their international footing—not only with the U.S.A., but with the world. You had your moment in the anti-American sun. High noon revealed you as powerless and inept.


For Germany, this divorce will offer some advantages. American combat forces soon will begin to leave German soil permanently, followed in good time by our logistics facilities, which are simply more difficult to shift. This will be to Germany's benefit practically and psychologically—and very much to the benefit of America's armed forces, which have become nothing but a cash cow for greedy organizations ranging from your railways to your labor unions.

NATO will survive, of course. Along with the European Union, it's an indispensable employment agency for Europe's excess bureaucrats. But other bilateral and multilateral military arrangements will take precedence in Washington's strategic calculations.

On the negative side, Germany will lose almost all of its diplomatic influence beyond continental Europe—and Berlin never had much, at least since 1945. The world will take your Euros, but will not take you seriously.

You have asserted your independence from America. Now you have it. Good luck.

We won our war, easily, despite your protests and without your help. And do not flatter yourself with rhetoric about refusing to be America's vassals. No one in the United States questioned Germany's right to decide for itself whether or not to support our efforts to depose Saddam Hussein. Germany had every right to decline to participate.

But it was the way you did it that infuriated us.

Bundeskanzler Schroeder astonished us. We long had recognized him as a political charlatan, but the extent of his demagogy and his amateurish inability to foresee the consequences of his ranting still came as a surprise to us. We see Mr. Schroeder as a man utterly without convictions—a man without qualities—a political animal so debased that he resembles no one so much as he does European caricatures of small-time American politicians. His opportunistic anti-Americanism seemed all for effect, without substance or genuine belief.

Yet, in other respects, Schroeder proved quintessentially European: He criticized but failed to offer meaningful solutions of his own. He chose slogans over ideas, convenience over ethics, and portrayed small-minded selfishness as political heroism. What qualities might better describe twenty-first-century Europe?

Germany has come a long way downhill from Adenauer and Schmidt to Gerhard Schroeder.

Most difficult of all for us to stomach were remarks from members of the German government comparing President Bush to Hitler. Now, does anyone reading this newspaper believe that's an honest comparison? And was it fitting coming from a German official?

One thinks not. Americans heard the echo of Joseph Goebbels.

Then there were all the demonstrators waving signs equating the United States to the Nazi regime, as tasteless a display as Germany has managed since the last crematorium went cold.

Once our tempers cooled, we realized that all these Nazi comparisons weren't really about us. It was all about *you,* your guilt, and your evasions.

Perhaps the most revealing incident of the war came during a television interview with a young protester in Berlin after Baghdad had fallen. The reporter asked him what he thought of the images of Iraqis cheering U.S. Marines and toppling Saddam's statue. The young German said the scenes "annoyed" him.

Doubtless. Reality is annoying, indeed.

Oh, we know how you see us. You never cease telling us. We are uncultured, because we cannot recall the date of the first performance of *Das Rheingold.* We are heartless, since our society favors opportunity over security. We are naive, since we do not share your prejudices. We are warmongers, because we still believe some things are worth defending. And now we are

Nazis, because we moved to depose a dictator who had slaughtered his own people as well as his neighbors, while harboring terrorists and pursuing weapons of mass destruction.

Of course, you continue to buy our cultural products. Your brightest young people come to our shores to work. We Americans have moved beyond the racism that blights Germany and France (we look forward to meeting a German Colin Powell of Turkish ancestry in Berlin or an ethnic-Senegalese Condoleeza Rice in Paris), so we certainly do not share your prejudices. And after the events of September 11, 2001, we will not wait to be attacked, but will strike pre-emptively wherever we believe it to be necessary—and we shall do so without ever again asking Europe's permission. So we are, indeed, warmongers by European standards.

But what about the charge that Americans are the new Nazis?

I think I understand the sickness that afflicts you. I received my first insight as a young Army sergeant in a not-yet-reunified Germany a quarter-century ago. Although the event was ten years past, young Germans unfailingly brought up the My Lai massacre in Vietnam during our conversations. My Lai was one of two documented American atrocities in that war. Almost two hundred villagers were murdered. It was inexcusable, and we did not try to excuse it. But those young Germans grasped at the My Lai massacre with an alacrity that astonished me. To them, the two-hundred dead at My Lai canceled Auschwitz and Treblinka, six million murdered Jews, Gypsies, homosexuals, and dissenters. The message was, "See! You Americans are just as bad as we Germans were—maybe worse."

I did not find the comparison convincing.

Now, with Germany's Jews long since slaughtered or driven out (to America's great benefit, thank you), you attack Israel at

every opportunity, hanging on every Palestinian claim, no matter how absurd, and inventing Israeli atrocities. Americans see
Israelis as fighting for their existence against those who want
to exterminate them. You view Israelis as a reproach to your
past deeds, and you lash out at them. Clausewitz is no longer a
guide to your national behavior. Today, we need to consult Sig-
mund Freud. A Jew, of course.

The Israelis, too, have been called Nazis by your elected
politicians—indeed, "Nazi" seems to be your favorite insult. At
times it sounds to us as though everyone who isn't a German is
now a Nazi. Unless, of course, we are talking of Arabs who
murder Jews, in which case a good German speaks of freedom
fighters.

Here in America, Holocaust survivors live among us, as do
those aging GIs who opened the gates to Dachau. They have
been our fathers, our teachers and our neighbors. Is it any
wonder that we find your rhetoric repulsive? Hitler, at least,
was honest about his bigotry.

And now we must endure the ludicrous schizophrenia of
your present society, in which you alternate between insisting
that German guilt must have an end and indulging in revisionist history that equates the allied bombing campaign against
your cities or the sinking of ships ferrying submarine crews
with Nazi evils.

Your attempts to excuse the inexcusable merely remind us
that Germany deserved every bomb dropped upon its soil.
Bush the equivalent of Hitler? Show us the American death
camps, please.

As a lifelong admirer of German culture, you leave me in
despair. Your chancellor has transformed the worthy old
maxim "Be more than you appear to be" into "Appear to be
more than you are." Goethe's timeless query, "Germany. . . but

where is it?" has been answered with "Between France and Russia, duped by Chirac and coolly manipulated by Putin." And Faust has been outed as Professor Unrat.

*Auf wiedersehen,* Lili Marleen. It was great while it lasted.

And Marianne? Since no one took Germany seriously to begin with, Berlin had less to lose in *l'affaire Iraq* than Paris. France gambled with Dostoevskian abandon in the strategic casino and ended up bankrupt in the morning light.

President Chirac and his sorcerer's apprentice, Foreign Minister Dominique de Villepin, emerged as one of the most incompetent combinations in diplomatic history, two drunkards behind the steering wheel of policy. It astonishes us that the French actually believed that Paris could dictate terms to Washington.

Sorry. Gaul does not give orders to Rome.

We understood that Chirac was playing to the Arab world as well as to his domestic electorate. But the succession of French refusals to negotiate seriously or even to consider compromises at the United Nations, climaxed by France's announcement, in advance, that it would veto any further resolutions introduced by the United States or Britain, seemed suicidal to us.

And it was suicidal. The legacy of Charles de Gaulle perished in the Security Council. The tradition of permitting France a greater voice in trans-Atlantic decision-making than its place, power, or contributions merited is over, as dead as Jean-Paul Sartre or his idol, Josef Stalin. The Gallic cock crowed so loudly it fell off the fence and broke its neck.

Washington will no longer entertain the views of Paris on vital international issues. Nor will we risk another French veto on a matter we view as critical to our national security. And we will feed the United Nations the crumbs of strategy.

Far from expanding its influence, France has forced its collapse. A quick round of applause in Algeria is hardly worth the loss of America's ear. Briefly the champion of all the anti-American forces in the world, from Libya to North Korea, France is left unable to resolve the civil strife in Ivory Coast. And Paris will *not* be given a significant role in rebuilding Iraq.

France long has seemed to Americans to be the apotheosis of European hypocrisy. While defending Saddam Hussein from "American aggression," Mr. Chirac hosted Robert Mugabe in Paris in a pathetic attempt to expand French influence into Anglophone Africa. But I was in Zimbabwe when the visit occurred and the degree of fury the people of that country felt toward France for hosting Mugabe—whom they have nicknamed "Robodan Mugabevich"—guaranteed that the French will never be welcome between the Zambezi and the Limpopo.

France seems to us an aging whore desperate to attract even the most diseased customers.

But, above all, it is French naiveté that leaves us shaking our heads. How could they so misjudge the situation? Aren't the French supposed to be terribly clever and devious? How could they be so clumsy, and on such a grand scale?

The short answer is that, like Arabs, they believed their own fantasies. In addition to the forlorn illusion that France is still a great power, Mr. Chirac and Mr. de Villepin utterly misjudged George Bush. They had called him a cowboy for so long that they came to believe there was nothing to the man. And they were wrong.

I did not vote for President Bush. But, after 9/11/01, I was glad he was our president. Had Al Gore been in the White House, we would have done the European thing and formed a committee to ask how we had brought disaster upon ourselves.

President Bush led a galvanized nation into a series of deliberate, carefully considered actions that have broken the back of one terrorist organization after another while removing a brutal, backward theocracy from one country and a blood-encrusted dictatorship from another.

And America is not finished. We will no longer subscribe to the European system in which dictators may do as they wish with impunity within their own borders—your insistence on respect for national sovereignty simply means that Hitler would have been perfectly acceptable had he only killed German Jews. And we will not follow the traditions of kings and Kaisers in which heads of state are exempt from personal punishment, no matter their crimes. We will go after the truly guilty, not the masses. And no amount of insults hurled from beneath the Brandenburg Gate or from the Place de la Concorde will deter us.

We are finished with your delight in weeping over past holocausts while you remain unwilling to act to prevent or interrupt new holocausts. Srebrenica is the European model. Baghdad is ours.

President Bush is a Texan, as Europeans never fail to remind us. But the intelligence services of France and Germany seem to have failed to understand the character of Texans. They don't speak artfully, but they act resolutely. They aren't relativists. Texans believe there is a difference between right and wrong. And when you insult a Texan to his face while betraying his trust, he is not going to take it kindly. Confronting a Texan in public is always ill-advised, unless you intend to fight it out to the end—and have the means to do so. Texans don't even care where Europe is on the map.

We Americans are all Texans now. You have left us no choice.